KDE For Linux® For D

D0763883

Window Manipulations

To do this:	Do this:
Move a window	Click and drag the window's title bar
Resize a window	Point to the window border. When the pointer changes to an arrow pointing to a perpendicular line, click and drag the window border
Minimize (iconify) a window	Click the Iconify button (usually a small dot or dash) in the window's title bar
Maximize a window	Click the Maximize button (usually a box) in the window's title bar
Close a window	Click the Close button (usually an X) in the window's title bar
Make a window sticky (retain its position onscreen when you switch to other virtual desktops)	Click the Sticky button (usually a push pin) in the window's title bar
Move a window to a different virtual desktop	Right-click the window's title bar, choose To Desktop and then the desktop number from the pop-up menu that appears
Move a window when its title bar is inaccessible	Press and hold Alt as you click and drag anywhere on the window
Kill a window that won't close normally	Press Ctrl+Alt+Esc. When the pointer changes to a skull and crossed bones symbol, click the window you want to kill

Global Keyboard Shortcuts

To do this:	Press this key combination:
Close a window	Alt+F4
Kill a window	Ctrl+Alt+Esc
Open the Execute Command box	Alt+F2
Open the Task Manager window	Ctrl+Esc
Switch to virtual desktop 1	Ctrl+F1
Switch to virtual desktop 2	Ctrl+F2
Switch to virtual desktop 3	Ctrl+F3
Switch to virtual desktop 4	Ctrl+F4
Switch to virtual desktop 5	Ctrl+F5
Switch to virtual desktop 6	Ctrl+F6
Switch to virtual desktop 7	Ctrl+F7
Switch to virtual desktop 8	Ctrl+F8

KDE For Linux® For Dummies®

Cheat Sheet

Standard Keyboard Shortcuts

To do this:	Press this key combination:
Close the window	Ctrl+W
Copy selected text or object to the clipboard	Ctrl+C
Create a New document or file	Ctrl+N
Cut the selected text or object and place it on the clipboard	Ctrl+X
Move cursor to the beginning of the current document	Ctrl+Home
Move cursor to the end of the current document	Ctrl+End
Open the file Open dialog box	Ctrl+O
Open the Find dialog box or feature	Ctrl+F
Paste the contents of the clipboard into the current document at the cursor location	Ctrl+V
Print the current document	Ctrl+P
Quit the current document or application	Ctrl+Q
Save the current document or file	Ctrl+S
Scroll to the next page	PageDown
Scroll to the previous page	PageUp
Undo the last operation	Ctrl+Z

Copyright © 2000 IDG Books Worldwide, Inc. All rights reserved.

Cheat Sheet $2.95 value. Item 0658-7.

For more information about IDG Books, call 1-800-762-2974.

For Dummies®: Bestselling Book Series for Beginners

TM

BESTSELLING BOOK SERIES

References for the Rest of Us! ®

Are you intimidated and confused by computers? Do you find that traditional manuals are overloaded with technical details you'll never use? Do your friends and family always call you to fix simple problems on their PCs? Then the *...For Dummies*® computer book series from IDG Books Worldwide is for you.

...For Dummies books are written for those frustrated computer users who know they aren't really dumb but find that PC hardware, software, and indeed the unique vocabulary of computing make them feel helpless. *...For Dummies* books use a lighthearted approach, a down-to-earth style, and even cartoons and humorous icons to dispel computer novices' fears and build their confidence. Lighthearted but not lightweight, these books are a perfect survival guide for anyone forced to use a computer.

> *"I like my copy so much I told friends; now they bought copies."*
> — Irene C., Orwell, Ohio

> *"Quick, concise, nontechnical, and humorous."*
> — Jay A., Elburn, Illinois

> *"Thanks, I needed this book. Now I can sleep at night."*
> — Robin F., British Columbia, Canada

Already, millions of satisfied readers agree. They have made *...For Dummies* books the #1 introductory level computer book series and have written asking for more. So, if you're looking for the most fun and easy way to learn about computers, look to *...For Dummies* books to give you a helping hand.

1/99

KDE For Linux® FOR DUMMIES®

by Michael Meadhra, Kate Wrightson, and Joe Merlino

IDG Books Worldwide, Inc.
An International Data Group Company

Foster City, CA ◆ Chicago, IL ◆ Indianapolis, IN ◆ New York, NY

KDE For Linux® For Dummies®

Published by
IDG Books Worldwide, Inc.
An International Data Group Company
919 E. Hillsdale Blvd.
Suite 400
Foster City, CA 94404
www.idgbooks.com (IDG Books Worldwide Web site)
www.dummies.com (Dummies Press Web site)

Library of Congress Catalog Card No.: 99-67161

ISBN: 0-7645-0658-7

Printed in the United States of America

10 9 8 7 6 5 4 3 2 1

1O/QX/QR/QQ/IN

Distributed in the United States by IDG Books Worldwide, Inc.

Distributed by CDG Books Canada Inc. for Canada; by Transworld Publishers Limited in the United Kingdom; by IDG Norge Books for Norway; by IDG Sweden Books for Sweden; by IDG Books Australia Publishing Corporation Pty. Ltd. for Australia and New Zealand; by TransQuest Publishers Pte Ltd. for Singapore, Malaysia, Thailand, Indonesia, and Hong Kong; by Gotop Information Inc. for Taiwan; by ICG Muse, Inc. for Japan; by Intersoft for South Africa; by Eyrolles for France; by International Thomson Publishing for Germany, Austria and Switzerland; by Distribuidora Cuspide for Argentina; by LR International for Brazil; by Galileo Libros for Chile; by Ediciones ZETA S.C.R. Ltda. for Peru; by WS Computer Publishing Corporation, Inc., for the Philippines; by Contemporanea de Ediciones for Venezuela; by Express Computer Distributors for the Caribbean and West Indies; by Micronesia Media Distributor, Inc. for Micronesia; by Chips Computadoras S.A. de C.V. for Mexico; by Editorial Norma de Panama S.A. for Panama; by American Bookshops for Finland.

For general information on IDG Books Worldwide's books in the U.S., please call our Consumer Customer Service department at 800-762-2974. For reseller information, including discounts and premium sales, please call our Reseller Customer Service department at 800-434-3422.

For information on where to purchase IDG Books Worldwide's books outside the U.S., please contact our International Sales department at 317-596-5530 or fax 317-572-4002.

For consumer information on foreign language translations, please contact our Customer Service department at 1-800-434-3422, fax 317-572-4002, or e-mail rights@idgbooks.com.

For information on licensing foreign or domestic rights, please phone +1-650-653-7098.

For sales inquiries and special prices for bulk quantities, please contact our Sales department at 800-762-2974 or write to the address above.

For information on using IDG Books Worldwide's books in the classroom or for ordering examination copies, please contact our Educational Sales department at 800-434-2086 or fax 317-572-4005.

For press review copies, author interviews, or other publicity information, please contact our Public Relations department at 650-653-7000 or fax 650-653-7500.

For authorization to photocopy items for corporate, personal, or educational use, please contact Copyright Clearance Center, 222 Rosewood Drive, Danvers, MA 01923, or fax 978-750-4470.

is a registered trademark under exclusive license to IDG Books Worldwide, Inc. from International Data Group, Inc.

About the Authors

Michael Meadhra is an author and consultant who has written, co-authored, or contributed to more than 30 books, including *StarOffice For Linux For Dummies*, *Banking Online For Dummies*, and *Lotus SmartSuite Millennium Edition For Dummies*, all published by IDG Books Worldwide.

Joe Merlino is a technical writer and avid Linux hobbyist. He is also a library worker and contributor to the Open Source Digital Library System project. He dabbles in Perl and Unix shell scripting. He has been a contributor to *Linux Gazette,* contributed to *StarOffice For Linux For Dummies*, and is co-author of *StarOffice 5.0 for Linux Bible* from IDG Books.

Kate Wrightson is a technical writer with several years of Linux experience and over ten years of experience using UNIX. She works with university and college faculty to help them improve their teaching, especially through using technology in their classrooms and course preparation. She also spends time working with the USENET newsgroup creation process. Kate has published articles on topics ranging from the history of American higher education to clear business writing; she is the co-author of *StarOffice 5.0 for Linux Bible* from IDG Books and contributed to *StarOffice For Linux For Dummies*.

ABOUT IDG BOOKS WORLDWIDE

Welcome to the world of IDG Books Worldwide.

IDG Books Worldwide, Inc., is a subsidiary of International Data Group, the world's largest publisher of computer-related information and the leading global provider of information services on information technology. IDG was founded more than 30 years ago by Patrick J. McGovern and now employs more than 9,000 people worldwide. IDG publishes more than 290 computer publications in over 75 countries. More than 90 million people read one or more IDG publications each month.

Launched in 1990, IDG Books Worldwide is today the #1 publisher of best-selling computer books in the United States. We are proud to have received eight awards from the Computer Press Association in recognition of editorial excellence and three from Computer Currents' First Annual Readers' Choice Awards. Our best-selling ...*For Dummies*® series has more than 50 million copies in print with translations in 31 languages. IDG Books Worldwide, through a joint venture with IDG's Hi-Tech Beijing, became the first U.S. publisher to publish a computer book in the People's Republic of China. In record time, IDG Books Worldwide has become the first choice for millions of readers around the world who want to learn how to better manage their businesses.

Our mission is simple: Every one of our books is designed to bring extra value and skill-building instructions to the reader. Our books are written by experts who understand and care about our readers. The knowledge base of our editorial staff comes from years of experience in publishing, education, and journalism — experience we use to produce books to carry us into the new millennium. In short, we care about books, so we attract the best people. We devote special attention to details such as audience, interior design, use of icons, and illustrations. And because we use an efficient process of authoring, editing, and desktop publishing our books electronically, we can spend more time ensuring superior content and less time on the technicalities of making books.

You can count on our commitment to deliver high-quality books at competitive prices on topics you want to read about. At IDG Books Worldwide, we continue in the IDG tradition of delivering quality for more than 30 years. You'll find no better book on a subject than one from IDG Books Worldwide.

IDG BOOKS WORLDWIDE

John Kilcullen
Chairman and CEO
IDG Books Worldwide, Inc.

Steven Berkowitz
President and Publisher
IDG Books Worldwide, Inc.

Eighth Annual Computer Press Awards ≥ 1992

IX WINNER
Ninth Annual Computer Press Awards ≥ 1993

X WINNER
Tenth Annual Computer Press Awards ≥ 1994

Eleventh Annual Computer Press Awards ≥ 1995

IDG is the world's leading IT media, research and exposition company. Founded in 1964, IDG had 1997 revenues of $2.05 billion and has more than 9,000 employees worldwide. IDG offers the widest range of media options that reach IT buyers in 75 countries representing 95% of worldwide IT spending. IDG's diverse product and services portfolio spans six key areas including print publishing, online publishing, expositions and conferences, market research, education and training, and global marketing services. More than 90 million people read one or more of IDG's 290 magazines and newspapers, including IDG's leading global brands — Computerworld, PC World, Network World, Macworld and the Channel World family of publications. IDG Books Worldwide is one of the fastest-growing computer book publishers in the world, with more than 700 titles in 36 languages. The "...For Dummies®" series alone has more than 50 million copies in print. IDG offers online users the largest network of technology-specific Web sites around the world through IDG.net (http://www.idg.net), which comprises more than 225 targeted Web sites in 55 countries worldwide. International Data Corporation (IDC) is the world's largest provider of information technology data, analysis and consulting, with research centers in over 41 countries and more than 400 research analysts worldwide. IDG World Expo is a leading producer of more than 168 globally branded conferences and expositions in 35 countries including E3 (Electronic Entertainment Expo), Macworld Expo, ComNet, Windows World Expo, ICE (Internet Commerce Expo), Agenda, DEMO, and Spotlight. IDG's training subsidiary, ExecuTrain, is the world's largest computer training company, with more than 230 locations worldwide and 785 training courses. IDG Marketing Services helps industry-leading IT companies build international brand recognition by developing global integrated marketing programs via IDG's print, online and exposition products worldwide. Further information about the company can be found at www.idg.com. 1/24/99

Authors' Acknowledgements

Publishing a book such as this one is a cooperative endeavor — and we don't mean just cooperation between the coauthors, whose names are listed on the cover. There's also the cooperation between the authors and the publisher, IDG Books Worldwide, and between the many people who make up that fine company. The IDG staff who had a hand in creating this book are listed on the Publisher's Acknowledgements page. The authors wish to acknowledge all those individuals and the rest of the staff of IDG who made this book possible. In addition, we want to specifically mention the following folks that we have worked with more directly.

Thanks to David Mayhew, Acquisitions Editor, for his vision and hard work to make this book a reality. Our Senior Project Editor, Pat O'Brien, and Copy Editors Jerelind Charles and Tonya Maddox polished our prose. The technical editor, Mike Pilone, made sure it was accurate. Thanks, guys.

We especially want to thank our agent, David Fugate, and the Waterside Productions crew for finding us the opportunity to do this book and for assembling the author team to tackle it.

Publisher's Acknowledgments

We're proud of this book; please register your comments through our IDG Books Worldwide Online Registration Form located at http://my2cents.dummies.com.

Some of the people who helped bring this book to market include the following:

Acquisitions, Editorial, and Media Development

Project Editor: Pat O'Brien

Acquisitions Editor: David Mayhew

Copy Editor: Jerelind Charles

Technical Editor: Michael Pilone

Media Development Editor: Marita Ellixson

Associate Permissions Editor:
Carmen Krikorian

Editorial Manager: Rev Mengle

Media Development Manager:
Heather Heath Dismore

Media Development Coordinator:
Megan Roney

Production

Project Coordinator: E. Shawn Aylsworth

Layout and Graphics: Jill Piscitelli,
Brent Savage, Brian Torwelle,
Dan Whetstine, Erin Zeltner

Proofreaders: Laura Albert, Corey Bowen,
Melissa D. Buddendeck, John Greenough,
Marianne Santy, Charles Spencer,
Toni Settle

Indexer: Tech Indexing

Special Help:
Amanda Foxworth

General and Administrative

IDG Books Worldwide, Inc.: John Kilcullen, CEO; Steven Berkowitz, President and Publisher

IDG Books Technology Publishing Group: Richard Swadley, Senior Vice President and Publisher; Walter Bruce III, Vice President and Associate Publisher; Joseph Wikert, Associate Publisher; Mary Bednarek, Branded Product Development Director; Mary Corder, Editorial Director; Barry Pruett, Publishing Manager; Michelle Baxter, Publishing Manager

IDG Books Consumer Publishing Group: Roland Elgey, Senior Vice President and Publisher; Kathleen A. Welton, Vice President and Publisher; Kevin Thornton, Acquisitions Manager; Kristin A. Cocks, Editorial Director

IDG Books Internet Publishing Group: Brenda McLaughlin, Senior Vice President and Publisher; Diane Graves Steele, Vice President and Associate Publisher; Sofia Marchant, Online Marketing Manager

IDG Books Production for Dummies Press: Debbie Stailey, Associate Director of Production; Cindy L. Phipps, Manager of Project Coordination, Production Proofreading, and Indexing; Tony Augsburger, Manager of Prepress, Reprints, and Systems; Laura Carpenter, Production Control Manager; Shelley Lea, Supervisor of Graphics and Design; Debbie J. Gates, Production Systems Specialist; Robert Springer, Supervisor of Proofreading; Kathie Schutte, Production Supervisor

Dummies Packaging and Book Design: Patty Page, Manager, Promotions Marketing

◆

The publisher would like to give special thanks to Patrick J. McGovern,
without whom this book would not have been possible.

◆

Contents at a Glance

Cartoons at a Glance

By Rich Tennant

page 233

page 131

page 273

page 5

page 83

page 311

Fax: 978-546-7747
E-mail: richtennant@the5thwave.com
World Wide Web: www.the5thwave.com

Table of Contents

Introduction

● ●

*A*s the twenty-first century comes smoking up out of the lamp, it offers computer users a whole new range of choices. Operating systems, for example — it isn't just a Windows-or-Mac world anymore. Actually, it never was. The mighty UNIX operating system has been around since Cold War days, and it still underpins the operation of the Internet. Although UNIX and its specialized offspring — in particular, Linux — have been getting a lot of press lately because of their low cost and high reliability, they all have that pesky command-line interface. Normally that would mean you have to be a pretty decent typist — and learn an exotic vocabulary of command words — to use Linux well. Most computer users who have a fondness for point-and-click — and a raging allergy to typing commands at a tiny prompt on a big dark screen — have been out of luck. Up to now, that is.

As Linux has gained popularity in the last few years, KDE has emerged to ease the heartbreak of windowless computer use. It's a graphical user interface! It's an award-winning innovation! It's a dessert topping! (Kidding.) And you hold in your hands the key to mastering KDE and making the Linux genie do your bidding. Rejoice and read on.

About This Book

KDE For Linux For Dummies eases you into the exciting new world of KDE by walking you through the features, capabilities, and oddities that make KDE similar (but not identical) to the graphical user interfaces you may have used before.

Who Should Read This Book

If you enjoy the convenience and efficiency of a window-style interface, but get a little queasy when you think about how much space it takes up on your hard drive, then Linux, KDE, and this book are for you. If you're already a seasoned Linux network administrator, and want to look into implementing KDE as one way to make peace with your users — whatever platform they're running — you've come to the right place. If you've just been handed a memo that announces a mass migration from Windows to Linux and KDE — or if you've been intrigued with the Linux phenomenon but intimidated by all the finger-gymnastics needed to run it, relax. Your interface is ready and your guidebook awaits.

How This Book Is Organized

Use this book in the way that makes the best sense to you. You can, as the King of Hearts said to the White Rabbit in *Alice in Wonderland,* "begin at the beginning . . . and go on till you come to the end . . . then stop." If you'd rather jump around in the book to chase after particular topics — or even read it all again for good measure when you're done — go right ahead. (We won't tell a soul.) Here's a rundown on what you'll find inside.

Part I: Getting Started

If you've used Windows or a Macintosh, you've used a graphical user interface. Which means you've got a leg up on KDE. If you haven't, you're in for a treat. Part I shows you the basic KDE operations, tours the desktop, and demonstrates the highly effective management of windows and files (you don't even have to cultivate seven new habits).

Part II: Making KDE Look Right

KDE gives you the features, options, and general wherewithal to set up your interface so it works for you and looks like it means business. Part II shows you how to set up your panel, customize your desktop, and get the most out of using KDE's themes.

Part III: Getting Down to Business

Part III unlocks the secrets of getting connected and using KDE on the Internet. You have a look at the applications and utilities available for work or play, and get the lowdown on keeping the peace when you're working with non-KDE applications.

Part IV: Under the Hood

The Linux community is a pretty self-reliant crew. They know they have no giant corporation to call when things go wrong. Of course, the upside is that they don't have to spend big bucks on the long-distance tech-support line while some machine plays them elevator music. As a Linux user, you can easily get a comfortable knowledge from your fellow users of how the underlying operating system works. Part IV gets you started, providing a basic guided tour through Linux, and checks you out on those shiny new Linux controls you get in the KDE Control Center.

Part V: The Part of Tens

Here's the KDE version of an exclusive *For Dummies* feature — a collection of distilled wisdom arranged in convenient groups of ten: ten really handy things to know before you have to learn them from experience, ten places you can turn for help, ten KDE toys for the pure fun of it, and the ten KDE themes you don't even have to turn in to your English teacher.

Part VI: Appendixes

The KDE/Linux community is your best friend. And they don't even charge you for it. Part VI shows you how to get hold of and install KDE, where to find more expertise on the Internet, and a catalog of the goodies you'll find on the CD-ROM that accompanies this book.

Icons in This Book

Along your way through *KDE For Linux For Dummies,* you'll find some friendly road signs in the form of these icons:

The Tip icon identifies shortcuts, not-so-obvious answers, and useful ways of looking at KDE and Linux.

The Warning icon calls your attention to possible pitfalls that lurk in the world of KDE and Linux as they do everywhere in cyberspace. Take heed.

The Technical Stuff icon conjures up techie issues, details, and info you may want to know about (if you want to frighten the techno-ignoramuses in your midst). Or you might not. If you leave the finer tech details to your friendly IT department, no one will think the worse of you. Honest.

Next best thing to an alarm watch, and a whole lot more polite. These icons highlight the . . . er . . . *highlights* of using KDE.

Where to Go from Here

By the end of this handy tome, you can take what you learn here in any of several directions — further into the world of the Linux community, deeper into the secrets of operating systems, or off into the new possibilities that KDE sets before you. For a glimpse of two possible places to go next, you might want to try these books from IDG Books Worldwide, Inc.:

✔ For more about the history, mystery, and delights of Linux, dive into *Linux For Dummies,* 2nd Edition, by Jon "maddog" Hall (ISBN: 0-7645-0421-5). As Executive Director of Linux International, he's sent his report from the front lines.

✔ If your company is making the move to a networked computing environment that uses the Linux operating system (very chic these days), get hold of *Linux Administration For Dummies* by Michael Bellomo (ISBN: 0-7645-0589-0). You'll be glad you did.

Let's get started!

Part I
Getting Started

The 5th Wave   By Rich Tennant

In this part . . .

As with any newfangled gadget (or, for that matter, any oldfangled gadget you're just starting to use), KDE takes a bit of orientation and practice. Fortunately, if you're familiar with Macintosh or Windows computers, you already know how a graphical user interface can make a computer a whole lot less agonizing to use — provided you know your way around.

This part stands proudly and nonchalantly on Square One, ready to show you the ropes. It takes you through the basic KDE operations, shows you what does what on the desktop, and gets you to managing windows and files with the best of 'em. It's amazing how much more sense it all makes when you've got the basics down. But you knew that.

Chapter 1

Getting Your Hands Dirty

· ·

In This Chapter

▶ Defining KDE

▶ Understanding basic skills: window functions, KDE mouse tricks, and more

▶ Starting KDE

▶ Touring the desktop

▶ Getting to know the icons

▶ Hanging out at the (task) bar

▶ I have *how many* desktops?

▶ Exiting KDE

· ·

*I*f you live in a big city, you probably see tour buses once in a while. The people on these buses know that one of the best ways to get to know a place is to take a quick tour. On that tour, they see the most important aspects of the new city, and learn a bit about getting around. Later, if the tourists want to revisit or explore an area they saw from the bus's window, they have a pretty good idea of where to go and what to do.

This chapter is your KDE tour bus. We start with a brief introduction to KDE — what it is and what it does — and then take a spin through the basic functions you need in order to get the most from KDE. You tour the panel, taskbar, and icons, as well as practice getting into and out of KDE. After you're done with this chapter, you'll be able to get around your desktop with no problem, and you'll be set for the more complicated stuff that you discover in the rest of the book.

Try to read this chapter in front of your computer. You get the hang of KDE faster if you can look up from the page and see what we're talking about. The pictures in the chapter are helpful, but you can figure out more if you click along with us.

For those of you new to Linux and other UNIX-based operating systems, we recommend that you get a good book about your operating system. We provide enough Linux information to make using KDE simple, but Linux itself is outside the scope of this book. If you're used to Windows or Macintosh systems, but you just bought a Linux CD and installed a new operating system that uses KDE as its basic desktop, you may be looking for more specific information about your OS. In this book, we focus mostly on KDE. Sometimes we talk about the operating system underneath KDE, but only as it relates to the desktop environment. Two books that serve as a good starting point are *UNIX For Dummies,* 4th Edition by John Levine and Margaret Levine Young, and *Linux For Dummies,* 2nd Edition by Jon "maddog" Hall, both published by IDG Books Worldwide, Inc.

If you're familiar with Linux, but you've never used a graphical interface (or you're just new to KDE), there's helpful information here as well.

Ladies and Gentlemen: KDE!

Okay, so you're ready to go. You've installed a UNIX-based operating system on your computer, and you're ready to jump into the wonderful world of open source software. But . . . hey! This is all command-line stuff. Didn't the computing world get rid of command lines back in the ancient DOS ages?

Well, sort of. But remember, UNIX-based operating systems are the heart and soul of geek culture. To hardcore tech-types, you have no reason to point and click at anything — the command line was even good enough for Bill Gates once upon a time, and it still works just fine, so why change it?

But *you* are not necessarily a geek. You're interested in the speed and power of open source software, sure, but not if the software is going to be harder to use and less easy to understand than what you used before. You want the combination of power and simplicity. KDE, my friend, is for you. KDE is a *graphical user interface,* or GUI (pronounced gooey, just like caramel clusters). So are Windows and the Macintosh operating system. If you've used either Windows or the Mac OS in the last five or ten years — and who hasn't, really? — you're a GUI pro. Different kinds of GUIs work with the X Window System, and you've chosen KDE, which is one of the most reliable and fully-featured of the Linux GUIs available right now.

KDE is one of three components that puts that friendly graphical look on top of the power of Linux or other UNIX-based operating systems.

- ✔ Linux is the first component, because it's the operating system that makes the computer run.
- ✔ KDE is the final component, because it's the specific GUI that you've chosen.

✔ The middle component is something called the *X Window System.*

The X Window System, which is often just called X, is a set of programs that work with your operating system to translate UNIX commands into graphic images.

X is incredibly complicated and not the sort of thing that you will need to mess with, probably ever. X is important to know about, though, if only to sound incredibly intelligent and thoroughly geeky at cocktail parties.

Before we jump into action-packed touring, here's what KDE is and is not:

✔ KDE is the *interface* between you and the computer. After you click an icon on the desktop, KDE sends a certain command to the operating system and the computer responds. You can use KDE to change the way your monitor displays information, and you can use various KDE tools to make your computer do what you want.

✔ KDE isn't an operating system. You don't have to use special KDE versions of your favorite programs, and KDE doesn't change anything about the way your system runs. And, even though you can find desktop themes that make it look as if you're running a Mac or a Windows 98 machine, you're still running Linux or another UNIX-based operating system. KDE just puts a friendlier face on it.

KDE stands for the K Desktop Environment. Really. The K doesn't mean anything in particular.

Who's in charge of KDE?

KDE exists through the volunteer labor of hundreds of computer programmers around the world, who use the Internet to swap ideas and code that go into the program. KDE is an *open source* program, which means that the guts of the program are freely available for anyone to work with. (So is Linux.) One of the benefits of using open source software is that the software is subjected to tons of testing by actual users, not just by people paid to test the software — so, if you find a bug or you have a great idea for a future version of the software, you can send in your input. For those of you who have the sneaking idea that "free" doesn't always equal "good," you can rest assured. KDE has even caught the eye of Ziff-Davis, a major computer magazine publisher, who named KDE the "Innovation of the Year 1998/1999" in the software category. You want to check in on www.kde.org regularly for news updates, new versions, and nifty programs to add to your computer.

Basic Skills: What You Already Know

Before you get started with a tour through KDE, we need to quickly mention basic computer skills. We're assuming that you've used a mouse and that you've used some sort of windowed desktop environment before. Here's a quick list of basic mouse moves that we assume you already know:

- ✔ Moving the mouse on its mousepad moves the mouse pointer on your monitor screen.

  In KDE, the mouse pointer is a large X, rather than the Mac or Windows arrow.

- ✔ Clicking the left mouse button once *selects* whatever item is underneath the mouse pointer on the screen. The selected file or program hasn't opened yet, but it's next on deck. For example, you can select an icon, a filename, or an option in a menu.

- ✔ *Double-clicking*, or clicking the left mouse button two times quickly, *chooses* the item under the mouse pointer. When you choose an icon by double-clicking it, you're telling the computer to open this program right away. If you double-click a filename, the computer knows that you want to open the file within the correct program, and launches the program as well.

- ✔ Clicking the right mouse button once usually brings up a hidden menu with additional options. For example, if you *right-click* the plain KDE desktop, a hidden menu pops up with options including Logout, Help, Screenlock, and various ways to arrange open windows.

- ✔ Clicking a selected item once, holding the left mouse button down, and moving the mouse across the pad, *drags* the selected item across the screen. Releasing the left mouse button *drops* the item in its new location. You can *drag and drop* icons, filenames, or almost anything you can select by clicking or highlighting.

- ✔ Clicking the left mouse button and holding the button down, and then moving the mouse pointer across a certain portion of text, *highlights* the selected text. If you've highlighted the wrong text, just click the left mouse button outside the highlighted area to *deselect* it.

- ✔ Highlighting text allows you to do various things to the highlighted block of text. You can *cut* the text, thus removing the entire block from the document. Or, you can *copy* the text, leaving the block in place, but making a copy that you can place elsewhere. You can also *paste* the text into a new location after you either copy or cut it.

If you use a different kind of *pointing device* with your computer, such as a trackball or an input tablet, you need to know how to do all these basic mouse moves with your specific device. Most people a use mouse, so we use mouse-specific terminology throughout the book.

And, here's the information about desktops and windows we assume you know:

✔ The colored background of the screen is the *desktop*. Like a regular desk's top that you have in your office or at home, you can pile file folders and documents on top of it. Also, like a regular desk's top, it can become a terrible mess. Graphical interfaces use the desktop concept to make it easier for you to remember how the computer's organizational system works, because you automatically associate your computer desktop with your ordinary desk and how it works (or, at least, how it's supposed to work).

✔ After you open a program or a document, it appears within a *window* on the screen. The window is smaller than the entire screen, and can be resized. (For those burning with desire to resize windows, check out Chapter 3 — working with windows is slightly different in KDE than in other operating systems, but not much.)

✔ A *program window* contains a program that you've started. This program can be a calculator, a spreadsheet, your e-mail, or a horrendous brain-eating program like solitaire. You can have multiple program windows open at the same time.

✔ A *document window* contains a file that you've created in a certain program. The most common example is a text document that you've created in a word-processing program. You can also have multiple document windows open at the same time.

✔ You can have more than one window open at a time. (This feature is what makes windowed desktop environments so much better than command-line interfaces.) The windows just pile up on the screen as you open them, overlapping, and sometimes hiding each other.

✔ The window on the very top has the *focus*, which means that it's the *active window*. You can tell the window has the focus because its *titlebar* (that line along the top of the window with the name of the program or document) is highlighted. If you want a different window to have the focus, click its titlebar. The window comes to the front and assumes the focus.

KDE has a couple of mouse tricks that make basic window management a bit faster, as well. Many items on the desktop, including the desktop itself, have *context menus* that you can access by clicking the right mouse button if the mouse cursor is over the item. The options on these menus change from item to item, which makes them *context-sensitive*.

Start It Up

Now you can get started with your whirlwind tour through KDE.

We're assuming that you've already located and installed KDE on your system, or that it was pre-installed when you arrived at the machine; if you haven't, jump to Appendix A to find out where to get KDE and information on installing it. As soon as you've got KDE set up, come back and start here.

Be sure that you use KDE as a *normal user* on your system. When you installed Linux, you should have created both user accounts and a special super-user account called *root*. Don't log in as root just to play with KDE — save root for when it's needed. The root account is the system administration account, and it has the authority to change everything about the operating system — even the basic processes that make the machine work. If you work with KDE in your user account, you can't break anything critical. One of the great features of Linux and other UNIX-based operating systems is that each user has a separate account with dedicated disk space to work in, and those user spaces are separate from the programs that really run the computer. If you're working in a user account, you really have to try hard to do anything that permanently harms the computer. If you're working as root, you can cause damage a lot more easily.

Your machine probably is turned on and waiting patiently for you at the login prompt. If not, go ahead and boot up now.

1. **Log into your machine using your user account name and password.**

   Depending on the Linux distribution you chose while installing, or if you've already installed and configured KDE, you may see a *graphical login* instead of a shell login prompt. A graphical login is a more pleasing welcome from your computer than the white-on-black of a shell prompt. If you'd like to set up a graphical login for your system, we explain the procedure in Chapter 14. Log into a computer with a graphical login by typing your user account name and password, and skip ahead to the "Touring the Desktop" section.

   If you haven't yet configured your system to use KDE as your default GUI, refer to Appendix A for more information on the usekde script. This script copies some basic files, which KDE needs in order to run properly, into your home directory.

2. **After you log in at the shell prompt, type** startx.

   You use this command every time you want to open KDE. The startx command actually starts up the X Window System, but after you ran the usekde script, you set X to run KDE as your default desktop environment. You can actually configure X to run KDE automatically, every single time you boot up the computer by changing a few lines of code deep in the guts of Linux. See Chapter 13 for a down and dirty discussion of *run-level,* or how your computer knows which programs to run first.

A bunch of text scrolls up the screen, and then everything goes dark, (well, goes gray, but that doesn't sound quite as dramatic). How long the screen *stays* dark depends on how much memory you've got installed in the computer. (Computer graphics, like employees, are easily cajoled into working faster and better if you throw money at them.)

3. **Wait for the KDE desktop to appear, as shown in Figure 1-1.**

If something went wrong in your KDE setup, or if you haven't run the `usekde` script yet to tell the X Window System that you want KDE as your default desktop environment, you may get a surprise after typing `startx`. Instead of KDE, you may get another window manager, such as Fvwm. If this happens, just exit out of the graphical environment (try right-clicking on the desktop — an Exit or Logout command is often in the context menu). Then go back to Appendix A and reconfigure KDE.

Icons   Taskbar

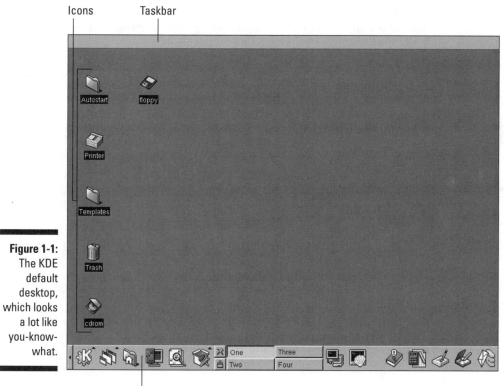

Figure 1-1:
The KDE
default
desktop,
which looks
a lot like
you-know-
what.

Panel

Touring the Desktop

The first time you run KDE, it appears with a basic desktop configuration (refer to Figure 1-1). (And yes, it sure does look a heck of a lot like Windows 95, doesn't it?)

If you don't like the default look, don't worry. Chapters 6 and 7 are all about desktop design, theme management, and doing heavy-duty cosmetic surgery on your desktop. For now, though, work with the default KDE desktop.

That gray horizontal bar running along the bottom of the screen is the *panel.* Use the buttons on the panel to start programs, which find files, launch applications, or control KDE itself. You will get to know the panel very well, because it's the central nervous system of KDE. Read Chapter 5 for more information about the panel and how to customize it.

KDE also puts some icons along the left side of your desktop. These icons enable you to run some common *utility programs,* or little programs that do important tasks behind the scenes. You can use the icons to create new files, remove old ones you don't want any more, print, or move files between CD-ROMs, diskettes, and your hard drive. See the "What Are All These Icons For?" section of this chapter for a description of each icon and its basic function.

Along the top of the screen, you see the *taskbar.* If you've used Windows 95 or Windows 98, you're already familiar with taskbars. We discuss the KDE taskbar in the "Hanging Out at the (Task) Bar" section of this chapter. Basically, you can use the taskbar to manage various applications and windows that you have open at the same time.

All of these facets are customizable. You can move them to different places on the screen, collapse them so you don't have to see them, or line them up neatly. Chapters 5, 6, and 7 contain a lot of information and ideas to help you tailor KDE to your own tastes.

One other feature that we should mention at this point is KFM, the KDE File Manager. KFM works like Windows Explorer or the Mac OS Finder. KFM is a graphical representation of the computer's file system, and it shows all the files in your *home directory,* the directory associated with your user account. Like Explorer or Finder, KFM shows your directory as a collection of folders and files. Think of KFM as an electronic file cabinet, because that's the way it was designed to work. You can drag files from one folder to another, or open windows that show the contents of various folders.

What Are All These Icons For?

Take a closer look at the desktop. Along the left side, you see six icons (refer back to Figure 1-1). These icons are super-duper shortcuts to some frequently used commands, and using them well can really speed up your desktop management skills (one of those fancy terms that really means "keeping your desk clean").

You can also create your own icons for programs that you use frequently by clicking the Template icon. Creating your own icons eliminates some of the searching that you have to do if you start programs from the KDE menu.

 Double-clicking the Autostart icon pops open a window where you can put links to programs on your hard drive. KDE makes sure that, after you start KDE, all the programs linked to the Autostart folder start automatically.

You need to remember two important aspects about Autostart, though.

✔ If you're running a Linux system, and you're the only user, you simply may not restart KDE very frequently.

UNIX-based computers have amazing *uptimes* compared to Windows computers. It's not unusual for a machine running Linux to go for a month or two without needing to be restarted. So, if you put programs here that you need every day, you're probably going to need to open them manually anyway. (If you don't live alone, or you have multiple users on this machine, you log out of KDE every time you end a session, so that Autostart is more helpful for you. Logging out is a good habit anyway — you never know when your cat is going to learn to type and send spam out under your e-mail address.)

✔ You don't have to link every single program to Autostart.

We've heard of people who set up Autostart that way. Every time they launch KDE, the poor machine spends time just opening programs . . . the word processor, the calendar, the accounting program, the graphics program, all the utility programs, the database, all the games, and so forth. You can always open programs just by finding them in the panel and clicking, so that you really don't need to add much to Autostart — maybe Netscape and your calendar, if those are the two programs you always open after you start a new session anyway.

 Double-clicking the Printer icon opens the printer configuration screen. On that screen, you can set up your printer for various kinds of paper, the direction you want text to print, and other basic printer information. Despite its name, the Printer icon doesn't actually send your files to be printed. Commands such as that are usually sent from inside a particular program. For example, if you're working on a letter or report, you tell the computer to print it by issuing the word processor's print command.

If you want to create new desktop icons to speed up the process of opening your favorite programs, you'll love the Template icon. Clicking the Template icon opens a window that contains a bunch of sample files for different kinds of desktop icons. You can use these samples to create new desktop icons that look and act like the sample files, and then edit the new icons by right-clicking on them and using the context menus.

 Here's a basic one. Trash can equals garbage, right? Yep! KDE puts a Trash icon on your desktop so that you have a convenient place to put files you want to delete. Just like a Macintosh Trashcan or a Windows Recycle Bin, the KDE trash icon provides a convenient link to a folder that holds files until you delete them permanently. You can drag file icons from open windows and drop them on the trash icon, or you can double-click the trash icon to open the Trash folder window and drag files between any open window and the Trash window. Files will remain in the Trash folder until you empty it. See Chapter 4 for more information on deleting files.

 Linux handles deleted files differently than Mac or Windows. You can use a special utility program to recover deleted files from Mac or Windows machines, even after you've emptied the Trash can or the Recycle Bin. This is *not* true for Linux and other UNIX-based systems! As soon as you empty the KDE trash folder, those files are permanently erased from your hard drive, and you have no way to get them back. If you're not sure you really want to toss something, put a copy on a diskette. You can always clean the diskette later.

 The final two icons work only if you are logged in as *root*. Yes, we told you to use this chapter in your regular user account and not as root. However, the Linux default settings allow only the root account to *mount* CD-ROM or floppy disk drives.

Mounting is a UNIX term that means making the file system on a disk available to the whole system. Unlike Windows or Mac, you can't just shove a disk into the floppy drive and use it in Linux. You need to mount the floppy drive first.

 If you want to change the default settings so that regular user accounts can mount drives, go to Chapter 13, where mounting file systems is discussed in excruciatingly correct detail. Changing your default setting will save you some time if you use lots of CDs or floppies in your user account.

 Double-click the CD icon to mount the CD-ROM drive. If you're not logged in as root, an error message pops up telling you to go away until you're root.

Like the CD icon, the Diskette icon lets you mount the 3.5" floppy disk drive. Remember, if you're not root, KDE won't let you do this.

Getting to Know the Panel

Some of the greatest books written for kids feature old houses with secret panels everywhere, so that the reader can imagine hiding behind the wall or sneaking through the house without anyone knowing. Unfortunately, the KDE panel isn't a way to creep through your computer without being noticed, but the panel is sure a handy way to run programs and get KDE set up. If you want more information about the panel than this brief introduction contains, refer to Chapter 5.

The panel, shown in Figure 1-2, is the heart of KDE. You can use the panel to launch just about any program that you have loaded on your computer, and you can customize it as much as you want. The panel is that long gray bar that runs along the bottom of the desktop. If you don't like the panel there, you can move it. Remember, you can easily change things in KDE.

Figure 1-2:
A closer
look at the
panel.

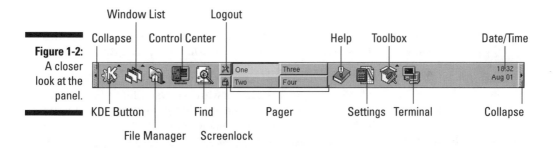

If you read this chapter and wonder why your panel doesn't have all these buttons, check to see that you have fully extended the panel. If your monitor is too small for the default KDE desktop size, KDE automatically hides some panel icons under others without telling you.

To *collapse* the panel, look for narrow textured bars with arrowheads. If you click one of these bars, the panel disappears behind it. Click the bar again to bring the panel back. You've just collapsed your panel, which means that you've hidden it temporarily. Hiding your panel is really useful if the panel just keeps getting in your way and you're about ready to scream. Collapse the panel, do your work, and bring it back after you're done.

The *KDE logo icon* is right next to the left-hand textured bar. If you click this button, KDE displays the main KDE menu, shown in Figure 1-3. The KDE menu works like the Start menu in Windows 95 or Windows 98, so the KDE menu may already be a familiar sight to you.

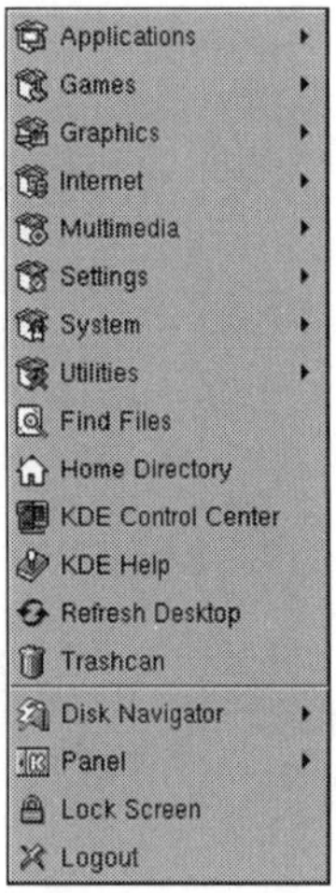

Figure 1-3:
The KDE
menu.

Throughout the book, we refer to the KDE menu as the first step in a series of actions. When you see the phrase "open the KDE menu," use this button to do so.

At the top of the KDE menu, you see items with arrows pointed to the right. The arrow means that item has a *submenu,* or additional choices that appear to the right of the KDE menu if you hold the mouse pointer over the arrowed item. Move your mouse pointer over one of the items with a submenu and take a look at what's there. Items without an arrow don't have submenus; if you hold your mouse pointer over a non-arrowed item, nothing happens. You need to click that item, which starts the named program. These items are usually programs that you use so frequently that you need one-click access instead of burrowing through a bunch of folders to find the right program.

If you forget what a particular desktop icon or command does, let your mouse tell you. Put the mouse pointer over the icon and just let it sit there for a moment. Don't click. A little box appears with the icon's label, which is usually enough of a reminder.

Move on and check out some of the other items in the menu. The KDE menu divides program items into convenient categories to make it easy for you to browse and find them.

The *Window List icon* has three windows on it. Click the icon to make the Window List appear on your screen. The Window List shows all the open windows on your screen, and makes it easier to manage a large number of open windows than trying to drag them around the screen so that you can see all the titlebars. To manage your open windows, click the icon to open the Window List, select the name of the window you want to work on from the list, and then click OK. The window you choose moves to the top of your pile of open windows.

 The *KFM icon* has a file folder and a tiny little house on it. This button opens *KFM,* or the KDE File Manager. KFM is a graphical directory of all the files in your *home directory.* KFM works like Windows Explorer in Windows 95 or the Mac OS Finder. In Linux, each user keeps personal files in an individual home directory, which is the part of the computer's landscape that's all yours. You can imagine white picket fences and climbing roses if you want, or barbed wire and "Do Not Trespass" signs. It's up to you.

To *customize* KDE to fit your needs perfectly, use the Control Center icon to open the Control Center. The Control Center handles all the changes to KDE's basic configuration, including functions such as moving the panel or changing the look of the desktop. See Part II for detailed coverage of the many options you find in the Control Center.

 The *Find Utility icon* is recognizable by the cute little pawprints. Find is a really useful button. Just pop Find open, type the name of the file or program you're looking for, and let Find, well, find it for you. Find is covered in more depth in Chapter 4.

The *Toolbox icon* contains links to a bunch of system utilities, which are described in more detail in Chapter 10. These system utilities are little programs that affect how your computer works. You don't have to use these, although you can do some pretty neat things inside the Toolbox.

 If you're running KDE on a machine that's part of a network, and you're not the network administrator, ask before you start fooling around in the Toolbox. Some networks are really picky, and changes to one machine can affect everyone's computer. Your network administrator will appreciate you asking.

Next to the Find Utility icon, you see two tiny buttons stacked on top of each other. The Logout button is the one on top. If you click this button, your KDE session ends, and you end up at a command-line prompt in your home directory. See the "So Long, Farewell: Exiting KDE" section of this chapter.

The button below the Logout button activates screenlock, which is a souped-up version of a screensaver. If you click the Screenlock button, your screensaver starts up right away. Unlike the regular screensaver, though, you have to type your screenlock password to get back to the desktop. See Chapter 10 for a discussion of screenlock and whether it's an option you need.

 The *Pager icon* is really a series of four buttons marked One, Two, Three, and (bet you can't guess it) Four. The Pager controls your *virtual desktops.* Usually, the One button is pressed down, because the One desktop is the basic one everyone uses. You read about virtual desktops in the "I Have *How Many* Desktops?" section of this chapter, and we discuss multiple desktops in more detail in Chapter 3.

 You click the *Terminal icon* if, for any reason, you need to issue commands directly to the operating system. A *terminal window* appears, which is a window that contains a shell prompt. Terminal windows emulate plain old character-based interfaces; you can use them to work directly with Linux, or you can use them to run programs that are purely character-based. Chapter 12 includes some tips about running text-based programs and using terminal windows. You generally won't use this icon much, because KDE makes it easy to handle operating system commands through other interfaces. However, knowing this button is there if you need it is good.

 Clicking the *Online Help icon* opens the KDE help browser, which includes answers to hundreds of common problems and topics. If you run into a problem or have a burning question, click this icon to activate the help browser, and use the browser links to get to the answer you need. You should know, though, that the KDE online help does not allow you to search or use a comprehensive index to the help files. You may have to poke around a bit before you find the answer you're searching for. Chapter 2 discusses the online help system in more detail.

The very last feature you see on the panel is the current date and time. KDE gets this information from your system settings, so if your system's confused about the date or time, the panel will be confused, too. We discuss setting the clock in Chapter 5.

Hanging Out at the (Task) Bar

In the default desktop shown in Figure 1-1, the KDE taskbar appears at the top of the screen. If you've ever seen or used Windows 95 or Windows 98, you've seen a similar tool. The taskbar allows you to see, with a quick glance, what programs are currently running on your computer. The taskbar does this by displaying a button for each open application. Take a look at Figure 1-4 to see the taskbar in action. Because you have a button for each open program, you can close all your windows, or layer them directly on top of each other, without losing track of what's running.

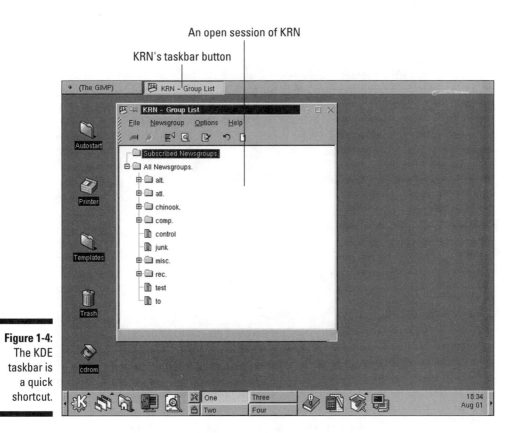

An open session of KRN

KRN's taskbar button

Figure 1-4:
The KDE
taskbar is
a quick
shortcut.

Whenever you start an application or open a new window, KDE places a cor-responding button on the taskbar. That new button carries a small icon and the application's name. Refer to Figure 1-4 to see the open KRN's button on the taskbar. If you want to bring that window to the top of the windows on the desktop, click the corresponding button in the taskbar. The window magi-cally appears.

One of the most helpful uses of the taskbar is for people who like to have multiple applications running, but only one window visible at a time: Click the small dot in the window's titlebar to close all the windows (except the one you want to work in.) The window disappears from the desktop, leaving only its button in the taskbar to remind you that it exists. Figure 1-5 shows a desktop with three running programs, all visible only in the taskbar. If you need a program again, just click the correct button in the taskbar to reopen it. You can get a reminder of what you've got running just by looking at the taskbar.

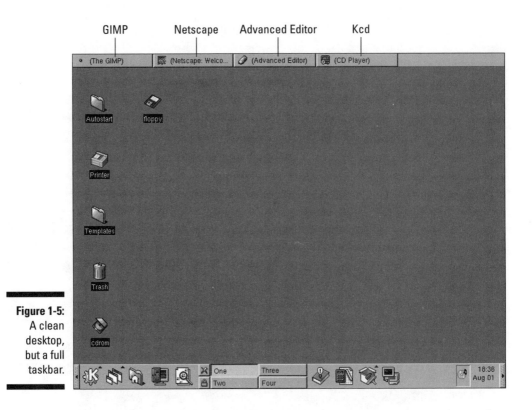

Figure 1-5:
A clean
desktop,
but a full
taskbar.

You can also control the various applications you're running by using the taskbar, without necessarily having to open each window. Just right-click the corresponding taskbar button. A small menu of options appears, with which you can control the behavior of the corresponding window or program. All these options are described more fully in Chapter 3.

- ✔ **Maximize** returns the program to the desktop, expanded to its fullest possible size.

- ✔ **DeIconify** returns the program to the desktop, if you had minimized the program or chosen the Iconify command to close the window, just leaving the button in the taskbar.

- ✔ **Sticky** makes the program's window appear on all your virtual desktops, not just one.

- ✔ **Onto Current Desktop** moves a program from one virtual desktop to another.

- ✔ **Iconify Other Windows** minimizes all other open windows, leaving this program as the only open window.

- ✔ **Close,** as you probably guessed, closes the program window and exits the program.

As with almost everything else in KDE, you can customize and move the taskbar to make it meet your needs. See Chapter 5 for more help on doing this.

I Have How Many Desktops?

Now that you've got the KDE desktop under control, both in concept and in practice, allow us to complicate things by talking about *virtual desktops*. In one sense, the desktop on your screen is already virtual; after all, it's not a real desk, it just looks like one. In Linux-speak, though, a virtual desktop is a whole new piece of electronic office furniture.

Imagine that your office is large enough to contain three more desks, giving you four desktops for your work. Now, imagine those additional desks inside your computer — all of a sudden, you have new clean desktops to manage your programs and documents. By default, KDE gives you four virtual desktops. If you need more, you can configure up to eight . . . and what are you doing that needs more than eight desktops, anyway?

Why on earth would you want to do this? Well, sometimes keeping various kinds of windows on separate desktops is useful. Separate desktops can help you stay organized and keep one desktop from getting so cluttered that you can't do anything. For example, say you have a word-processing program window open on desktop 1, and you really need to look something up on the Web to add to your document. Running Netscape on the same desktop as the word-processing program may be too much of a distraction . . . admit it, haven't you gotten sucked into surfing the Web when you should be working? So, you switch to a new desktop. You start Netscape on that separate desktop, where it will be the only program running, look up the item you need, and head back to the first desktop and your document.

"Okay," we hear you say, "but where the heck *are* these desktops? I only see one when I look at the screen." Well, look back at the Pager icon in the panel. See how the pager has four buttons in a block? Each of those buttons represents a desktop. You can tell which one you're on by which button is depressed, or shaded around the edges. To switch between virtual desktops, press the Pager buttons.

If the concept's still a bit fuzzy, take a minute to play with it. You can also read Chapter 2, which has a lot more information about desktops in general, including virtual desktops. Here's a little exercise to work with using the KNote utility, which is included in the default KDE installation.

1. **Click the Two button in the Pager icon.**

   Doesn't look like much happened, does it? The desktop still looks the same, and everything's identical except that the Two button is depressed instead of the One button. Something really did happen, though. You're looking at desktop 2 instead of desktop 1, and they just happen to be exactly the same.

2. **From the KDE menu, choose Utilities⇨KNotes.**

   A small yellow window labeled `knote 1` appears, as shown in Figure 1-6. This window is an electronic version of those yellow sticky notes we all have plastered over our desks, phones, books, walls, and any other surface they'll stick to.

3. **Click inside the note and type "Hi, I'm Desktop Two."**

4. **Click the One button in the Pager icon.**

   The note disappears, because you're back on desktop 1. The note still exists — just not here.

5. **Click the Window List icon on the panel.**

   A list of all your desktops appears. See there, under Desktop 2? It says "Note: knote 1."

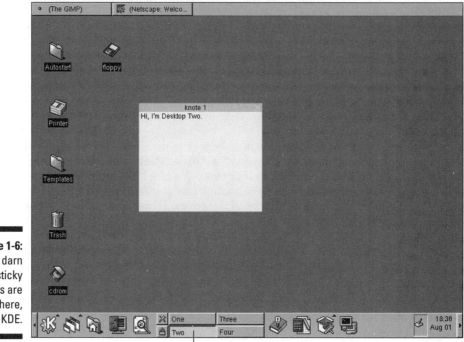

Figure 1-6:
Those darn sticky notes are everywhere, even in KDE.

Desktop Two's Pager button pressed down.

6. **Click the Two button in the Pager.**

   The note is there, just where you left it. You can get rid of it, if you like, by clicking the X button in the title bar.

7. **Click the One button in the Pager icon to return to desktop 1.**

The taskbar contains items for all the programs you have open, regardless of which desktop they're on. If you click the item for a program that's on a different desktop, the taskbar automatically takes you to that desktop. Using the taskbar is a quick and easy way to shift between desktops without having to cycle through them with the Pager buttons.

So Long, Farewell: Exiting KDE

After you're done with this session of KDE fun, you need to exit out of the desktop environment to get back to a shell prompt so that you can log out of the machine, or back to a graphical login if you've set one up.

1. **Log out of KDE using one of the following options:**

   - **Click the Logout button on the panel.**

   - **Click the K button on the panel and choose Logout from the KDE menu that appears.**

   - **Right-click the desktop and then choose Logout from the pop-up menu that appears.**

   KDE displays the Session prepared for logout dialog box. This dialog box lists the programs that are running and gives you the opportunity to abort the logout, return to those programs and save your work.

2. **Click Logout to confirm that you want to close KDE.**

   KDE disappears from your screen and returns you to the plain text environment of the Linux shell prompt.

Don't forget to log out of your shell account after you exit KDE! Leaving KDE doesn't mean that you've logged out. Leaving yourself logged in is an invitation to cruel hijinks and mischievous pranks that can embarrass you or worse. *Log out, log out, log out!*

Chapter 2

Getting Around the Desktop

- -

In This Chapter

▶ Running your programs in KDE

▶ Using the icons on your KDE desktop

▶ Working with the KDE equivalent of a Start menu

▶ Using the Window List to find the right window

▶ Helping yourself to KDE Help

- -

*I*n the physical world, your office desk is the work surface where you spread out the projects you're working on. The KDE desktop serves a similar purpose — it's the work surface where you spread out the tools and documents you work with on your computer. Over the years, you've no doubt discovered the appropriate ways to use the tools available on your office desk. (You've probably discovered a few ways to use some of the things on your desk as fun distractions as well.) In this chapter, you discover how to use the tools you find on the KDE desktop.

Launching Applications

KDE provides a convenient working environment for your Linux computer by furnishing a graphical user interface for the operating system. But for desktop workstations (as opposed to servers), it's the application software, not the operating system, that really does the day-to-day work you use a computer for. For example, word-processing programs enable you to create letters, reports, proposals, and other documents; spreadsheets enable you to create budgets and statistical analysis and do other number-crunching projects; database programs keep track of everything from client lists to product inventories; Web browsers and e-mail programs enable you to access information and communicate on the Internet. Therefore, one of the most important functions of KDE is to provide convenient ways to launch the application programs you use every day.

KDE does, indeed, make launching applications easy. The primary KDE program launch pad is the KDE menu, accessible by clicking the panel button with the KDE logo on it. But choosing a program from the menu isn't the only way to launch applications in KDE. In fact, you can use several techniques. Here's a summary of the techniques:

- ✓ Choose a program from the KDE menu. (We explain this technique in detail in this section.)
- ✓ Double-click the program's desktop icon. (Program icons are covered in the next section of this chapter.)
- ✓ Click the program's panel button. (For more information, just keep reading.)
- ✓ Double-click an icon for a program file or a document file in a KFM window. (See Chapter 4 for information on launching programs and opening document files with the KDE file manager, KFM.)
- ✓ Execute a command from the KDE desktop. (Read on to find out how.)
- ✓ Access the Linux command line from a terminal window and type the commands to start the program. (See Chapter 12 for the details on accessing the Linux command line from a terminal window.)

Running programs from the KDE menu

One of the prominent features of the KDE desktop panel is a button that you can click to display a menu of the applications available to run in KDE. It works very much like the Windows 95 or 98 Start button, complete with the cascading submenus that are so familiar to Windows users. The KDE menu enables you to conveniently start a program with just a couple of mouse clicks.

The KDE panel button with the KDE logo on it goes by a variety of names, such as *K* button, *KDE* button, and *KDE logo* button; but we just call it the *KDE Menu* button because that's what appears when you click it. The menu itself is sometimes referred to as the *KDE application starter menu,* but *KDE menu* seems more succinct, so we use that term in this book.

Before you start criticizing the KDE menu as being too Windows-like, consider how simple and efficient it is at organizing a large assortment of programs and making them easily accessible. After all, why not use the successful features of other user interfaces — especially when it makes learning KDE easier for multitudes who have previously used Windows. And don't forget that KDE offers several other ways to launch programs, so you don't have to use the KDE menu if you don't want to.

To launch a program using the KDE menu, follow these simple steps:

1. **Click the KDE Menu button in the panel.**

   The KDE Menu button is the one with the KDE logo (a big K and a gear) on it. The button is normally located at the left end of the panel. When you click the KDE Menu button, the KDE application starter menu appears.

2. **Point to a menu item (such as Applications) with a right-facing arrow.**

   Pointing means to move the mouse pointer over the menu item and let it rest there for a second or so. A cascading submenu appears, as shown in Figure 2-1.

3. **Click the desired program in the submenu.**

   KDE closes the menu and launches the selected program. Normally, the program appears in its own window on your desktop although some utilities might show up in the panel or other locations. Depending on the speed of your system and the size of the selected program, the program may appear immediately or it may take nearly a minute to show up on your desktop.

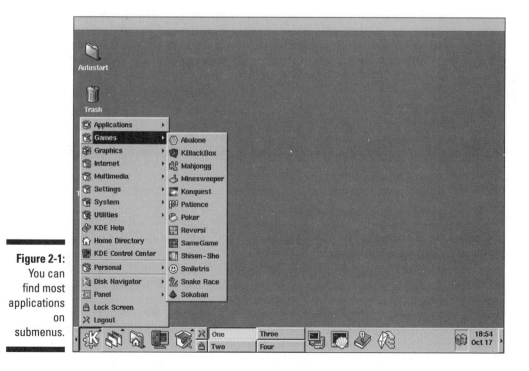

Figure 2-1:
You can
find most
applications
on
submenus.

This technique works for all the standard KDE utilities, games, and other applications listed on the default KDE menu. It also works for applications that you add to the KDE menu manually or with the Appfinder utility (more on customizing the KDE menu in Chapter 5). In some cases, choosing an item from the KDE menu or one of its submenus doesn't really launch a true application, but rather opens a KDE configuration dialog box, issues a system command, or does something of that sort instead.

A few items on the KDE menu don't have arrows indicating the presence of submenus. Examples on the default KDE menu include KDE Help, Home Directory, Lock Screen, and Logout. Clicking one of these menu items invokes an action immediately instead of opening a submenu.

Launching a program with a desktop icon

In your physical office, you probably keep most of your tools and materials stored in your desk drawers, where they remain out of sight but are relatively easy to access when you need them. But the stuff you use the most is sitting out on your desktop where it's instantly available.

KDE enables you to organize your computer desktop in much the same way. Most of your programs are accessible from the KDE menu — out of sight but accessible with about three mouse movements (click the KDE Menu button, point to expand the appropriate submenu, and then click a menu item to launch the program). However, for the programs you use the most, you can create desktop icons that sit in full view on your computer desktop and are available with a single click of your mouse.

Desktop icons are simply links to files and resources stored elsewhere. The icon can link to a program file, a shell script, a directory, a document file, an Internet URL, or a file system device. If the link is to a document file and KDE knows what application is associated with the document type, it can automatically launch the appropriate program to open the file.

Using a desktop icon to launch a program is simplicity itself; there's only one step involved:

1. **Click the desktop icon for the item you want to open.**

   KDE immediately takes the appropriate action to open the item associated with the desktop icon.

For example, the Trash icon on your desktop is a link to a special subfolder of your home directory where KDE temporarily stores files that you want to delete. Clicking the Trash icon launches the KFM file manager program and displays the contents of the Trash folder.

The default KDE desktop starts out with an assortment of desktop icons — mostly links to special-purpose folders (such as Autostart) and system devices (such as cdrom). However, you're not stuck with this meager selection of icons. You can create your own desktop icons for the programs and documents you use the most. We show you how in the "Working with Desktop Icons" section of this chapter.

Launching a program with a panel button

Icons on your desktop aren't the only way you can instantly access your applications in KDE. You can also use panel buttons to launch programs. In addition to the KDE Menu button and the other special buttons such as the Window List, Toolbox, and virtual desktop buttons, the KDE panel is home to an assortment of buttons for individual applications and utilities.

When you install KDE, it typically starts out with the panel that is populated with a set of program buttons for utilities such as KVT, Konsole, KHelp, KCalc, KNotes, KEdit, and KMail. Like so many other things in KDE, the selection of panel buttons is customizable. You can easily remove program buttons from the panel, add buttons for other applications, and move or rearrange the buttons on the panel. We show you how in Chapter 5.

Launching a program with a panel button couldn't be any simpler. You just click the button, and KDE instantly launches the associated application or utility. There are no menus to navigate or other selections to make — KDE just opens the program as fast as your system can access the related files.

There's a real advantage to launching programs from panel buttons as opposed to desktop icons. Desktop icons are often obscured behind the various windows that might be open on your desktop, whereas the panel usually remains visible on top of any open windows. Having the panel always visible makes panel buttons accessible without the need to first move or minimize (iconify) windows in order to uncover desktop icons. On the other hand, this advantage may not be as pronounced if you have your panel collapsed or configured to autohide (slip out of sight when it's not in use). If the panel isn't visible, you need an extra mouse action to bring the panel into view before you can click a panel button to launch your application. (Collapsing and expanding the panel is covered in Chapter 1, and setting the panel to Autohide is covered in Chapter 5.)

Instant access to typed commands

Sometimes the fastest way to launch a program is to just issue a typed command. This is especially true if you're a veteran Linux/UNIX command line user or if you need to launch an infrequently used program for which you haven't set up a KDE icon, button, or menu item. Of course, you could launch one of the KDE terminal emulation utilities (KVT or Konsole) and use it to interact with the operating system command line. (See Chapter 12 for more information on using the command line in a terminal window.)

Issuing commands in a terminal window works, but KDE offers a simpler alternative for issuing commands that you can type on a single line. Just follow these steps:

1. **Right-click the desktop and choose Execute Command from the pop-up menu that appears.**

   KDE opens the Command box as shown in Figure 2-2.

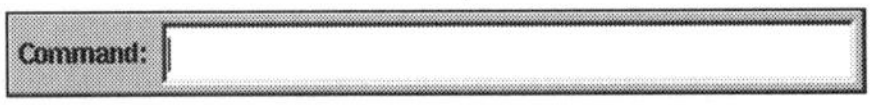

Figure 2-2:
Type a
command to
launch a
program.

Command: [   ]

2. **Type the command to launch your program and then press Enter.**

   KDE closes the Command box and passes the command to the operating system. Linux executes the command and launches your application. If you properly typed the command to launch a KDE or X Window program, the program window appears.

Be careful with commands you type in the Command box. Any command you enter is executed immediately and, unlike typing a command in a terminal window, you won't see any error messages or other warnings that your command generates. The results of mistyping a command to launch a program are usually harmless (it doesn't work and you have to try again), but using the Command box to enter system commands or to launch command-line programs may have unpredictable results.

Working with Desktop Icons

Desktop icons are those little symbols, such as folders and a trash can, that start out on the left side of the default KDE desktop. Chapter 1 identifies the desktop icons you find on the default KDE desktop. They include icons for the Autostart and Templates folders, the Trash folder, and the CD-ROM and Floppy drives. But, as Figure 2-3 shows, you're not stuck with that limited assortment of icons. Just as you have an assortment of tools and papers on your physical desk, you can have an assortment of desktop icons on your KDE desktop so the files, folders, and programs represented by those icons are always within easy reach.

When you click a desktop icon, the effect is the same as if you clicked the icon for the file or other resource represented by the icon — KDE launches the program and/or opens the file or folder. For example, if you click a desktop icon for a folder, KDE opens a KFM window and displays the contents of the linked folder. If you click an icon for a World Wide Web URL, KDE opens your Web browser (usually KFM), which then retrieves and displays the Web page found at the address recorded in the icon's link file. If you click a desktop icon for a text file, KDE launches your text editor and loads the text file for editing.

How does KDE know what program to use to open your file when you click a desktop icon for a text file or other file type? It identifies the file's MIME type by its extension and uses the application that is associated with that MIME type to open the file. See Chapter 4 for information about associating specific programs with file types.

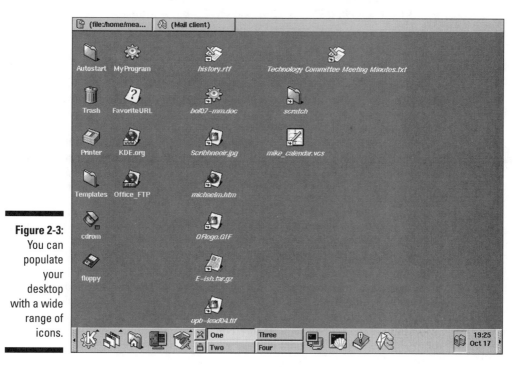

Figure 2-3:
You can populate your desktop with a wide range of icons.

You can create desktop icons for all sorts of files and system resources, including the following:

- ✔ **Files**: A link to any document or other file on your system. Clicking a file icon opens the file in the appropriate program.

- ✔ **Folders**: A link to a directory anywhere in the file system. Clicking a folder icon opens a KFM window displaying the contents of the folder. Of course, to use the link, the target directory must be part of a mounted file system and you must have the proper access permission.

- ✔ **File System Device**: A link to a mountable device or directory such as floppy disk, CD-ROM drive, hard drives, and file systems from other machines. Clicking a device icon opens a KFM window and displays the contents of the device — if the device is already mounted. Otherwise KDE attempts to mount the device first and displays an error message if you lack the proper permissions to mount the device.

- ✔ **FTP URL**: The Internet address for the directory on an FTP (File Transfer Protocol) server. Clicking an FTP icon launches your FTP program and attempts to access the FTP address.

- ✔ **Application**: A link to an executable program (including shell scripts). Clicking an application icon launches the program.

- ✔ **Internet Address URL**: The address for a generic Internet resource. Clicking an Internet Address icon launches the appropriate program and attempts to access the URL.

- ✔ **World Wide Web URL**: The Internet address for a Web page. Clicking a Web address icon launches your Web browser and loads the Web page.

The KDE desktop icons are actually graphic representations of link files stored in the Desktop subfolder of your home directory. The KDE link file specifies what icon to display and defines a link between the desktop icon and the file, program, or system resource the icon represents, but KDE doesn't actually store the target of the link (or even a copy of it) on your desktop.

Arranging icons

KDE starts out with the default desktop icons arranged in a neat column on the left side of your desktop. But you don't have to leave the icons there any more than you have to leave the items on your real-world desk arranged the way they were when you first walked into your new office. You can rearrange your desktop icons any time you want.

- ✔ To move an icon, just click the icon and hold the left mouse button down as you drag the icon to a new location. Release the mouse button to deposit the icon at its new home.

When you move an icon on your desktop, it may not stay exactly where you put it. KDE sets up an invisible grid on the desktop, and the icon automatically jumps to the nearest grid intersection when you move it. The grid helps keep icons from overlapping and makes it easy to maintain some semblance of order on your desktop. See Chapter 6 for information on adjusting the desktop grid setting.

✔ To have KDE automatically arrange your desktop icons for you, right-click the desktop and choose Arrange Icons from the pop-up menu that appears; then click Yes to confirm that you really want to rearrange your desktop icons. KDE arranges your icons into neat columns starting at the upper-left corner of the desktop.

You may get a bit of a surprise when you let KDE arrange your desktop icons for you: The columns of icons may start farther out from the edge of the desktop than you expect. KDE positions the icons to leave room along the edges of the desktop for the panel and taskbar; therefore, if you configured the KDE panel or taskbar to be positioned on the left side of the desktop, the icons will be displaced to the right, toward the center of the desktop, even if the panel and taskbar are hidden at the time you rearrange the icons.

Creating your own desktop icons

The desktop icons that appear on the default KDE desktop merely hint at what you can do with icons on your desktop. You can freely create, edit, and remove desktop icons to build a custom desktop environment that matches your own working style, complete with icons for the programs you use, the files you're working on, and the Web sites you visit daily.

Creating a new desktop icon

The technique you use to create a desktop icon varies somewhat depending on the kind of icon (or rather, on the kind of item the icon is linked to). Perhaps the simplest kind of desktop icon to create is a shortcut link to a file or folder. To create such an icon, follow these steps:

1. **Open a KFM window and navigate to the directory containing the file to which you want to create a link.**

   Make sure the file that you want to access with the desktop icon is displayed in the KFM window. (See Chapter 4 for information on using the KFM file manager utility.) The file can be a word-processing document, a spreadsheet file, a text file, or anything else you want. It can even be a folder. Also make sure that some portion of the KDE desktop is visible — don't maximize the KFM window or allow all the KDE desktop to be obscured by other open windows. Minimize, resize, or move windows as needed to have access to both the contents of the KFM window and the desktop.

2. **Click the file icon and drag it out of the KFM window while holding the mouse button down. Release the mouse button to drop the file icon on a blank portion of the desktop.**

   A pop-up menu appears, giving you the choice of Copy, Move, or Link.

3. **Choose Link.**

   KDE creates a desktop icon linked to the selected file. The icon displays a small arrow in the lower-left corner to indicate that it's a shortcut or link instead of the original file. The text label beneath the icon is a copy of the name of the file or folder to which the link points. Figure 2-4 shows a newly created desktop icon.

In addition to a simple link to a file or folder, you can create several other kinds of desktop icons, such as icons for Web pages and other Internet resources and icons for file system resources. The following steps describe the process for creating a desktop icon for a Web page URL:

1. **Right-click the desktop and choose New⇨World Wide Web URL from the pop-up menu that appears.**

   A dialog box appears as shown in Figure 2-5 prompting you for the name of the New World Wide Web URL. The default is `WWWUrl.kdelnk` — the default filename of the link file that makes the desktop icon work.

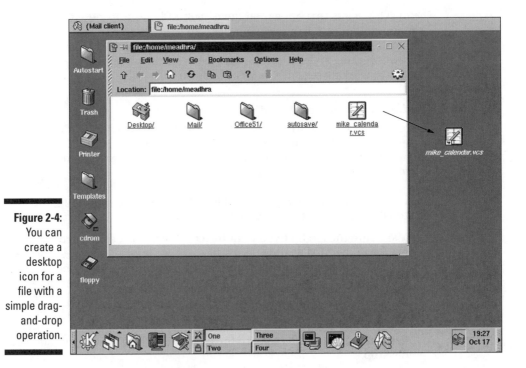

Figure 2-4: You can create a desktop icon for a file with a simple drag-and-drop operation.

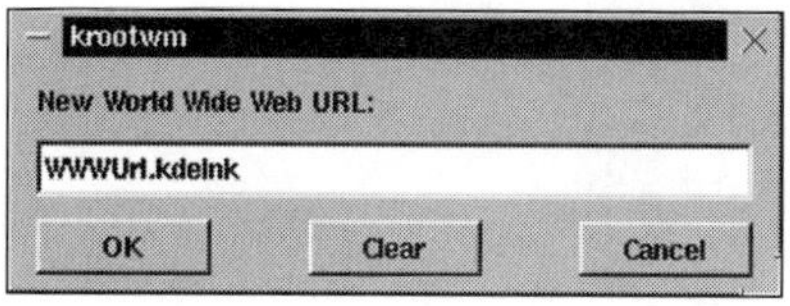

Figure 2-5:
Name your
new desk-
top icon.

krootwm ✕

New World Wide Web URL:

WWWUrl.kdelnk

| OK | Clear | Cancel |

2. Edit the filename and click OK.

You can change the WWWUrl portion of the filename to just about anything you want, but it's best to leave the .kdelnk portion of the filename
intact. KDE automatically strips off the .kdelnk extension and displays
the rest of the name as the label under the desktop icon. After you click
OK, the name dialog box disappears and KDE adds the new icon to your
desktop and opens a properties dialog box for the icon as shown in
Figure 2-6.

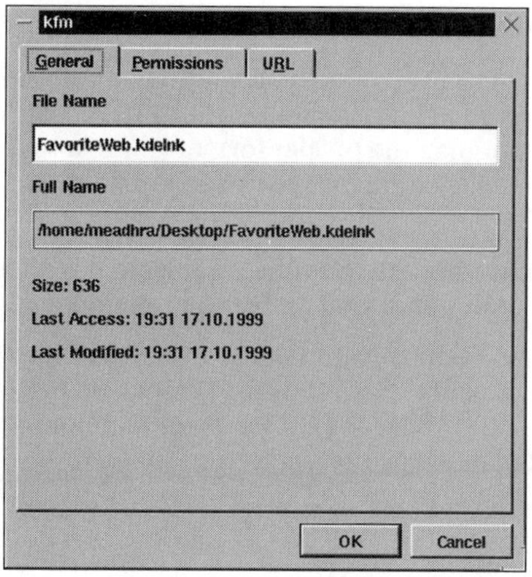

kfm ✕

| General | Permissions | URL |

File Name

FavoriteWeb.kdelnk

Full Name

/home/meadhra/Desktop/FavoriteWeb.kdelnk

Size: 636

Last Access: 19:31 17.10.1999

Figure 2-6:
Edit the
properties
of your new
desktop
icon.

Last Modified: 19:31 17.10.1999

| OK | Cancel |

3. Edit the settings on the General tab as needed.

You have another opportunity to change the name of the icon by editing
the contents of the File Name box.

4. Click the URL tab.

KDE displays the settings shown in Figure 2-7.

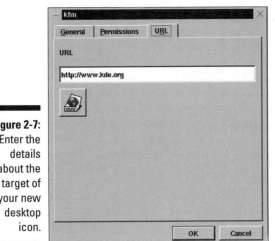

Figure 2-7:
Enter the
details
about the
target of
your new
desktop
icon.

5. **Type the Web page address in the URL text box.**

   Enter the full address of the Web page you want your Web browser to retrieve and load when you click the new desktop icon. Be sure to enter the address carefully and use the proper format (for example, `http://www.kde.org`), and not the common shortened version (such as `www.kde.org`).

6. **(Optional) Click the button with the icon on it, select a different icon from the Select Icon dialog box that appears, and click OK.**

   This step enables you to select an alternate symbol for KDE to display as the desktop icon. Pick a symbol from the many displayed in the Select Icon dialog box (see Figure 2-8) by clicking the icon you want and then clicking OK to close the Select Icon dialog box and return to the KFM dialog box where you were defining the properties of the desktop icon link.

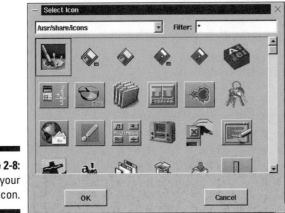

Figure 2-8:
Pick your
own icon.

7. **Click OK.**

KDE closes the properties dialog box and records the settings for the desktop icon. The desktop icon is ready to use. You can simply click the icon to begin loading the target Web page into your Web browser.

You can use essentially the same technique to create other kinds of desktop icons such as icons for file system devices, applications, and other Internet resources. Just select the appropriate icon type in place of the World Wide Web URL in Step 1. You can choose File System Device, FTP URL, Application, or Internet Address URL. Then, in Steps 4 and 5, select the corresponding tab in the properties dialog box and fill in the appropriate settings as prompted.

Naturally, the settings for a link to a file system device or an application are a little different from the settings for a Web page or other Internet URL, but the basic idea of defining a link is the same. In order to define an icon for a file system device, you need to be familiar with device addresses and mount points. And to define all the settings for an application, you need to know a little about MIME types and the files associated with the application, in addition to the name of application's executable file.

Editing a desktop icon

You can make changes to desktop icons any time you want. For example, you can select a different icon for display on the desktop. Simply right-click the icon you want to change and choose Properties from the pop-up menu that appears. A dialog box appears, where you can edit all the same settings you used to define the icon and its link in the first place. (See Steps 3 through 6 in the procedure for creating a desktop icon.) Edit the settings as needed and then click OK to close the dialog box and record your changes.

Removing desktop icons

If you have too many icons cluttering your desktop, it's easy to get rid of a few of them. To remove an icon from your desktop, just drag it onto the Trash icon. The icon disappears from the desktop and the link file is stored in the Trash folder until you delete it permanently by emptying the trash. To remove an icon permanently in one step, right-click the icon and choose Delete from the pop-up menu that appears, and then confirm the action by clicking Yes in the KFM Warning box that appears.

Removing a desktop icon only removes the icon and its link file — it doesn't affect the original file, folder, file system device, or URL referenced by the link.

Getting Around with the Window List

If you're like most people, your real world desk soon gets cluttered with books, folders, and papers for your various projects. Finding the item you want often takes a little shuffling to excavate it from a stack of other items.

Similarly, your KDE desktop can quickly get cluttered with numerous open windows that often obscure other windows. In addition, you might have minimized some windows so that they aren't visible on your desktop at all. Add the prospect of multiple virtual desktops that may be lurking out of sight, each populated with its own assortment of windows, and you have a situation that could make locating a particular window a challenge.

Fortunately, KDE provides a tool that greatly simplifies the job of finding any window on any of your KDE desktops. The Window List button in the panel gives you instant access to any window — it's a sort of index of all the open windows on your KDE system. To use the Window List, follow these steps:

1. **Click the Windows List button in the panel.**

   KDE displays a pop-up menu listing all the open windows, organized by desktop. (See Figure 2-9.)

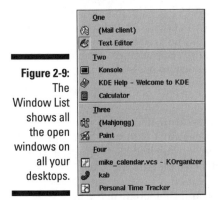

Figure 2-9:
The Window List shows all the open windows on all your desktops.

2. **Select a window name from the Window List menu.**

   KDE instantly brings that window to the foreground, switching desktops if necessary.

The Window List and the taskbar both perform similar functions. You can select an open window by clicking its button on the taskbar or by selecting the window name from the Window List menu.

The taskbar (described in Chapter 1) has the advantage of being visible on-screen all the time (if you choose to configure it that way instead of hiding it from view). As a result, you can select a window with the taskbar with a single click on the corresponding taskbar button. However, as the taskbar gets crowded with buttons for numerous windows, the button labels are often truncated due to lack of space, which can make it difficult to identify which button is linked to which window.

The Window List, on the other hand, provides a much more complete description of each window, even when the menu is populated with numerous windows. On a crowded desktop, the better descriptions shown in the Window List make identifying the window you want much easier and more than offset the extra click required to pop up the Window List and then select the window from the menu.

Getting Help

Help is never far away when you're using KDE. Even if you're using your laptop computer on a deserted island and you don't have this book, you can still get instant advice on how to use KDE and its many features. That's because the KDE online documentation is never more than a couple of mouse clicks away.

If you're an experienced Linux/UNIX user, you're undoubtedly accustomed to having online documentation available in the form of man pages. And a few man pages are devoted to KDE. However, the bulk of the KDE documentation is available in a much more attractive and accessible form. The KDE online help files are stored in HTML format (the same format used for Web pages), and a special Kdehelp utility is included to display both traditional UNIX-style man pages and the HTML-formatted KDE Help documents. The Kdehelp utility (shown in Figure 2-10) is accessible from many places within the K Desktop Environment and using it to view help documents is as simple as viewing Web pages in your browser.

- ✔ To open Kdehelp from the desktop, right-click the desktop and choose Help On Desktop from the pop-up menu that appears.
- ✔ To open Kdehelp from the panel, click the KDE Help button.
- ✔ To open Kdehelp from the KDE menu, choose KDE Menu➪KDE Help.
- ✔ To open Kdehelp from almost any program window, choose Help➪Contents.

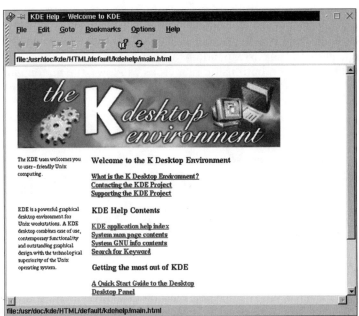

Figure 2-10:
KDE Help is
readily
accessible
and easy
to use.

Regardless of how you access the Kdehelp utility, the result is the same: The Kdehelp window appears, displaying the help document associated with the part of KDE you were using when you opened Kdehelp. For example, if you access Kdehelp from the desktop, you get the generic KDE Help index, but if you access help from within a KFM window, you see the help files for the KFM file manager utility.

✔ To navigate within a KDE Help document, click an underlined link to view the related information. It's just like following links on a Web page displayed in your Web browser.

✔ To move back or forward through the Help pages you've viewed, click the Previous or Next buttons in the Kdehelp toolbar.

✔ To display the Contents page, click the Contents button in the Kdehelp toolbar.

✔ To load another help file, choose File➪Open, select a file from the Open dialog box that appears, and then click OK to close the dialog box and display the file.

✔ To search for a help topic by keyword, choose File➪Search to display the KDE Help Search page shown in Figure 2-11, enter the search term in the Enter Keywords box, select the checkboxes to define the scope of the search, and then click Submit Search. Kdehelp displays the results of your search as a list of links. Click a link to display the related page.

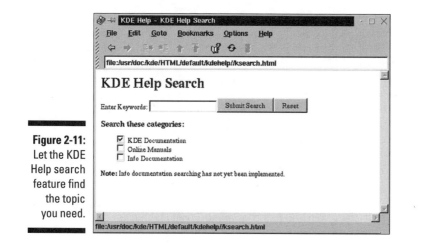

Figure 2-11:
Let the KDE
Help search
feature find
the topic
you need.

Chapter 3

Managing Windows with KWM

*1*magine, if you will, a large castle or manor house with scores of windows. In the days before central air conditioning, one member of the household staff might be assigned the responsibility for managing all those windows: opening some for ventilation, closing others to keep out drafts and rain, shuttering the windows against a storm, and opening drapes to welcome the warmth and light of the sun.

But the windows on your KDE desktop are very different from the windows in a building — they show views of computer programs instead of the countryside surrounding the house, and information flows through your KDE windows instead of air and light. Still, when the number of windows gets large enough, you need a staff member devoted to managing them. The KDE Window Manager, or KWM, is the member of the KDE staff that has that responsibility.

KWM does its work quietly, working unobtrusively in the background. You don't see KWM anywhere on your desktop, but you see the effects of KWM's work everywhere on your desktop. KWM controls the placement and appearance of every window. KWM gives KDE much of its distinctive look and feel.

Like a good household staff member, KWM performs most tasks routinely, but also dutifully takes instructions from the lord of the manor. In this chapter, you discover how to issue those instructions to KWM.

What's a Window Manager?

Unlike monolithic operating systems, such as Windows and Mac OS, the desktop environment you are coming to know as KDE is composed of several layers of mix-and-match components. Your Linux (or UNIX) operating system kernel and its supporting drivers and programs create the foundation layer. The next layer is the X Window System server and client software that creates a basic graphical interface for your system. Then come the KDE components that complete the graphical user interface and give it the look and feel that you experience as the K Desktop Environment. These components include KWM, the KDE Window Manager; KPanel, which creates the KDE panel; KFM, the KDE File Manager; and a bunch of miscellaneous components collectively known as the KDE extensions.

A *window manager* is an X Window program that handles drawing window components such as borders, titlebars, and buttons. It also handles moving and sizing windows, manages their placement on the desktop, and controls much of the appearance of that desktop.

The window manager really provides a service to applications and to application developers. Thanks to the window manager, each application doesn't have to include separate code for handling details of window sizing, borders, and so on. As a result, applications can be smaller and almost all the windows you see on your desktop look and act the same. As a bonus, you can customize window details such as the color of the active window's titlebar in a central location instead of having those attributes set by each program individually.

KWM does all the tasks expected of a standard X Window manager, plus it provides multiple desktops to work on and enables features such as dragging files to and from the desktop and between windows. Of course, KWM is designed specifically to work with KDE and other KDE components. Together they create the complete KDE environment.

Because KWM is a separate program, you can use another window manager (such as Enlightenment or Another Step) if you really want to. However, other window managers don't have the tight integration with the rest of KDE that KWM enjoys. Conversely, you could theoretically use KWM as a generic window manager for X Window, but KWM can't really perform up to its potential without the rest of KDE.

You don't have to change window managers to change the appearance of your desktop. You can customize KWM in many ways, and you can use themes to make major changes quickly and easily. If you like the looks of a different window manager, you may be able to emulate it with a KDE theme. (See Chapter 7 for more information on using themes.)

Anatomy of a KDE Window

The key elements of a graphical user interface — program windows with title-bars, and so on — are pretty standard and familiar to most computer users. A KDE window, such as the one shown in Figure 3-1, may look a little different from its counterpart in Windows or Mac OS, but most of the parts are easily recognizable.

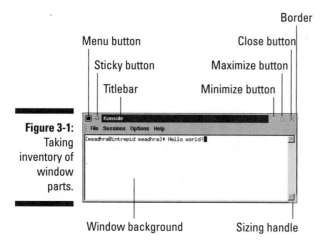

Border

Menu button   Close button

Sticky button   Maximize button

Titlebar   Minimize button

Figure 3-1: Taking inventory of window parts.

Window background   Sizing handle

Here's a quick rundown on the main parts of a KDE window:

 ✔ **Titlebar:** The colored bar that runs across the top of the window normally displays the name of the program and/or the filename of the document that appears in the window. The titlebar also serves as a "handle" that you can drag with the mouse pointer to move the window.

 ✔ **Border:** Defines the edge of the window. The border also serves as a sizing handle that you can drag with the mouse pointer to expand or contract the size of the window on a given side.

 ✔ **Close button:** Click this button to close the window and exit the application or document that is running within the window.

 ✔ **Maximize button:** Click this button to automatically expand the size of the window to fill all the available space on your desktop. If the window is already maximized, the complementary Restore button replaces this button (usually labeled with two stacked rectangles). Clicking the Restore button returns the window to its previous unmaximized size and position.

✔ **Minimize button:** Also known as the Iconify button. Click this button to remove the window from your desktop without exiting the program within the window. After you click the Minimize button, the program continues to run, but is represented only by a button on the KDE taskbar and a listing in the Window List, not by an open window on any desktop.

✔ **Sticky button:** Click this button to toggle Sticky mode on or off. If you make a window sticky, it appears in the same place on all of your virtual desktops instead of being available on only one virtual desktop.

✔ **Menu button:** Click this button to open a menu of window management commands. The default Menu button (labeled with a plain horizontal line) is normally replaced by an icon for the program running within the window. But regardless of the appearance of the Menu button, clicking it has the same effect.

✔ **Sizing handle:** Click and drag the sizing handle at the lower-right corner of the window to resize the window along both the horizontal and vertical axis at the same time.

✔ **Window background:** The interior of the window is the domain of the program running within the window. The application controls everything that appears within the window including the menus, toolbar buttons, status bar, and the contents of the main work area. KWM doesn't do anything except set the default colors for the window background, text, menu text, and selected items.

KDE is a highly customizable environment, and that customization extends to the appearance of the buttons and other components of the KDE windows. Figure 3-1 shows a KDE window using the default KWM settings. Your windows may look very different — especially if you use themes to modify the appearance of your KDE desktop. The window borders may be rendered to look like thick metal pipes and the titlebar buttons may carry different symbols. However, despite cosmetic differences, the KDE window components still work the same.

The KDE Custom Window Shop

You may be quite content to stick with the default settings of KDE for controlling the appearance and behavior of your KDE windows and desktop. For the most part, the KDE developers have done an excellent job of selecting sensible defaults that create a highly usable windowing system. However, if you're the type who just loves to tinker with your system, KDE gives you ample opportunity to do so. You can manipulate an amazing array of settings to control almost every imaginable detail of window management. Although a few aspects of window design (such as specifying the image files used to render window borders and buttons) require hand-editing arcane configuration files (and are those beyond the scope of this book), most of the custom window settings are readily available in a series of convenient dialog boxes.

You can find most of the custom window controls on various tabs of the KDE Control Center in dialog box. To open the KDE Control Center dialog box, use one of the following techniques:

✔ Click the KDE Menu button and then choose KDE Control Center.

✔ Click the KDE Control Center button on the panel.

After the KDE Control Center dialog box appears, you can use the index tree on the left side of the dialog box to select the tab you want to work on. The following sections of this chapter detail the settings you can adjust on each of the tabs.

Configuring the titlebar

Perhaps the most prominent feature of any window is its titlebar. You can adjust several aspects of the titlebar appearance by following these steps:

1. **Open the KDE Control Center dialog box.**

   Click the KDE Control Center button on the panel or choose KDE Menu⇨KDE Control Center. The KDE Control Center dialog box appears.

2. **Choose Windows⇨Titlebar.**

   The Titlebar tab appears, as shown in Figure 3-2.

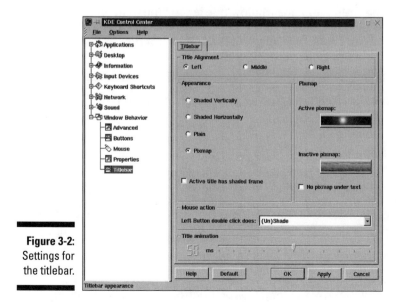

Figure 3-2:
Settings for
the titlebar.

3. **Adjust the settings on the Titlebar tab as needed.**

You can adjust the following settings:

- **Title Alignment:** The three radio buttons in this area enable you to select the alignment of the title within the titlebar. You can select Left (the default), Middle, or Right.

- **Appearance:** The options in this area define the kind of background that appears in the titlebar. Select Shaded Vertically to specify a color blend from top to bottom in the titlebar. Select Shaded Horizontally (the default) to make the color blend go left to right. Select Plain to specify a solid color titlebar and select Pixmap to display an image as the background of the titlebar.

- **Pixmap:** If you select the Pixmap option in the Appearance area, the options in the Pixmap area become available. Click the Active Pixmap and Inactive Pixmap buttons to open dialog boxes where you can select image files to use for the background of the active and inactive window titlebars. Select the No Pixmap Under Text option to suppress display of the image as a background for the title text.

- **Mouse Action:** Select an action from the Left Button Double-Click Does drop-down list box to define what happens if you double-click the titlebar. The default, (Un)Shade, causes the window to collapse so that only the titlebar remains visible, thus occupying less space on the desktop. Double-click the collapsed window titlebar to reverse the effect and restore the window to its normal size.

- **Title Animation:** If a window title is too long to fit in the titlebar, KWM automatically scrolls the title back and forth in the titlebar. You can control the speed of the scrolling action by dragging the Title Animation slider left or right.

4. **Click the Apply button.**

KDE applies the settings to your desktop and windows.

Configuring the buttons

The titlebar buttons are an important feature of KDE windows. They provide quick access to the most-used window controls. You can rearrange the buttons to place the buttons in the positions that are most convenient for you. Here's how:

1. **Open the KDE Control Center dialog box.**

Click the KDE Control Center button on the panel or choose KDE Menu⇨KDE Control Center. The KDE Control Center dialog box appears.

2. Select Windows⇨Buttons.

The Buttons tab appears, as shown in Figure 3-3.

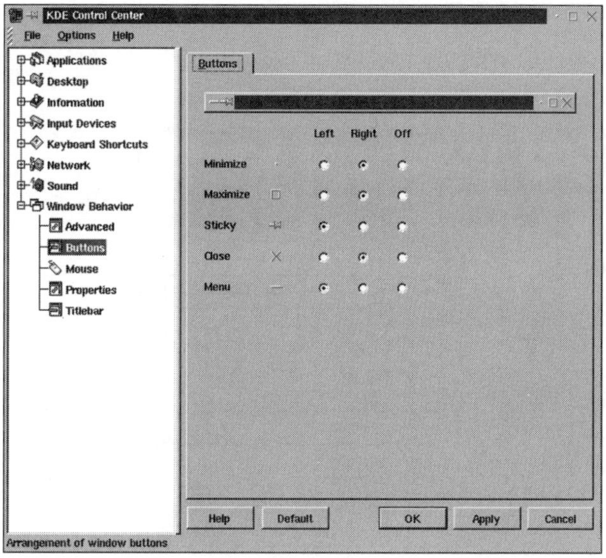

Figure 3-3:
Controlling
which
titlebar
buttons go
where.

3. Select the position for each of the titlebar buttons.

You can set the position for each of the five titlebar buttons (Minimize, Maximize, Sticky, Close, Menu) by selecting one of three radio buttons (Left, Right, Off). The sample titlebar near the top of the Buttons tab previews your selections.

You can't put more than three buttons at either end of the titlebar. If you attempt to place a fourth button on one end, KWM automatically turns off one of the other buttons at that end. You need to reselect another location for the disabled button.

4. Click the Apply button.

KDE applies the settings to your desktop and windows.

Configuring mouse button actions

KWM provides a multitude of options for controlling what happens when you click a window with the mouse pointer. Depending on which mouse button you click, where you click the window, and whether the window is active or inactive, the mouse click can raise a window to the foreground or lower it to the background, move or resize the window, or pass the click to the application within the window. And all these details are configurable. Follow these steps to change the mouse settings:

1. **Open the KDE Control Center dialog box.**

   Click the KDE Control Center button on the panel or choose KDE Menu⇨KDE Control Center. The KDE Control Center dialog box appears.

2. **Choose Windows⇨Mouse.**

   The Mouse tab appears, as shown in Figure 3-4.

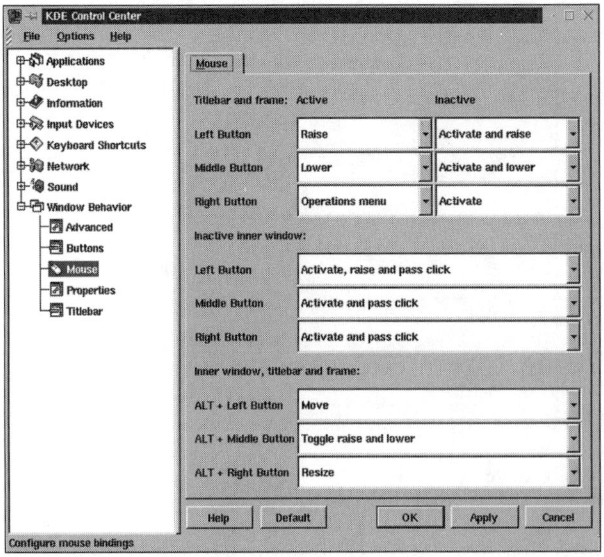

Figure 3-4: You can customize the behavior of your mouse so completely that users other than you are bound to be flummoxed.

3. **Adjust the settings on the Mouse tab as needed.**

   To change a setting, select an option from the drop-down list box corresponding to the mouse button and window area that you want to adjust. The options are organized into the following window areas:

   • **Titlebar and Frame:** Just as you may expect, these settings apply when clicking on the titlebar or border of the active and inactive windows.

   • **Inactive Inner Window:** These settings control what happens after you click inside an inactive window. You have no corresponding option for controlling mouse clicks inside the active window because those mouse clicks are automatically passed to the application in the window.

   • **Inner Window, Titlebar and Frame:** The options in this area control actions that occur in response to clicking a window (anywhere on any window) while pressing the Alt key.

4. **Click the Apply button.**

   KDE applies the settings to your desktop and windows.

Configuring window management options

The window management options control factors such as where KWM places new windows, how focus shifts from one window to another, and whether KWM displays the window contents or just an outline of windows as you move or resize them. To adjust the window properties options, follow these steps:

1. **Open the KDE Control Center dialog box.**

   Click the KDE Control Center button on the panel or choose KDE Menu⇨KDE Control Center. The KDE Control Center dialog box appears.

2. **Choose Windows⇨Properties.**

   The Options tab appears, as shown in Figure 3-5.

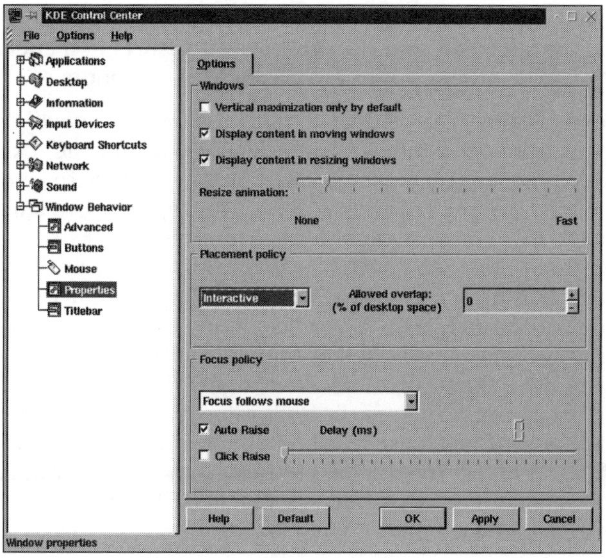

Figure 3-5:
Settings for
the window
properties
options.

3. **Adjust the settings on the Options tab as needed.**

   You can adjust the following settings:

   • **Vertical Maximization Only By Default:** Select this option to instruct KWM to change the height, but not the width, of a window when you click its maximize button. (The normal action is to maximize both height and width of a window.)

   • **Display Content In Moving Windows:** Select this option to show the contents of a window moving as you move the window. The default is to display only a transparent wireframe outline of the window as you move it — the window contents remain in the original position until you drop the window at its new location.

- **Display Content In Resizing Windows:** Select this option to show changes in the contents of a window as you resize the window. The default is to display only a transparent wireframe outline of the window as you resize it.

- **Resize Animation:** Drag the slider left or right to control the speed of the animated size change when you minimize or maximize a window. Drag the slider all the way to the left to make the change appear instantly.

- **Placement Policy:** Select an option from the drop-down list box to control the default placement of new windows. The default setting is Smart, which automatically positions new windows to minimize overlap. The Manual setting creates a window outline that moves with the mouse until you click to place the new window. If you select Interactive, the Allowed Overlap box appears, where you set the amount of window overlap that you deem acceptable. KWM places new windows automatically, if it can do so without exceeding the specified overlap; otherwise it resorts to manual placement. The other options are Cascade and Random.

- **Focus Policy:** The settings in this area control how KWM shifts focus from one window to another. The default is Click to Focus, which means you must click an inactive window to give it the focus. If you select Focus Follows Mouse, the focus shifts to a new window as soon as you move the mouse pointer over any visible portion of that window. The other options, Classic Sloppy Focus and Classic Focus Follows Mouse, are both minor variations of Focus Follows Mouse. If you select one of the Focus Follows Mouse options, you can also select Auto Raise to automatically raise a window to the foreground when it gets the focus. Drag the slider to adjust the delay before the auto raise feature takes effect. You can also select Click Raise to allow a click anywhere on a window (instead of just the titlebar) to raise it to the foreground. Auto Raise and Click Raise aren't available if Click to Focus is selected in the Focus Policy drop-down list box.

4. **Click the Apply button.**

    KDE applies the settings to your desktop and windows.

Configuring advanced window manager settings

The so-called advanced window manager settings aren't really any more advanced than any of the other KWM options. The advanced moniker is just a convenient label for some of the settings you're less likely to need to change. The settings control how KWM reacts to some shortcut keys and enable you to set up filters to specify special treatment for certain windows.

1. **Open the KDE Control Center dialog box.**

   Click the KDE Control Center button on the panel or choose KDE Menu⇨KDE Control Center. The KDE Control Center dialog box appears.

2. **Choose Windows⇨Advanced.**

   The Advanced tab appears, as shown in Figure 3-6.

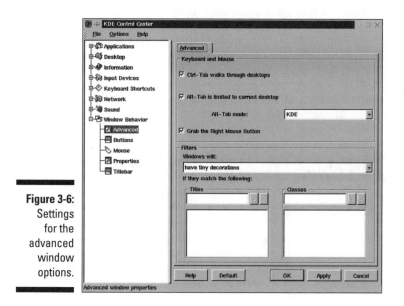

Figure 3-6:
Settings
for the
advanced
window
options.

3. **Adjust the settings on the Advanced tab as needed.**

   You can adjust the following settings:

   - **Ctrl-Tab Walks Through Desktops:** Select this option to use the Ctrl+Tab shortcut key to switch desktops.

   - **Alt-Tab Is Limited to Current Desktop:** Select this option to cause the Alt+Tab shortcut key to cycle through windows on the current desktop only. Otherwise, pressing Alt+Tab cycles through all the windows on all your virtual desktops.

   - **Alt-Tab Mode:** Select KDE or CDE to determine which windows KWM opens if you press the Alt+Tab repeatedly. KDE mode always switches back to the previous window. CDE mode always steps through the available windows sequentially.

     If you want to step through all available windows sequentially, press and hold the Alt key as you tap the Tab key repeatedly. This technique works in both KDE and CDE modes.

- **Grab the Right Mouse Button:** Select this option to give KWM first crack at right clicks, which are used to open context menus and for various window control functions. This option is selected by default. You only need to deselect it if you're using a non-KDE application that requires full-time access to the right mouse button.

- **Filters:** Use the settings in this area to define special treatment for windows with certain titles or X class names. Select an option from the Windows Will drop-down list box and then build a list of window titles or classes to get the special treatment by typing a name in the Titles or Classes text boxes and clicking the plus (+) button to add the name to the respective list box.

4. **Click the OK button.**

    KDE closes the KDE Control Center dialog box and applies the settings to your desktop and windows.

Getting Real Work Done on Virtual Desktops

One of KWM's chores is to manage your virtual desktops, which give you more space to spread out application windows. Although you can see only one desktop at a time, KWM can manage up to eight virtual desktops and keep track of what windows are open on what desktops. You can switch back and forth between the different desktops to access the windows running on each one. Chapter 1 introduces the concept of virtual desktops and Chapter 5 details how to control the number of desktops that are available and their names.

To switch desktops, you can use any of the following techniques:

- **Click one of the desktop pager buttons in the panel.** By default, the desktop pager buttons are labeled One, Two, and so on. Clicking one of the buttons displays the corresponding desktop and its collection of windows (if any).

- **Click a taskbar button for a window that isn't on the current desktop.** KWM automatically switches to the virtual desktop where the window resides and opens the window.

- **Click the Window List button on the panel and choose a window from the menu that appears.** KWM automatically switches to the virtual desktop where the window resides and opens the window.

- **Press Ctrl+Tab to switch to the next virtual desktop in sequence.** Press Ctrl+Tab repeatedly to step through the available desktops. (The Ctrl-Tab Walks Through Desktops option must be selected on the Advanced tab of the KDE Control Center in order for this technique to work.)

As an alternative to the standard techniques for switching desktops and moving windows between desktops, you can try the KPager utility program. To launch KPager, choose KDE Menu⇨System⇨Desktop Pager. The KPager window appears, displaying thumbnail representations of each of your desktops. Double-click on a desktop in KPager to switch to that desktop. Dragging windows from one desktop to another in KPager has the effect of moving the window on your virtual desktops as well.

Border patrol — using active and magic borders

KWM's active desktop feature enables you to switch desktops by simply dragging the mouse pointer to the edge of the desktop. Here's how you can enable and configure the active border option:

1. **Choose KDE Menu⇨Settings⇨Desktop>Borders.**

   The Window Manager Style dialog box appears with the Borders tab displayed, as shown in Figure 3-7.

   (You can also get to these same settings in the KDE Control Center by selecting Display⇨Borders.)

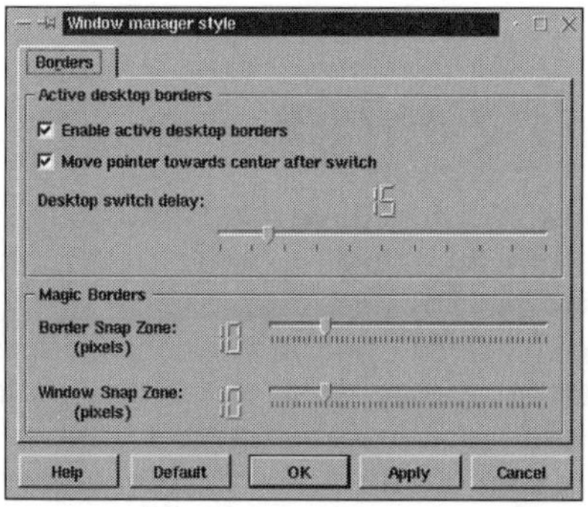

Figure 3-7:
Setting the
active
border
option.

2. **Select the Enable Active Desktop Borders option.**

3. **Select the Move Pointer Towards Center after Switch option.**

   If you select this option, KWM automatically positions the mouse pointer near the center of the new desktop after switching desktops.

4. **Drag the Desktop Switch Delay to set the switch sensitivity.**

   This setting is a short delay after the mouse pointer contacts the edge of the current desktop before KWM switches desktops.

5. Click OK.

KDE closes the Window Manager Style dialog box and activates the active desktop feature.

The Border Snap Zone and Window Snap Zone settings at the bottom of the Borders tab allow you to adjust the size of the snap zone that runs around the perimeter of the desktop (the Border Snap Zone) and around the outside edge of each window (the Window Snap Zone). If you want to disable the snap zone feature, drag both sliders to 0.

Moving windows between desktops

One way to control the desktop on which a window resides is to switch to the desired desktop before opening the window. But if a window is already open on a different desktop, you can move the window by

  ✔ Right-clicking the window's titlebar and choosing To Desktop⇨Two.

  ✔ Clicking the menu button in the window's titlebar and choosing To Desktop⇨Two.

These examples move the current window to desktop Two. To move the window to a different desktop, select the desired window name.

Making your window sticky

If you are using multiple desktops, you may have a window that you always want to remain available no matter which desktop you're using currently. KWM enables you to address that need by making a window *sticky,* which means that the window sticks to the same spot on your screen regardless of what desktop you switch to. Another way to think of it is that a sticky window appears in exactly the same location on all your virtual desktops. To make a window sticky, you can use any of the following techniques:

  ✔ Right-click the window's titlebar and choose Sticky from the pop-up menu that appears.

  ✔ Click the menu button in the window's titlebar and choose Sticky from the menu that appears.

  ✔ Click the Sticky button in window's titlebar.

To reverse the sticky effect, you can use any of the same techniques, except that the command that appears on the menu of a sticky window is UnSticky.

Chapter 4

A Place for Your Stuff — the KFM File Manager

*O*ver the years, a variety of tools have been developed to help you manage the mounds of books and paper that are associated with the projects you work on in your real-world office. And it's a good thing too! Without file folders, binders, shelves, and filing cabinets to keep things organized, most of us would be drowning in a sea of paper.

Managing your computer files is no less of a challenge. Fortunately, KDE provides you with a powerful tool — the KDE File Manager — to help you meet and master the file management challenge. The KDE File Manager, better known as KFM, is your electronic filing cabinet. It creates easy-to-use graphic representations of your entire computer file system and enables you to manipulate files and folders by clicking and dragging onscreen icons instead of typing arcane commands at the command line. Even fans of the command-line interface will find KFM faster and easier to use for many file management tasks.

This chapter shows you how to use KFM (and its companion program, Find Files) to manage and manipulate files. But KFM is more than a file management utility — it's also a Web browser (we cover that aspect of KFM in Chapter 9).

Where Are My Files?

In your physical office, if you need to get a file or document that isn't already open on your desktop, you go to the file cabinet and pull open a drawer. If you need to work with a file in KDE, the place to go is KFM — your electronic filing cabinet.

KFM enables you to navigate your entire computer file system, as well as manage and manipulate your files and folders. KFM is your virtual filing cabinet; and it's also your virtual copy machine, file mover, trash can, shredder, and more. KFM makes full use of KDE's desktop features by offering the capability to drag and drop file icons between windows — whether to another KFM window, the KDE desktop, or a different program window. It's a true graphical user interface to your file system.

KFM is the KDE counterpart to the Windows Explorer and the Macintosh Finder. KFM fulfills the same basic purpose as Explore and Finder — and uses some of the same familiar conventions for graphically representing the files and folders of your computer's file system. If you previously used the Windows or Macintosh file management utilities, you already have a head start toward understanding how to use KFM.

Opening KFM is easy. It's a tool you'll probably use frequently, so the KDE developers provide a number of ways to open a KFM window. You can use any of the following techniques to open a KFM window:

✔ Click the Home Directory button on the panel.

✔ Click the KDE Menu button and choose Home Directory.

The KDE Menu button is the panel button with the KDE logo K and gear on it. It's normally located at the left end of the KDE panel. Clicking the KDE Menu button causes KDE to display a list of programs on the KDE menu (sometimes called the *application starter menu*). Refer to Chapter 1 for more about using the KDE Menu button and its menu.

✔ Click any folder's desktop icon (for example, Templates or Autostart).

✔ Click the KDE Menu, point to Disk Navigator, and then choose any of the folder or device items on the Disk Navigator submenu.

✔ Right-click the desktop and choose Execute Command, type a path name in the Command box, and press Enter.

✔ Click any desktop icon for a file-system device such as a CD-ROM or floppy. (If the device isn't already mounted, use KDE to mount it before opening KFM — provided you have permission to mount the device.)

When you open a KFM window, it automatically displays the contents of your home directory (as shown in Figure 4-1) unless you specified an alternate directory by clicking a desktop icon or choosing a menu item for a different folder. For example, if you click the Home Directory panel button, KFM displays your home directory — the one assigned to your login name. But if you click the Templates desktop icon, KFM displays the contents of the Templates folder instead.

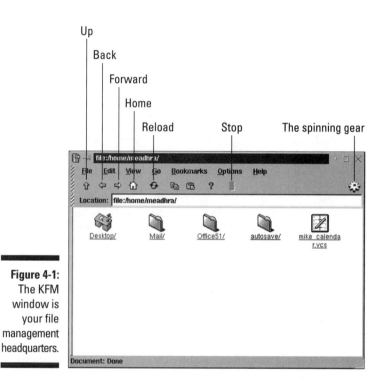

Figure 4-1:
The KFM
window is
your file
management
headquarters.

In Linux and other UNIX variants, each user is normally assigned a separate directory in which to store personal files. Typically, your home directory is a subdirectory of /home and the directory name matches your logon user ID. For example, the home directory for the user *meadhra* is /home/meadhra. This home directory is the one KFM displays by default and it's where you store all your documents and other files. The operating system and KDE also store a number of personalized configuration files in your home directory and in several subdirectories.

The tilde character (~) is a filename wildcard that is shorthand for your home directory. You can use it when typing pathnames to make it easier to enter the path to a file or subfolder in your home directory. For example, instead of typing the full path and filename `/home/username/docs/MyDoc.txt`, you can simply type `~/docs/MyDoc.txt`.

Navigating

Using KFM to navigate your file system is like using your car to drive around in a city. Driving the car is the easy part. Finding your way around on the city streets is the challenge. If you know the layout of the city and you're familiar with the streets, you can get from place to place easily, but if you're a stranger in the city, the streets seem like a confusing maze.

As with your car, KFM has a few simple controls that you'll master easily. (Finding out how to use KFM is a lot easier than learning how to drive. We show you how, and besides, you don't have to learn to parallel park KFM.) When you take KFM out for a spin around your file system, how easily you find your way among the files and folders depends on how well you know your file system. As soon as you venture beyond the local neighborhood of your home directory, the Linux file system can be as confusing to a newcomer as the streets of a strange city. As with some of the newest cars that include navigation aids such as GPS (global positioning satellite) receivers and moving map displays, KFM includes features to help you discover and explore your files and folders — but nothing takes the place of familiarity with the local streets and with your file-system layout.

Actually, using KFM to navigate your file system is similar to using a Web browser to navigate a Web site. If you can surf the Web, you already know the basics of surfing your file system. Here's a summary of the KFM navigation tools:

> ✔ Type a path name in the Location box below the KFM toolbar to display the contents of that directory in the KFM window. As with a Web browser, KFM always displays the full path name of the current directory in the Location box, even if you use another navigation technique to open the directory.

Office51/

> ✔ Click a folder icon (or the underlined text name of the folder) to open the folder and display the contents of the selected directory in the KFM window.

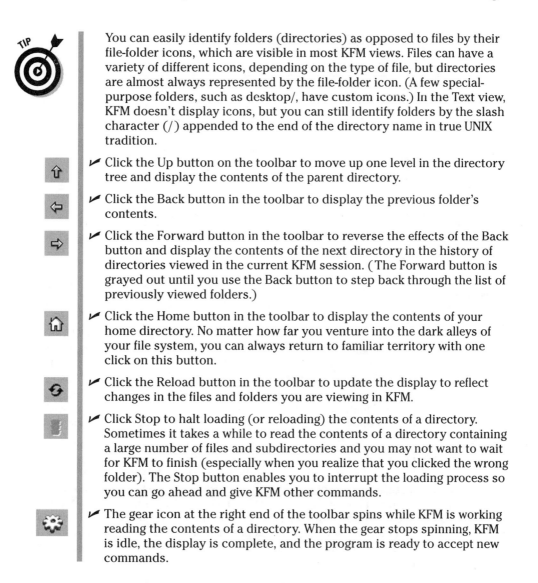

You can easily identify folders (directories) as opposed to files by their file-folder icons, which are visible in most KFM views. Files can have a variety of different icons, depending on the type of file, but directories are almost always represented by the file-folder icon. (A few special-purpose folders, such as desktop/, have custom icons.) In the Text view, KFM doesn't display icons, but you can still identify folders by the slash character (/) appended to the end of the directory name in true UNIX tradition.

✔ Click the Up button on the toolbar to move up one level in the directory tree and display the contents of the parent directory.

✔ Click the Back button in the toolbar to display the previous folder's contents.

✔ Click the Forward button in the toolbar to reverse the effects of the Back button and display the contents of the next directory in the history of directories viewed in the current KFM session. (The Forward button is grayed out until you use the Back button to step back through the list of previously viewed folders.)

✔ Click the Home button in the toolbar to display the contents of your home directory. No matter how far you venture into the dark alleys of your file system, you can always return to familiar territory with one click on this button.

✔ Click the Reload button in the toolbar to update the display to reflect changes in the files and folders you are viewing in KFM.

✔ Click Stop to halt loading (or reloading) the contents of a directory. Sometimes it takes a while to read the contents of a directory containing a large number of files and subdirectories and you may not want to wait for KFM to finish (especially when you realize that you clicked the wrong folder). The Stop button enables you to interrupt the loading process so you can go ahead and give KFM other commands.

✔ The gear icon at the right end of the toolbar spins while KFM is working reading the contents of a directory. When the gear stops spinning, KFM is idle, the display is complete, and the program is ready to accept new commands.

Getting Different Views of Your Files

KFM gives you several ways to customize how the program represents the files and folders shown in the KFM window. You're not stuck with the default arrangement shown in Figure 4-2. You can choose from one of four different views and select other options to control such things as whether KFM displays hidden files.

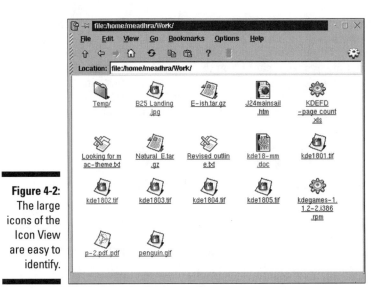

Figure 4-2:
The large
icons of the
Icon View
are easy to
identify.

✔ **Icon View** — When you first start the KDE file manager, the KFM window appears and displays the contents of your home directory as rows of large icons — one icon for each visible file and folder within the directory. (Refer back to Figure 4-2.) The icons are large and easy to see, which also makes them easy to click and drag with your mouse. Each icon is labeled with the file or folder name beneath the icon. If you're using a different KFM view and want to switch back to Icon View, choose View➪Icon View.

✔ **Long View** — If you need to see more detailed information about your files and folders, Long View (shown in Figure 4-3) is the way to go. Instead of rows of large icons, the display consists of a table-style listing of your directory's contents. Each file or folder appears on a separate line that starts with a small icon and the file or folder name on the left and includes the file's access permission mask, owner, group, size, and modification time and date. Choose View➪Long View to switch KFM to this detailed display mode.

✔ **Short View** — If you like the small icons and compact list style of the Long View, but don't need all the detailed information about each file or folder, then choose View➪Short View to see a display similar to the one in Figure 4-4.

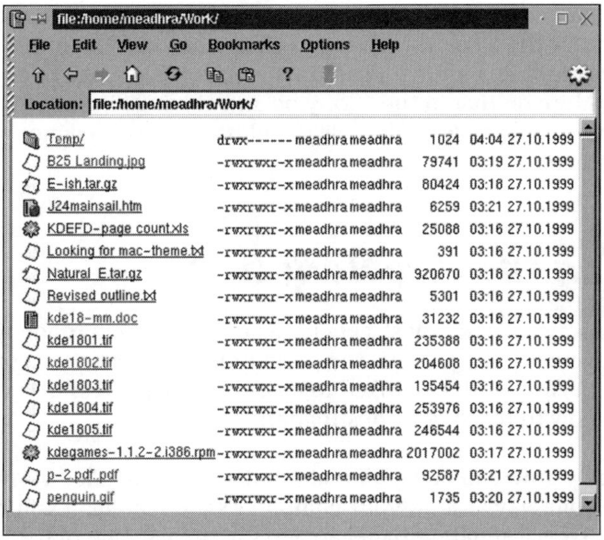

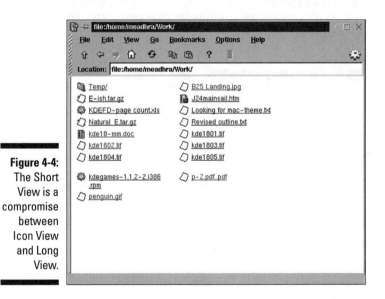

Figure 4-3:
The Long
View shows
more
details.

Figure 4-4:
The Short
View is a
compromise
between
Icon View
and Long
View.

✔ **Text View** — The Text View is essentially the same as the Long View, except without the icons at the left end of each row. The absence of icons enables KFM to render a long directory display a little faster, but the speed difference between Text View and other views is seldom a major issue. Basically, Text View is for purists who just prefer the traditional text-based file listing. To invoke Text View, choose View⇨Text View.

No matter which view you choose, you still work with the files and folders in the KFM window the same way. You can click icons or filenames to open the selected files or folders and you can drag icons or filenames to copy and move files. (More on that in the "Copying and Moving Files" section of this chapter.) The view changes only how the files are displayed, not what you can do with them.

Climbing the directory tree

Finding your way around city streets is easier with a good roadmap. In these days of fancy electronic gadgets, the premier luxury cars often come equipped with GPS receivers linked to electronic maps to show you where you are and how to reach your destination.

KFM includes a powerful navigation aid that serves a similar purpose in helping you find your way around your computer's file system. If you choose View⊃Show Tree, a separate panel appears in the left side of the KFM window that displays a hierarchical listing of the file-system directory tree as shown in Figure 4-5. Repeat the same command to remove the tree panel from the KFM window.

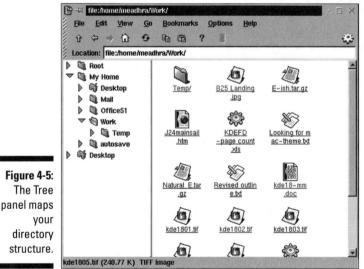

Figure 4-5:
The Tree panel maps your directory structure.

KFM's tree display uses a collapsible outline format to show the nested directories and subdirectories that make up your computer's file system. The arrowhead symbols to the left of each directory name enable you to expand or collapse the directory tree to show or hide the subdirectories within a given directory.

✔ Click a right-pointing arrow to expand the tree listing and show the subdirectories nested below the that directory.

✔ Click a down-pointing arrow to collapse the tree listing and hide any sub-directories.

✔ Click a directory name in the tree listing to display the contents of that directory in the main panel on the right side of the KFM window.

✔ The open file-folder icon beside a directory name indicates the selected directory.

When you select a directory in the tree list, KFM displays the contents of the selected directory in the right side of the KFM window. However, if you click a folder name in the right side of the KFM window, click the Home button on the toolbar, or use any other navigation technique to change directories, KFM doesn't necessarily update the tree list to indicate which directory is open. *Don't rely on the tree list to show the location of the current directory unless you activate the Tree View Follows Navigation option.*

✔ Use the scroll bar on the right side of the tree display to scroll through the tree listing.

✔ Right-click a directory name in the tree list to open a pop-up menu of options that enable you to do things such as open, copy, and delete the directory. Most of your options for manipulating directories in the main panel of the KFM window are also available on this pop-up menu.

The KFM directory tree panel includes a top-level branch labeled My Home and another top-level branch labeled Desktop. These are links to your home directory (/home/username/) and Desktop subdirectory (/home/username/Desktop/) rather than real branches on the directory tree. They appear on the tree list to provide convenient access to these oft-used directories so you don't have to expand the Root branch in order to drill down to your home directory and Desktop. Note that your home directory is labeled My Home instead of its real path name.

Showing thumbnails

If you work with a lot of image files, you'll appreciate the way KFM displays thumbnail previews of each image in Icon View. For identifying images, a picture — even a small one — almost always beats the most descriptive file name.

To activate thumbnails, choose View⇨Show Thumbnails. Then, when you view the contents of a folder that contains image files, KFM displays a small preview image of each image file instead of the normal generic file icon, as shown in Figure 4-6. The Show Thumbnails command is a toggle — to deactivate it, just choose the same command again.

Figure 4-6:
Thumbnails
enable you
to preview
image files.

The Show Thumbnails option works only with the large icons in Icon View, not the small icons in Long View or Short View. The small icons in the other views are too small to make useful preview images anyway. Also, before KFM can display a thumbnail preview, the image must be in a file format KFM can display at the appropriate size for an icon. If KFM can't display a file's image format (or can't adjust the image to icon size), the program displays the generic file icon for the file type instead of a thumbnail image.

Revealing hidden files

When you view the contents of a directory in KFM, typically you see only a portion of the files and subdirectories stored there. In addition to the files you see in the normal directory listing, some directories contain many more files and subdirectories that remain invisible — hidden from view.

On a UNIX-style operating system, file and directory names that start with a period are omitted from normal directory listings. As a result, these files are effectively hidden. Often configuration files and other system files or directories are hidden in this way, especially when stored in the same directories as documents and other files that a user routinely accesses. Although hiding files can enhance security somewhat, the real purpose of hidden files isn't to keep those files secret. Hiding configuration and system files simply reduces the on-screen clutter in your directories so you don't have to look through a bunch of seldom-used configuration files in order to locate your programs and documents.

KFM normally keeps hidden files out of sight and doesn't display the file-names or icons for hidden files or directories in the main KFM window or in the tree panel. However, if you need access to those hidden files, you can choose View⇨Show Hidden Files to force KFM to reveal all. When you enable the Show Hidden Files option, KFM displays *all* the files and subdirectories in the current directory, including the "dot" files. Previously hidden directories also become visible in the directory tree panel if it is active. Figure 4-7 shows a KFM window with hidden files visible. Compare it to Figure 4-5, which shows the normal view of the same directory.

Figure 4-7: KFM can display files that are normally hidden from view.

Peeking inside archive files

Traditionally, backup copies of files are stored in the UNIX tape archive (.tar) or compressed tape archive (.tar.gz) formats, which condense the data and file descriptions from multiple original files into each archive file. But archive files aren't just for backups any more. Archives and compressed archives are also used for other purposes such as packaging all the files for a program installation into a single *tarball* (geek jargon for a .tar archive file) for distribution. KDE themes are distributed as compressed archives. And just about anything you download over the Internet is likely to be in a com-pressed archive as well.

Of course, you need a special utility program to create an archive file. The most common command-line utility is named, appropriately enough, tar. A KDE utility — Archiver — provides a graphical tool for creating archive files. You can use these same tools to view the contents of archive files and extract component files from the archive and restore them to separate, individual files that you can then use just like a copy of the original.

However, you don't have to resort to using separate utilities to work with archive files. KFM can do the job. Here's how:

1. **Click an archive file (with the .tar or .tar.gz extension) in a KFM window.**

   KFM opens the file and displays its contents in the KFM window. It's just like opening a folder. In fact, KFM normally displays the contents of the archive as a single folder.

2. **Click the folder icon.**

   KFM displays a list of the files and subfolders contained within the archive. Figure 4-8 shows an example of KFM displaying the contents of a compressed archive file — in this case, a theme. Note the path name in the location bar. The part following the # character is within the archive file.

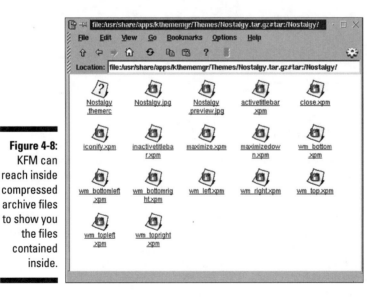

Figure 4-8:
KFM can reach inside compressed archive files to show you the files contained inside.

3. **Click or drag individual files to open or copy them.**

   You can do pretty much anything with the files within the archive that you can do with files in a regular folder. You can open most documents and you can copy files from the KFM window to other locations. The principal exception is running a program from an archive. In order to run a program, you must first copy the program file and its supporting files from the archive to a regular folder on your hard drive so the operating system can find and access all the necessary files.

Changing the appearance of the file manager

As with most KDE features, you can customize the appearance of the KFM window. The preceding sections of this chapter show you how to change the view, show thumbnails, and add the tree panel to the KFM window. But that's not all you can do. Check out these configuration options:

- ✔ Choose Options⇨Show Menubar to remove the menus from the KFM window.

  There is no easy way to restore the menu bar to a KFM window after you turn it off. Your best bet is to close the menuless KFM window and open another KFM window with its default settings intact.

- ✔ Choose Options⇨Show Statusbar to remove the status bar from the bottom of the KFM window. Choose the command again to restore the status bar.

- ✔ Choose Options⇨Show Locationbar to toggle the Location bar (the one with the big Location or address box) on or off.

- ✔ Choose Options⇨Show Toolbar to remove the toolbar from the KFM window. Choose the command again to restore the toolbar.

- ✔ Choose Options⇨Configure File Manager to open the KFM Configuration dialog box. The settings on the Font and Color tabs enable you to select the fonts and colors KFM uses to display file lists in the KFM window.

  The most interesting settings are on the Other tab, shown in Figure 4-9. There you can specify the default programs to use as your terminal emulator and text editor. Another useful setting is the Tree View Follows Navigation option. Select this option to force KFM to automatically update the Tree panel to show the current directory selection, even when you navigate to a different directory by clicking a folder in the right panel of the KFM window. (Personally, I don't understand why this option isn't enabled by default. It should be!) After adjusting the settings, click OK to close the KFM Configuration dialog box and apply the settings.

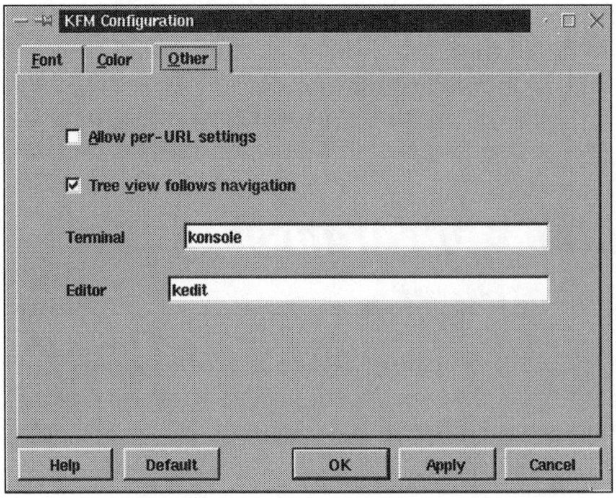

KFM Configuration

Font | Color | Other

☐ Allow per-URL settings

☑ Tree view follows navigation

Terminal | konsole |

Editor | kedit |

Help | Default | OK | Apply | Cancel

Figure 4-9:
The KFM
Configuration
dialog box
contains
some
important
settings.

✔ When you get KFM configured the way you like it, choose Options⇨
Save Settings to make the current KFM configuration the default. New
KFM windows will then appear with the same view and other configuration settings as the current KFM window, instead of the original installation defaults.

Creating a New Folder

Creating new document files is something that you probably do in your various application programs. But creating the folders in which to store those
documents is a job for KFM. To create a new folder, follow these steps:

1. **Open KFM and navigate to the location where you want to create the
   new folder.**

   You can use any of the techniques mentioned elsewhere in this chapter
   to open a KFM window and to navigate to the directory in which you
   want to create the new subfolder.

   In order to create a new folder, you must have appropriate access permissions for the directory where you are creating it. If you are logged on
   under a regular user name, you are generally restricted to creating new
   folders in your home directory and its subdirectories. If you are logged
   on as the superuser, root, then you can create folders anywhere in the
   file system.

2. **Choose File⇨New⇨Folder or right-click the KFM window and choose
   New⇨Folder from the pop-up window that appears.**

   KFM opens the dialog box shown in Figure 4-10, prompting you for the
   name of your new folder.

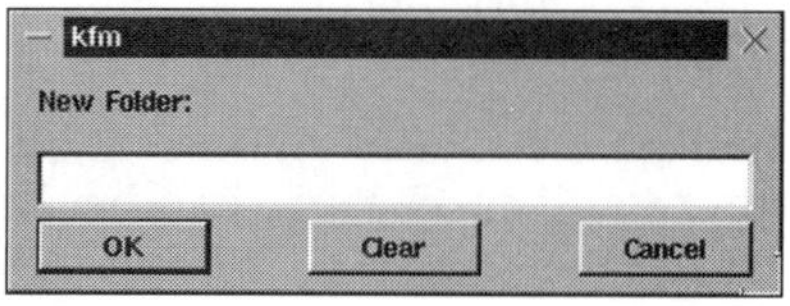

Figure 4-10:
Give your
new folder
a name.

kfm ✕

New Folder:

| OK | Clear | Cancel |

3. Type a name for the new folder and then click the OK button.

KFM closes the dialog box and creates the new folder. The folder name
and icon appear in the KFM window.

After you create a new folder, you can copy and move files into it (see the
"Copying and Moving Files" section of this chapter) and use the folder as the
location in which you create new document files.

When you create a new folder, it starts out with the access permissions set to
allow you, the owner, full access and to prevent all other users (except the
superuser) from accessing the directory. If you want to allow others to
access your new folder, you must change its permission settings. To do that,
follow these steps.

**1. Right-click the folder name or icon in the KFM window and choose
Properties from the pop-up menu that appears.**

KFM opens a dialog box where you can edit the properties of the selected
folder. (You can use the same technique to edit the properties — including
access permissions — for files as well as folders.)

2. Click the Permissions tab.

KFM displays the options shown in Figure 4-11.

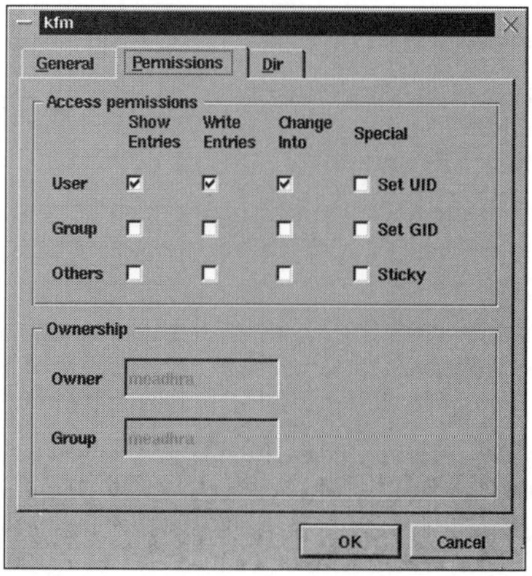

kfm ✕

General | Permissions | Dir

Access permissions

	Show Entries	Write Entries	Change Into	Special
User	☑	☑	☑	☐ Set UID
Group	☐	☐	☐	☐ Set GID
Others	☐	☐	☐	☐ Sticky

Ownership

Owner meadhra

Group meadhra

| OK | Cancel |

Figure 4-11:
Change the
permission
settings to
allow others
to access
your folder.

3. Click checkboxes in the Access Permissions area to select or deselect access permissions as needed.

The default settings shown in Figure 4-11 allow full access by the owner (you) but deny access to others. Add checkmarks to other boxes to grant various forms of access to other groups of users.

If you're logged on as a regular user, you can't change the ownership of a file or folder. So the Owner and Group settings are grayed out. To change those settings, you must be logged on as the superuser.

4. After adjusting the permission settings, click the OK button.

KFM closes the dialog box and changes the access permission settings for your folder.

Refer to Chapter 13 for more information on access permissions and on using KFM in superuser mode to perform file management tasks that you can't do as a normal user.

Copying and Moving Files

Perhaps the most common file maintenance task you'll do with KFM is to copy or move a file from one directory to another. KFM makes it easy to do. Whether you're moving or copying a file, the basic procedure is the same — and it's a simple drag-and-drop operation between two KFM windows. The following steps outline the procedure in detail:

1. Open a KFM window and navigate to the directory containing the file you want to copy or move.

If necessary, scroll the KFM window so the file you want to move is readily accessible.

2. Open a second KFM window and navigate to the destination directory.

Make sure the KFM window displays the directory into which you want to copy or move files. Position the window on your desktop so it will not be obscured by the other KFM window.

A quick way to open another KFM window is to click the gear icon at the right in the KFM toolbar. A new window appears displaying the contents of the same directory.

Normally, you copy or move files from one directory to another — hence the two KFM windows. However, you can also copy and move files directly to the KDE desktop. In that case, the second KFM window is not necessary.

3. Click the first KFM window's titlebar.

This brings the source KFM window to the foreground — gives it the focus.

If you want to copy or move multiple files at once, you can preselect a batch of files for processing. Press and hold the Ctrl key as you click each file that you want to copy or move in the next step. KFM highlights the selected files.

4. **Click and drag the file from the source KFM window to the destination window. Release the mouse button to drop the file on the destination window.**

   A small pop-up menu appears giving you the option to Copy, Move, or Link.

5. **To copy the file, choose Copy. To move it, choose Move.**

   Copying a file makes an exact copy of the file in the new directory and leaves the original file in its original location. Moving a file makes a copy of the file in the new directory and removes the file from the original location.

The third option (Link) on the pop-up menu that appears when you drag-and-drop a file from a KFM window creates a symbolic link file in the destination directory that points to the original file in the source directory. (Creating a Link is roughly equivalent to creating a shortcut icon in Windows.) Sometimes creating a symbolic link is preferable to creating a copy of a file. A link creates the appearance of having a copy of the file in the new location, but the link is usually much smaller than the original file and, because clicking the link actually opens the original file, there's no problem with two copies of the same information getting "out of sync." If you're not familiar with symbolic links, refer to a general Linux or UNIX book.

Deleting Files

Another common file maintenance chore is getting rid of outdated and otherwise unwanted files and folders. KDE provides two options for disposing of unwanted files. The KDE trash can enables you to remove files in such a way that you can later recover them if necessary. You can also remove files from your system permanently and completely with KFM's Delete command.

Trashing files

The KDE Trash appears on your desktop as a cute little trash can icon. However, the Trash is really a special-purpose folder (~/Desktop/Trash/) that serves as the temporary storage space for files and folders on their way to being removed from your system.

Placing a file or folder in the Trash folder is analogous to dropping papers into your office trash can. Files that are in the Trash are out of sight and out of mind, but they aren't yet out of your office. If you discover that you made a mistake and trashed the wrong file, you can dig into the trash can and retrieve it. When you're sure that you no longer need anything out of the Trash, you can empty the trash — permanently deleting files. The following list gives you some quick tips for using the KDE version of the trash can:

- ✔ Drag a file icon from the desktop or from a KFM window and drop it on the desktop Trash icon to move the file from its original location to the Trash folder.

- ✔ Right-click a file or folder icon in a KFM window and choose Move to Trash from the pop-up menu that appears. This also moves the file or folder into the Trash folder.

- ✔ Double-click the Trash icon on the desktop to open a KFM window displaying the contents of the Trash folder.

- ✔ To recover an individual file from the Trash, open the Trash folder and then click and drag the file icon out of the KFM window and drop it on the desktop or another KFM window.

- ✔ Right-click the Trash desktop icon and choose Empty Trash Bin from the pop-up menu that appears to permanently delete all the files stored in the Trash folder.

Putting files through the shredder

If you want to remove files or folders from your system without going through the two-step process of moving them to the Trash and then emptying the Trash, KFM enables you to do just that with its Delete command. But be careful, and be very sure that you really want to erase the file or folder. The Delete command is permanent. Using delete is kinda like running a paper through the shredder instead of just dropping it into the trash bin — there's no going back and retrieving the deleted file later.

Deleting a file or folder with KFM is easy. Just follow these steps:

1. **Open a KFM window and navigate to the directory containing the file or folder you want to delete.**

   You can also delete files and folders from the desktop without opening a KFM window.

2. **Right-click the file or folder icon and choose Delete from the pop-up menu that appears.**

   The KFM Warning box appears as shown in Figure 4-12. This is your last chance to change your mind before permanently removing the selected file from your system.

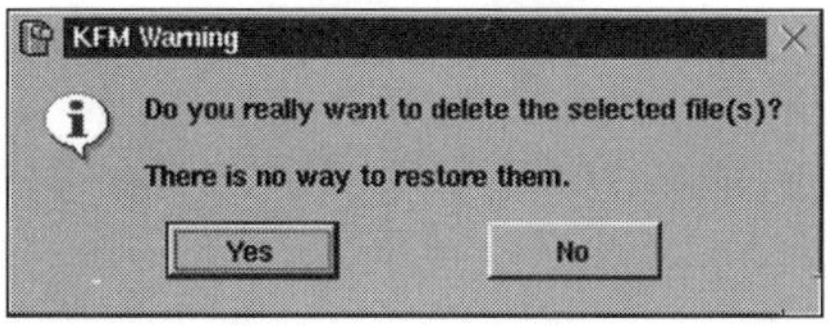

Figure 4-12:
KFM issues
a warning
before
deleting
the file.

> **KFM Warning** ☓
>
> (i) Do you really want to delete the selected file(s)?
>
> There is no way to restore them.
>
> [Yes]   [No]

3. Click the Yes button.

KFM closes the warning box and deletes the selected file or folder. It's outta here! Gone! Vamoosed!

Deleting a file removes the individual file from your system. But deleting a folder deletes not only the folder but also all the files and subfolders contained within that folder. That's a pretty drastic step. It's a good idea to open folders and check their contents before deleting them.

Opening Files in the Right Program

KFM enables you to explore your entire file system, going from directory to directory viewing the list of files in each folder. But you're not confined to looking at lists of filenames — KFM can also open files and launch programs.

To launch a program, click the program's executable file in a KFM window. KFM launches the program just as if you typed the program name at the command line. To open a document in a program of your selection, follow these steps:

1. Right-click a document icon in a KFM window and choose Open With from the pop-up menu that appears.

The dialog box shown in Figure 4-13 appears.

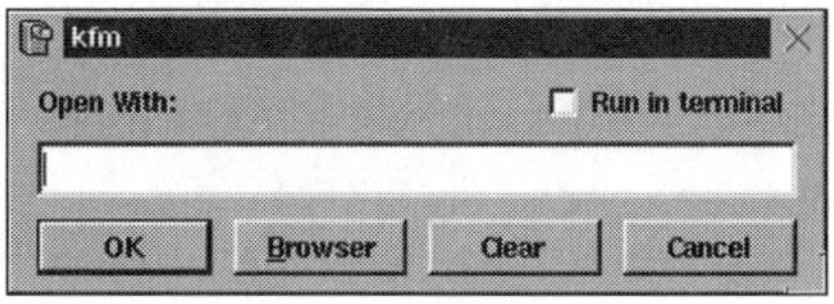

Figure 4-13:
You can
specify
what
program
KFM should
use to open
your file.

> **kfm** ☓
>
> Open With: ☐ Run in terminal
>
> [   ]
>
> [OK] [Browser] [Clear] [Cancel]

2. **Type a program name in the Open With text box.**

   Enter the name of the program you want to use to open the selected file. Be sure to use the name of the executable file, not the name as it appears on a menu somewhere. For example, type **kview** to use the KDE Image Viewer utility.

3. **Click OK.**

   KFM launches the program, which then loads the selected file.

To automatically open a document file in its parent program, click the document file in a KFM window. If KFM can identify the file type and its associated program, KFM launches the program and passes the file name to the program, so the program automatically loads the selected file.

If you want KFM to automatically launch the correct program when you click a document file, KFM must be able to identify the file type, and it must know what program to launch to open that file type.

A standard set of file type descriptions (called *MIME types*) and a set of default links between certain file types and some of the standard KDE utility programs, are both parts of the normal KDE installation. As a result, KFM starts out with a respectable number of file types that you can open with a single click. In addition, when you install new KDE programs, the installation routine should set up MIME types for the program's file types — and add links between those file types and the program so you can automatically open those files in the newly installed program.

Sometimes, you may need to create or customize the association between document file types and the application used to open them. You'll probably never need to create an actual MIME type from scratch; you probably won't even need to edit any existing MIME types. (So you're off the hook; this book won't drag you through creating MIME types.) If you want to use a specific program to open a particular kind of file, you may need to change the established links between the file type and the program KFM uses to open those files. You revise the application links by following these steps:

1. **Open a KFM window and choose Edit⇨Applications.**

   KFM displays the contents of a hidden subdirectory of your home directory, ~/.kde/share/applnk. This directory contains a series of link files and folders that correspond to the contents of the KDE menu.

2. **Navigate the subfolders to locate the application you want to change.**

   Open folders and subfolders as needed until KFM displays the icon for the link to the application you want to use to open the target file type.

3. **Right-click the application icon and choose Properties from the pop-up menu that appears.**

   A dialog box appears where you can edit the properties of the application link.

4. **Click the Application tab.**

   The settings shown in Figure 4-14 appear. The links between the application and the available file types are shown in the pair of list boxes near the bottom of the tab. The list box on the right shows all the available MIME types. The list box on the left shows the MIME types that are associated with this application.

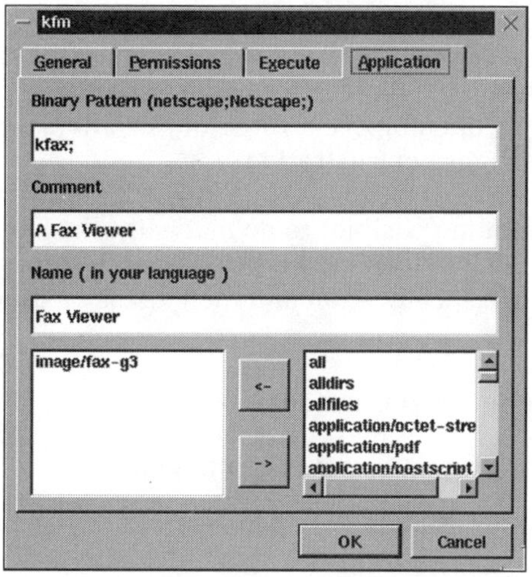

Figure 4-14:
Edit the list
of MIME
types
associated
with this
application.

5. **Select a file type in the list box on the right and click the <- button.**

   Select a MIME type by clicking it. When you click the <- button, the selected MIME type appears in the list box on the left, indicating that it is now linked to the current application type.

6. **Repeat Step 5 as needed for other MIME types.**

   You can also select a MIME type in the left list box and click the -> button to remove it from the list and thus remove the association between this application and the MIME type.

7. **After adjusting the list of MIME types, click OK.**

   KFM closes the dialog box and updates the associations between the application and the file types.

After adding an association between an application and a file type, you should be able to simply click a file icon for a file of that type and KFM will launch the application and automatically load the file. If KFM previously used a different application to open that file type, you may need to edit the properties for that application to remove the link to the file type in question. The idea is to remove any potential confusion about what program to use when opening the files.

Finding Lost Files

KFM can do an admirable job of managing any files you can display in a KFM window. However, locating a certain file in the complex directory structure of a typical Linux/UNIX system can be a real challenge. If you don't know where a file is located, the maze of nested directories-within-directories can make finding that file manually (by opening every directory in a KFM window and scanning its contents) an exercise in frustration.

But what is impractical (if not impossible) to do manually, the Find Files utility can do automatically. Find Files can methodically search through your file system looking for a given file specification and then display a list of the matches it finds.

To use the Find Files utility, follow these steps:

1. **Open the KDE menu and choose Utilities⇨Find Files.**

   The Find Files window appears as shown in Figure 4-15.

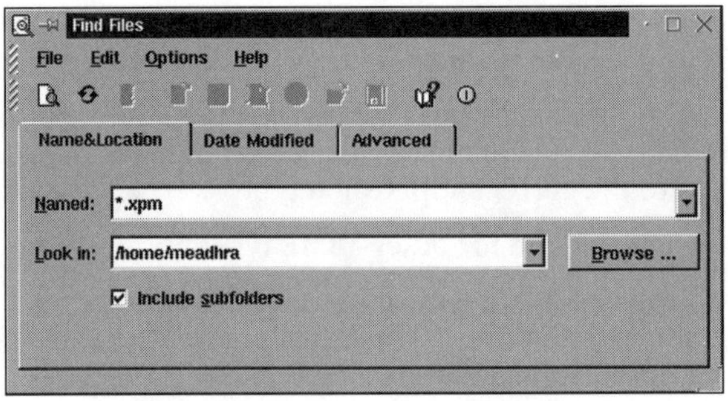

Figure 4-15:
The Find Files utility does just what its name implies.

2. **Type a file specification in the Named box.**

   You can enter a specific filename or use wildcards (***** and **?**) to define a search specification that may match multiple files.

3. Type the path name in the Look In box.

Enter a path name for a single directory or define the highest level of a directory tree branch that you want to search. To search the entire file system, enter the slash character (/).

4. Select (or clear) the Include Subfolders option.

As you probably guessed, this option controls whether Find Files confines its search to the specified folder or extends the search to all the subfolders as well.

5. If you need to further refine the search parameters, click the Date Modified or Advanced tabs and adjust the settings you find there.

You seldom need to use the Date Modified or Advanced settings, but they are there if you need them. For a normal search, select the All Files option on the Date Modified tab; and on the Advanced tab, select All Files and Folders in the Of Type drop-down list box — and make sure the Containing Text box is empty.

6. Choose File⇨Start Search.

Find Files begins searching your file system for files that match your specifications. After a few minutes, the Find Files window expands to display a list of the files it found, as shown in Figure 4-16.

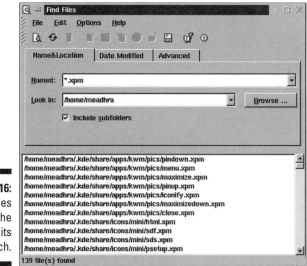

Figure 4-16:
Find Files
displays the
results of its
search.

7. Select a file from the list and choose File⇨Open Containing Folder.

A KFM window appears, showing the contents of the folder in which the selected file resides. Then you can use KFM to perform any normal file-maintenance chore on the selected file.

Instead of opening a KFM window, you can open the file directly from the Find Files window by double-clicking it. Alternatively, you can select the file and choose one of the other commands on the File menu — to delete the file, open its Properties dialog box, or add the file to an existing archive file.

Part II
Making KDE Look Right

The 5th Wave   By Rich Tennant

"Well, she's fast on the keyboard and knows how to load the printer, but she just sort of 'plays' with the mouse."

In this part . . .

1n some ways, the cyberworld is mercifully different from the real world. Case in point: Here, too, appearances matter — but in the world of KDE, you *can* master them — they actually have a practical reason beyond making an on-screen fashion statement.

This part shows you how to set up your Panel to your liking, design a desktop tailored to the way you actually work (what a concept!), and use KDE's themes to best advantage. Form follows function. Beautiful.

Chapter 5

Playing with the Panel

• •

• •

*I*f you settle into the driver's seat of a well-designed car, you find all the controls you need to drive the car arranged within easy reach on the wheel or the dashboard. The steering wheel and gearshift are not only at your fingertips — but the lights, turn signals, cruise control, heater, and even the radio are all readily accessible.

The KDE panel provides you with a similar level of convenient access to the command and control functions of your computer desktop. The panel enables you to launch programs, explore the file system, open virtual desktops, or log out with the click of a button. Just as the automotive dashboard, the panel even includes a convenient clock. You can use the taskbar to figuratively change gears by switching to another open window.

One big difference between a computer and automobile is that the computer is a much more versatile device. The tasks and tools required to drive a car are highly predictable, which enables engineers to develop a standard dashboard that is functional for nearly everyone. However, you perform a much wider variety of activities with the computer, such as checking e-mail, browsing the Web, writing letters and proposals, creating graphics, and much more. So, your computer dashboard — the KDE panel — needs to be customized to fit the way that you use it in order to make the panel the powerful and convenient tool that it should be.

As you discover in this chapter, KDE provides plenty of ways for you to customize the KDE panel and taskbar to tailor them to your preferences and working style.

Configuring the Panel and Taskbar

The KDE panel and taskbar start out in a standard location and configuration that is determined by the KDE developers. But you don't have to stick with the default setup. You can move both the panel and taskbar; you can hide them when they are not in use. You can change the size of the icons in the panel; you can edit the names that appear on the virtual desktop buttons. You can do all this and more.

A few simple changes in the panel and taskbar configuration can make a big difference in the appearance and usability of your KDE desktop.

Positioning the panel and taskbar

Perhaps the most obvious change you can make to the KDE panel and taskbar is to move them to another location on your desktop. The panel doesn't have to stay anchored to the bottom edge of the screen and the taskbar doesn't have to stay attached to the top. You can attach the panel to any one of the four sides of the screen. You can move the taskbar to the top, bottom, or top-left corner — or you can hide the taskbar completely. The choice is yours.

To reposition the KDE panel and taskbar, follow these steps:

1. **Click the KDE Menu button and choose Panel⇨Configure, or right-click the panel and choose Configure from the pop-up menu that appears.**

   The KPanel Configuration dialog box appears, as shown in Figure 5-1. The Panel tab is normally selected after you first open the KPanel Configuration dialog box. If not, click the Panel tab.

2. **Select one of the four radio buttons in the Location area.**

   This specifies the location of the KDE panel. You can position the panel on any one of the four sides of the desktop: top, bottom, left, or right. The default panel location is Bottom.

3. **Select one of the three size options in the Style area.**

   This option controls the size of the buttons in the KDE panel. You can choose the default size, Normal; a smaller, button size, Tiny; or a larger button size, ingeniously named Large.

   This option also indirectly controls the thickness of the KDE panel because the panel thickness adjusts automatically to accommodate the button size.

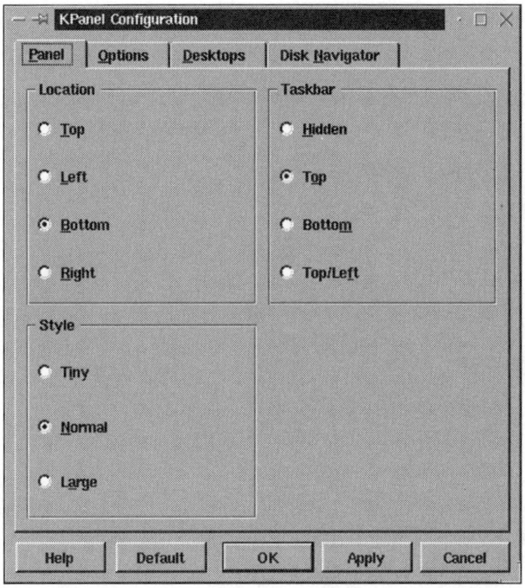

Figure 5-1:
Choose your preferred location for the KDE panel and taskbar.

4. **Select one of four radio buttons in the Taskbar area.**

   This option controls the location of the KDE taskbar. You have four choices:

   - **Hidden:** Suppresses display of the taskbar. If you don't like the taskbar, you don't have to use it. This is the choice for people who are using KDE on a low-resolution screen and can afford to devote screen space to the taskbar. (Hiding the taskbar is also the preferred option for KDE users who consider the taskbar just a little too Windows-like.)

   - **Top:** Positions the taskbar at the top edge of the screen (the default location).

   - **Bottom:** Positions the taskbar at the bottom edge of the screen or, if the panel is also located at the bottom, adjacent to the panel.

   - **Top/Left:** Positions the taskbar buttons in a column starting at the upper-left corner of the screen and continuing as far down the left side of the screen as necessary to accommodate a button for each running application.

5. **Click the Apply button.**

   KDE redraws the panel using the settings you specify.

Figure 5-2 shows a KDE desktop with the panel on the right side of the screen and taskbar in the top-left position. This is just one of the many combinations of panel and taskbar locations you can select. (Note that KDE automatically moves the desktop icons to the right to make room for the taskbar buttons.)

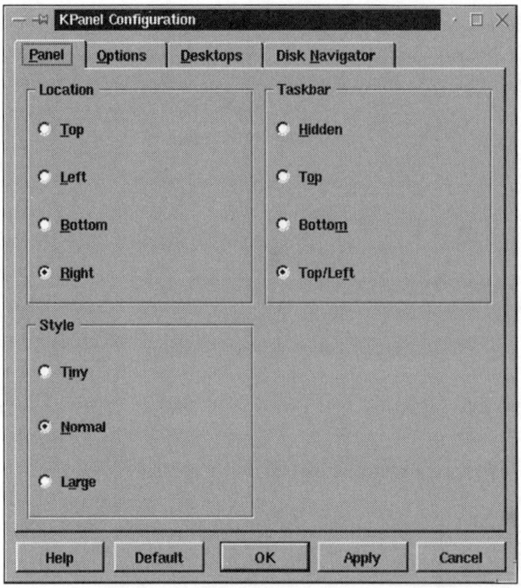

Figure 5-2:
Panel on the right and taskbar on the left — just one of many possibilities.

Playing hide and seek with the panel and taskbar

The KDE panel and the taskbar are both handy tools, but some people object to the amount of screen space they both consume — especially in the crowded confines of a low-resolution display. If you're concerned about devoting screen real estate to the panel or taskbar, you can configure KDE to automatically hide the panel or taskbar from view if they aren't being used. Here's how:

1. **Click the KDE Menu button and choose Panel⇨Configure, or right-click the panel and choose Configure from the pop-up menu that appears.**

   The KPanel Configuration dialog box appears.

2. **Click the Options tab.**

   The Options tab appears in the KPanel Configuration dialog box and displays the settings shown in Figure 5-3.

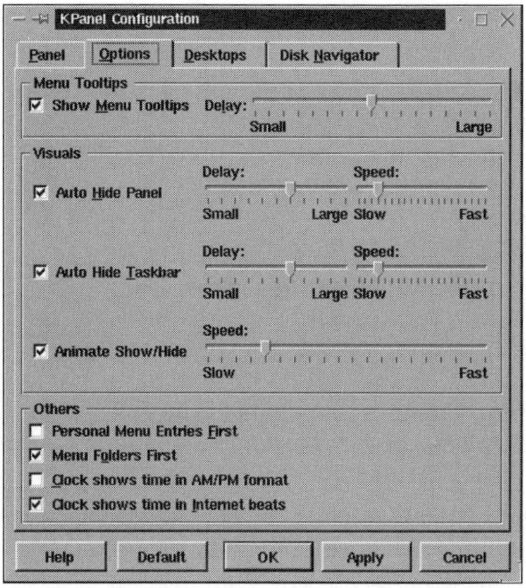

Figure 5-3:
The Auto
Hide feature
reduces the
screen
space
devoted to
the panel or
taskbar.

3. **Select (or deselect) the Show Menu Tooltips option and then adjust the Delay slider.**

   If you select the Show Menu Tooltips option, KDE displays a small pop-up box giving a short description of the button under the mouse pointer anytime you let the mouse pointer hover on a button for a second or so. The Delay slider controls how long the mouse pointer must hover on a button before the Tooltip box appears. Drag the Delay slider to the left to cause the Tooltip box to pop up quicker or drag the slider to the right to lengthen the delay before the Tooltip appears.

4. **Select (or deselect) the Auto Hide Panel option and then adjust the Delay and Speed sliders.**

   If you select the Auto Hide Panel option, KDE automatically collapses the KDE panel into the side of the desktop to which it is attached after you move the mouse pointer away from the panel. The panel becomes just a thin line at the edge of the desktop. This hiding action occurs after a short delay, the length of which is controlled by the Delay slider. KDE animates the hiding action, showing the panel slip into the side of the screen. The Speed slider controls the duration of the animation.

   To restore the hidden panel to its normal position on your desktop, simply move your mouse pointer over the thin line at the edge of the screen. The KDE panel resumes its normal size immediately.

5. **Select (or deselect) the Auto Hide Taskbar option and then adjust the Delay and Speed sliders.**

   The Auto Hide Taskbar option works the same as the Auto Hide Panel option described in Step 4.

6. **Select (or deselect) the Animate Show/Hide option and then adjust the Speed slider.**

This option controls what happens after you click the collapse buttons at either end of the KDE panel. If you deselect the Animate Show/Hide option, the KDE panel collapses instantly after you click one of the collapse buttons. If, on the other hand, you activate this option, KDE displays the collapsing panel as a smooth animation effect. The Speed slider controls the speed of the animation.

7. **Select (or deselect) the options in the Others area.**

You can activate or deactivate any combination of the following four options:

- **Personal Menu Entries First:** Changes the order of items on the KDE menu to place applications and menu folders you add to the menu above the default KDE entries.

- **Menu Folders First:** Displays individual applications above folders (submenus) in the KDE menu.

- **Clock Shows Time in AM/PM Format:** Changes the clock display in the panel from the default 24-hour (military time) format to the 12-hour, AM/PM format.

- **Clock Shows Time in Internet Beats:** Changes the clock display in the panel from normal time to Internet beats — a proposed universal time format in which the day is divided into 1,000 beats with 500 being noon.

8. **Click the Apply button.**

KDE redraws the panel using the settings you specify.

Check out the desktop shown in Figure 5-4. Neither the panel nor taskbar is showing, but they aren't far away. If you look closely at the top and bottom edge of the screen, you can see a thin line, which are the remnants of the panel and taskbar in hiding. Just pointing to one of these lines with your mouse brings the panel or taskbar back on-screen.

Naming the desktop pager buttons

Virtual desktops are a great way to get more space to spread out your windows. Instead of shuffling stacks of open windows on your computer desktop, you can create up to eight virtual desktops, each with a different collection of windows, and switch back and forth between them. You can keep your Web surfing on one desktop and your budget proposal on another.

But wait, is your e-mail program open on desktop Two or desktop Five? You can solve that problem by renaming the panel buttons you use to access your virtual desktops. To manage the number of virtual desktops and assign them meaningful names, follow these steps:

1. **Click the KDE Menu button and choose Panel⊏Configure, or right-click the panel and choose Configure from the pop-up menu that appears.**

   The KPanel Configuration dialog box appears.

2. **Click the Desktops tab.**

   The Desktops tab appears in the KPanel Configuration dialog box and displays the settings shown in Figure 5-5.

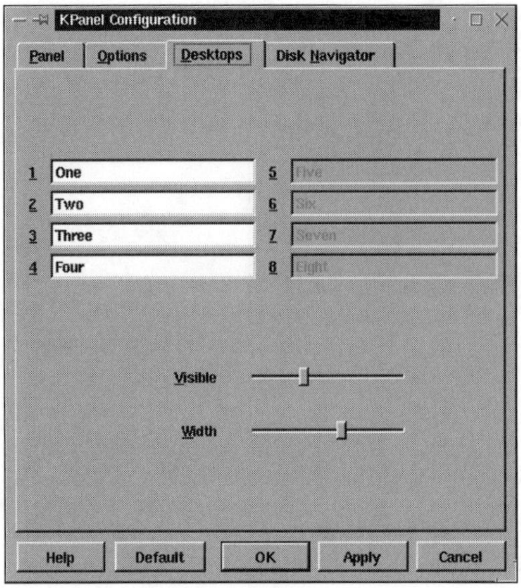

KPanel Configuration

| Panel | Options | Desktops | Disk Navigator |

1 One   5 Five
2 Two   6 Six
3 Three 7 Seven
4 Four   8 Eight

Visible ———⊟————

Width ————⊟———

| Help | Default | OK | Apply | Cancel |

Figure 5-5:
Assign your
virtual desk-
tops names
that relate
to the way
you use
them.

3. **Adjust the Visible slider.**

   Drag the slider to the left to decrease the number of desktop buttons visible in the panel. Drag the slider to the right to increase the number of buttons available.

4. **Adjust the Width slider.**

   Drag the slider left or right to decrease or increase the horizontal size of the desktop buttons on the panel.

5. **Double-click a desktop name in one of the numbered text boxes and type a new name.**

   You can rename your desktops from the default names (One, Two, and so on) to anything you want. Keep the names short so that they fit on the panel buttons.

   Try naming your desktops for the kind of work that you do on each desktop. For example, if you normally keep a Web browser open on one desktop and your e-mail program on another, you can name those desktops Web and Mail.

6. **Repeat Step 5 for each of the desktop names.**

7. **Click the OK button.**

   KDE closes the KPanel Configuration dialog box and redraws the panel using the settings that you specify.

Panel Ploys

The KDE panel starts out with a default assortment of buttons that provide one-click access to several useful utility programs. But the odds are that those buttons don't represent the programs and utilities that you use the most. You need to replace the default button selection with buttons you can use to launch the programs you use every day.

Only after you customize the panel with buttons for your favorite programs does the panel begin to live up to its potential for making your day-to-day computer use faster and easier. Fortunately, adding and rearranging panel buttons are among the fastest and easiest KDE customization tasks.

Adding buttons to the panel

KDE makes it very easy to add buttons to the panel. If you can access a program from the KDE menu, you can add its button to the panel. (To find out how to add a program to the KDE menu, see the "Adding Applications to the KDE Menu" section in this chapter.) To add an application button to the panel, follow these steps:

1. **Click the KDE Menu button and then choose Panel⇨Add Application.**

   KDE displays a submenu that duplicates the menu structure of your main KDE menu.

2. **Choose the application that you want to add from the submenu.**

   For example, to add a button for the Reversi game to the panel, the full menu selection is: KDE Menu⇨Panel⇨Add Application⇨Games⇨Reversi. The new button appears on the panel between the desktop buttons and the clock.

 The Windowlist and Disk Navigator buttons have their own separate menu commands that you can use to add or remove those buttons on the panel. Choose KDE Menu⇨Panel⇨Add Windowlist to add the Windowlist button to the panel. Choosing the command again removes the button. Similarly, you can use the Add Disk Navigator command to add or remove the Disk Navigator button.

Rearranging panel buttons

If you don't like the arrangement of the buttons on the KDE panel, move 'em. It's easy to do. Here are the simple steps for moving a panel button:

1. **Right-click the panel button and choose Move from the pop-up menu that appears.**

   The pointer changes to a four-headed arrow.

2. **Move the mouse to drag the button around on the panel and then click the mouse button to drop the button in its new location.**

   KDE automatically rearranges other buttons on the panel, scooting them over to make room for the button you moved.

To remove a button from the panel, right-click the panel button you want to delete and choose Remove from the pop-up menu that appears. KDE deletes the button from the panel immediately.

Docking maneuvers

Some applications have the capability to *dock* in the panel — that is, an icon for the application appears in a special part of the panel next to the clock. Figure 5-6 shows several icons in the dock area. Usually, the docked application is really a mini-application (called an *applet*) that needs to run in the background but remains accessible.

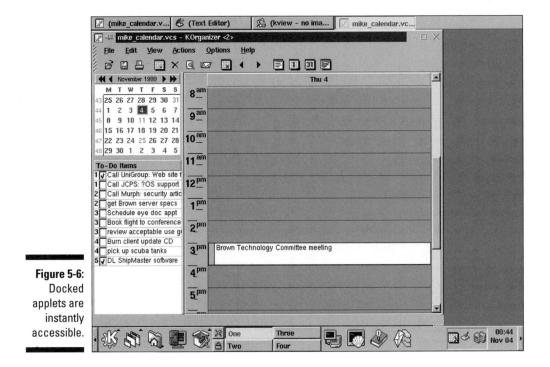

Figure 5-6:
Docked
applets are
instantly
accessible.

Docking ability must be programmed into utility, because it's not something you can control. Normally, a program places an icon into the panel dock automatically after you start the application. KNotes and the KOrganizer Control Applet are examples.

Sometimes docking is an optional feature of a program or utility, and you invoke it by selecting an option in a dialog box. For example, if you select the Dock Into The Panel option in the lower-left corner of the Background tab of the Display Settings dialog box, KDE adds the Display Settings icon to dock. To open the Display Settings dialog box, you simply click the icon in the dock.

Adding Applications to the KDE Menu

Unquestionably, the most versatile button on the KDE panel is the KDE Menu button. Other panel buttons enable you to launch individual programs and utilities. The KDE Menu button, on the other hand, enables you to launch any of the many programs that are installed on the menu. That's one powerful button.

The KDE menu comes preconfigured with menu items for all the standard KDE components. Other KDE-aware programs automatically add themselves to the KDE menu after you install the program. That means that most, if not all, of your KDE-specific programs are available on the KDE menu. However, you undoubtedly have other programs installed on your Linux/UNIX system that deserve a place on the KDE menu as well. After all, the KDE menu can't fulfill its promise as your one-stop command center for starting applications unless the KDE menu includes all your applications.

Like nearly everything else on the KDE desktop, you can customize the KDE menu to adapt it to your own needs. You can add and delete menu items and submenus and you can rearrange the menu to suit your preferences.

If you have already created a desktop icon or other `.kdelnk` file icon to launch an application, you can simply drag that icon from the desktop or from a KFM window and drop it on the KDE Menu button in the panel. KDE immediately adds the new menu item to the Personal submenu to launch that application. Later, you can use the Menu Editor to move the menu item to another location on the KDE menu.

Adding applications automatically

After you first install KDE, the idea of having to manually add a long list of your non-KDE programs to the KDE menu may seem like a daunting task. Fortunately, the KDE developers anticipated this scenario and created a utility program that will do the job for you automatically. Here's how:

1. **Click the KDE Menu button and choose System⇨Appfinder.**

   KDE opens a Terminal window and runs a script that scans your system looking for a long list of known applications. Depending on the size and speed of your system, the process can require anywhere from a few seconds to a few minutes. The Appfinder utility creates a Personal submenu on the KDE menu and automatically adds menu items to that submenu for the applications it finds on your system.

That's all there is to it. One simple step and you're done!

Appfinder may not find every executable program on your system, but it does a pretty good job of locating most of the standard inventory of applications included with the popular Linux distributions. After running Appfinder, you should be left with a fairly short list of applications that you need to manually add to the KDE menu.

Manipulating menus with the menu editor utility

The Appfinder utility is a fast and easy way to add applications to the KDE menu, but it doesn't provide any opportunity to really customize the menu. For that, you need to use the KDE Menu Editor utility. With it, you cannot only add applications to the menu, you can also add submenus and rearrange menu items. Menu Editor gives you complete control over the contents and arrangement of the KDE menu's Personal submenu and lets you make some changes to the KDE default menu as well.

To open the KDE Menu Editor utility, use the following technique:

1. **Click the KDE Menu button and choose Panel⇨Edit Menus.**

The Menu Editor window appears. Two menus appear in the window. The one on the left is the Personal submenu and the one on the right is the KDE Default menu. The standard menu items that appear at the bottom of the KDE menu (Disk Navigator, Panel, Lock Screen, and Logout) do not appear in the Menu Editor window because those items are permanent parts of the KDE menu and you can't edit them.

As you work with the Menu Editor, keep the following factors in mind:

✔ Click a submenu name to open or close the submenu.

✔ Pointing to a menu item or submenu causes it to look like a raised button. This indicates the item that will be changed or the location where a new item will be inserted.

✔ Right-click a menu item or submenu to pop up a menu of commands you can use on that item.

Building your own menus

You can use Menu Editor to add submenus to the Personal menu and to its submenus, but not to the KDE default menu. To add a submenu, follow these steps:

1. **Right-click anywhere on the Personal menu and choose New from the pop-up menu that appears.**

   A KMenuEdit dialog box appears

2. **Select SubMenu in the Type drop-down list box.**

   The unneeded options in the lower half of the dialog box disappear.

   You can use this same technique to create a new menu item for an application. In that case, you'd probably need some of those lower options. But these options don't apply to submenus, so they disappear after you choose the SubMenu type.

3. **Click the Name text box and type a name for the new submenu.**

   This is the menu name that appears on the KDE menu.

4. **To specify an icon for the submenu, type the icon's filename in the Icon text box.**

5. **Type an alternate description in the Comment text box.**

   This is the text that KDE displays in the pop-up Tooltip, which appears if you point to the submenu without clicking it.

6. **Click OK.**

   The Menu Editor closes the dialog box and adds the new submenu to the Personal menu in the Menu Editor window. You can click the submenu name to open the new submenu.

Adding applications with KFM

You can add applications to the KDE menu by simply dragging icons from a KFM window. Here's how:

1. **Open the Menu Editor window and display the contents of the menu and submenu where you want to add a new menu item.**

   You may need to open one or more submenus to get the target location of the new menu item visible. Move the Menu Editor window and/or the menus within the Menu Editor so that the target submenu won't be obscured by the KFM window that you open in the next step.

2. **Open a KFM window and position it so that the target submenu is visible in the Menu Editor window.**

3. **Display the application file in the KFM window.**

Navigate through the directory structure to display the filename and icon for the application's executable file.

4. **Click and drag the file from the KFM window and drop it on the target submenu in the Menu Editor window.**

The filename appears as an entry on the submenu in the Menu Editor window.

Rearranging menus

In addition to adding applications to the KDE menu, you can rearrange the menus to change the order of the items on a submenu, move items from one submenu to another, and delete submenus and menu items.

✔ To move a menu item within the same submenu, right-click a menu item (or submenu) and choose Select Item For Moving from the pop-up menu that appears. After the cross-hair cursor appears, use it to drag the selected item up or down the submenu list and drop the item in its new location. Menu Editor moves the other menu items to make room.

✔ To delete a menu item, right-click a menu item or submenu and choose Delete from the pop-up menu that appears. Menu Editor removes the item from the menu. If you Delete a submenu, you also delete its contents.

✔ To move a menu item from one submenu to another, right-click a menu item you want to move and choose Cut from the pop-up menu that appears. Then open the submenu to which you want to move the item, right-click the submenu where you want to insert the item, and choose Paste from the pop-up menu that appears.

After editing your KDE menu with the Menu Editor, don't forget to save your changes before closing the Menu Editor window. Choose File➪Save or click the Save button on the Menu Editor toolbar.

Chapter 6

Desktop Design

- -

In This Chapter

▶ Redecorating your desktop

▶ Having fun with screensavers

▶ Sounding off with system sounds

▶ Language lessons for KDE keyboards

- -

*M*ost people like to customize their office environment with personal touches of some kind.

Most people? What are we saying? *Everybody* does it! If you walk down the hall and find an occupied office or cubicle that doesn't have at least some personalized decorations, check the occupant's pulse.

KDE caters to this universal need to customize and control our environment by providing plenty of ways to tailor the KDE desktop to individual tastes and preferences. You can change the color of almost everything on the desktop, and you can select the sounds associated with various actions. You can customize the keyboard to work with your native language, and you can change the position of the buttons in the window titlebars. This chapter shows you how to do all of these things and more.

Redecorating the Desktop

Wouldn't it be nice if you could change the color of the walls in your office to fit your mood? While you're at it, you could plop down some new carpet, move in a different style desk, and replace all your desk accessories. When you're feeling like a traditionalist, you could surround yourself with hand-rubbed mahogany wood furniture and then switch instantly to a high-tech industrial style after you wake up from the dream (or was that a nightmare).

Unless you have a magic wand (and an unlimited budget), such changes aren't possible in the real world. But changes are possible in the virtual world of your computer desktop. KDE not only enables you to customize nearly every aspect of your desktop, the changes are so quick and easy to do that you can completely redecorate your desktop on a whim, anytime the mood strikes you.

Designing desktop color and wallpaper

KDE provides you with many ways to customize your desktop environment. Perhaps the single most striking change you can make is to select a different background for the KDE desktop. You can select a solid color, a two-color gradation or pattern; or you can use an image file to create the computer equivalent of wallpaper. If you choose the wallpaper option, you can use a single large image to cover your desktop, such as a mural (as shown in Figure 6-1), or you can repeat a smaller image many times to create a pattern.

To adjust your desktop background settings, follow these steps:

1. **Right-click the desktop and choose Display Properties from the pop-up menu that appears.**

   KDE opens the Display Settings dialog box. Normally, the Background tab is selected by default. If not, click the Background tab to display the options shown in Figure 6-2.

Figure 6-1:
This vegetarian desktop is just one of the many wallpaper effects you can try.

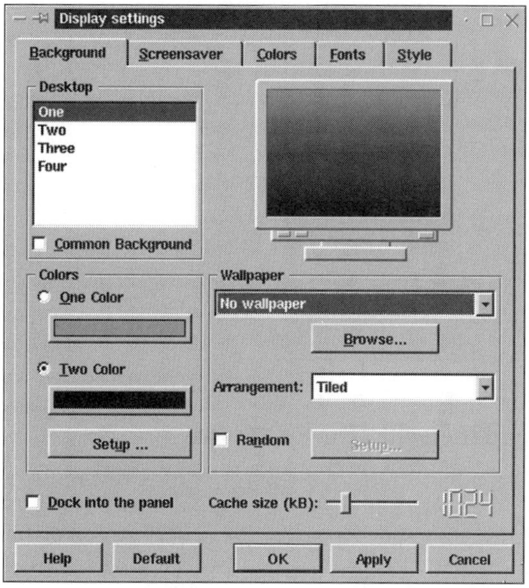

Figure 6-2:
The
Background
tab of the
Display
Settings
dialog box
gives you
lots of
options.

You can also access the same Background settings by choosing KDE
Menu⇨KDE Control Center to open the KDE Control Center dialog box
and select Desktop and then Background in the list box on the left side
of dialog box. The Background tab then appears on the right side of the
KDE Control Center dialog box.

**2. Select a desktop name in the Desktop list box or select the Common
Background checkbox.**

If you select a specific desktop, all the other settings on the Background
tab will apply to that desktop and not to the other desktops. This
enables you to create separate backgrounds for each desktop. If, on the
other hand, you select the Common Background option, the background
settings will apply to all the desktops — all your desktops will be
identical.

3. Select One Color or Two Color in the Colors area.

Select One Color to create a desktop background that is all one solid
color. Select Two Color to create a graduated background effect that
blends from one color to another or a two-color pattern. If you select the
Two Color option, the second color button and the Setup button become
active. (Both are grayed out if you select the One Color option.)

4. Select the One Color radio button.

The Select Color dialog box appears, as shown in Figure 6-3.

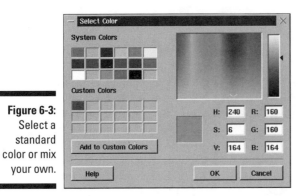

Figure 6-3:
Select a
standard
color or mix
your own.

5. **Select a color and then click the OK button.**

   You can select a System Color or a Custom Color by simply clicking one of the color boxes on the left side of the Select Color dialog box. To create a new color, click the color you want in the large spectrum box on the right half of the Select Color dialog box. A sample of the color appears in the preview box just below the spectrum. You can make the color darker or lighter by dragging the arrow pointer beside the value slider to the right of the spectrum box. For precise control, you can type numbers into the H, S, V or R, G, B text boxes. After creating a new color, you can add it to the Custom Colors palette by clicking the Add to Custom Colors button.

   After you make a color selection, the face of the One Color button changes to reflect your choice. The monitor-shaped preview box in the upper-right quadrant of the Background tab also changes to give you an idea of how your color selection will look on your desktop.

6. **If you chose the Two Color option in Step 3, click the Two Color button and select the second color.**

   Again, the Select Color dialog box appears. Select a system color or a predefined custom color, or create a new color, and then click the OK button to close the Select Color dialog box to record your choice. KDE updates the face of the Two Color button and the preview box to reflect your color choice.

7. **If you chose the Two Color option in Step 3, click the Setup button. Choose a blend direction or pattern from the Two Color Backgrounds dialog box, and then click the OK button to close the dialog box and record the setting.**

   After you click the Setup button, the Two Color Backgrounds dialog box appears, as shown in Figure 6-4. The three radio buttons enable you to choose between a vertical blend, a horizontal blend, or a pattern. If you choose one of the blends, KDE creates a graduated color background composed of intermediate shades and tints between the two colors you specify. If you choose the Use Pattern option, you can then select a pattern from the Pattern Name list. The Preview box shows the selected pattern. After making your selections, click the OK button to close the Two Color Backgrounds dialog box.

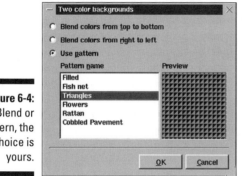

Figure 6-4:
Blend or pattern, the choice is yours.

8. **Select an image file from the Wallpaper drop-down list box.**

If you don't want to use wallpaper on your desktop, select the No Wallpaper option in the Wallpaper drop-down list box. Otherwise, select the name of the image file you want to use as desktop wallpaper. If the file you want to use doesn't appear in the list, click the Browse button to display an Open dialog box (the same kind of dialog box you use to open and file an application) and use the controls in the dialog box to locate and select an image file.

If you elect to use wallpaper and choose either a full-screen image or a smaller image that is tiled to fill the entire desktop, the background color setting becomes meaningless because none of the background will show. However, if you select a wallpaper image that does not fill the entire screen, the background color will create a frame around the wallpaper image and you will need to select a compatible color.

9. **Select a display pattern in the Arrangement drop-down list box.**

For full-screen images, you normally select Centered. For small images that you want to repeat as needed to fill the desktop, you normally select Tiled. However, the Arrangement drop-down list box contains a number of selections — mostly variations on these two themes. Try selecting different arrangement settings and watch the Preview box to see their effect.

For an interesting variation on the wallpaper idea, select the Random option. Then click the adjacent Setup button to open the Random Mode Setup dialog box, where you can select a whole directory full of image files and specify a delay to have KDE automatically change wallpaper every few minutes. Personally, we find many effects distracting, but who knows, you may like it.

10. **Unless you chose Common Background in Step 2, repeat Steps 2 through 9 for each of the other desktops.**

    After you select a new desktop on the Background tab, KDE applies the settings to the previous desktop. The effect is the same as if you clicked the Apply button.

11. **Click the Apply button or the OK button.**

    KDE applies the settings to your desktop, and if you clicked the OK button, closes the Display Settings dialog box.

Window dressing — color schemes

When you start redecorating your KDE desktop, you don't have to stop with the desktop background. Although the desktop background is the largest piece of screen real estate you can recolor, it's certainly not the only one. You can also control the colors KDE uses to draw application windows, dialog boxes, and the like. You can exercise individual control over details such as the titlebar color, titlebar text color, and window background. You can select the colors of each element individually, or you can choose one of several pre-defined color schemes. The choice is yours.

To select your window colors, follow these steps:

1. **Right-click the desktop and choose Display Properties from the pop-up menu that appears.**

    The Display Settings dialog box appears. (The step isn't necessary if the Display Settings dialog box is already open.)

2. **Click the Colors tab.**

    KDE displays the settings shown in Figure 6-5.

3. **Select a predefined color scheme from the Color Scheme list box.**

    The preview box in the top of the Colors tab shows a sample of the selected color scheme. The preview box makes it easy to check out the individual schemes without having to apply each one to your desktop. If you find a color scheme that you like, you can click the Apply button to apply it to your desktop, and skip the rest of this procedure.

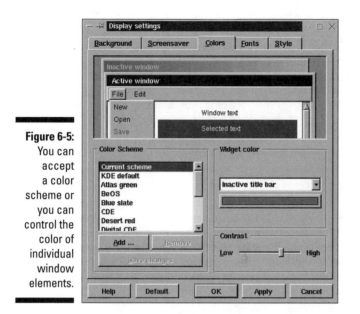

Figure 6-5:
You can
accept
a color
scheme or
you can
control the
color of
individual
window
elements.

4. **To change the color of an individual window element, select the element name from the Widget Color drop-down list box.**

   You can also select a window element by clicking the part of the window that you want to change in the preview box.

5. **Click the Widget Color button and choose a color from the Select Color dialog box that appears, and then click OK to close the Select Color dialog box.**

   The Widget Color button is the unlabeled button below the Widget Color drop-down list box. After you click the Widget Color button, the Select Color dialog box appears. Refer back to Figure 6-3 and to Step 5 of the "Designing desktop color and wallpaper" section for instructions on using the Select Color dialog box.

   After you select a color, the face of the Widget Color button and the corresponding portion of the preview box both change to reflect your new color choice.

6. **Repeat Steps 4 and 5 as needed to change the color of other window elements.**

   Continue adjusting the color of various window elements until you achieve the effect you desire.

7. **Click the Apply button.**

   KDE applies the current color settings to the windows and dialog boxes on your desktop. If you like what you see, you can save the current window color settings as a new color scheme.

8. **Click the Add button, type a name in the Add a Color Scheme dialog box that appears, and then click the OK button.**

   KDE creates a new color scheme containing the current window color settings. In the future, you'll be able to re-create these color settings by simply selecting the scheme name from the Color Scheme list box. If, instead of creating a new color scheme, you want to update the settings for the current color scheme, click the Save Changes button instead of the Add button.

Using the screensaver

Screensavers used to be essential tools to prevent *burn in* — a ghost image that would become permanently burned into the phosphors of a computer monitor if the same image remained on the screen too long. To prevent the problem, the screensaver kicks in after a predefined period of inactivity and replaces the normal screen image with a blank screen or a moving image that doesn't remain static long enough to cause burn in.

Modern computer monitors are highly resistant to burn in, but screensavers are more popular now than ever before. That's because screensavers do more than prevent burn in — they also protect your work from prying eyes if you leave your computer unattended for a few minutes. In addition to the practical applications of screensavers, they have a significant fun quotient as well. The moving images employed by screensavers can be amusing, and even hypnotic . . . or, mesmerizing . . . er, heh, wake up!

Of course, KDE includes an assortment of interesting screensavers for your enjoyment. To put screensavers to work protecting your system, follow these steps:

1. **Right-click the desktop and choose Display Properties from the pop-up menu that appears.**

   The Display Settings dialog box appears. (The step isn't necessary if the Display Settings dialog box is already open.)

2. **Click the Screensaver tab.**

   KDE displays the settings shown in Figure 6-6.

3. **Select a screensaver name from the Screen Saver list box.**

   The preview box in the top half of the Screensaver tab shows you approximately what your screensaver choice looks like.

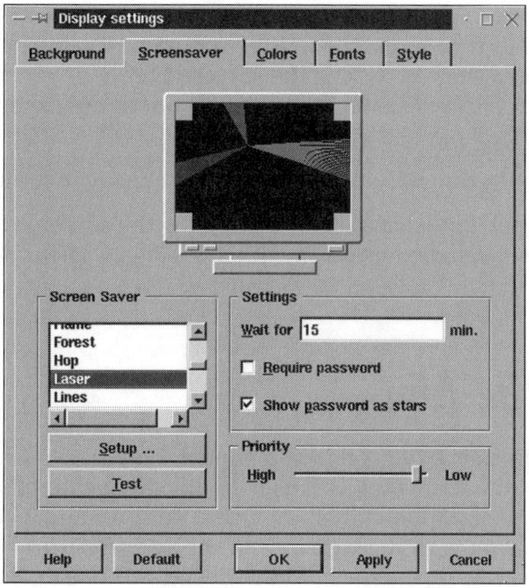

Figure 6-6:
Pick your
favorite
screensaver.

4. **Click the Setup button, adjust the settings in the dialog box that appears, and click the OK button to return to the Screensaver tab.**

   Each screensaver has a different dialog box that appears after you click the Setup button. The settings in the dialog box vary depending on what options are available for that screensaver. Typically, you can select how many objects are to appear on the screen and how fast they move. You may be able to specify colors or other settings. Some screensavers have no setup dialog boxes associated with them.

5. **Type a number in the Wait For text box.**

   This setting controls how long KDE waits after your last keyboard or mouse input before engaging the screensaver.

6. **If you want to require a password to disengage the screensaver, select the Require Password option and also the Show Password As Stars option.**

   If you do not engage in the Require Password option, any mouse movement or keyboard input disengages the screensaver and immediately returns your normal desktop to the screen. If you elect to use the password option, KDE displays a dialog box requesting your login password after you attempt to disengage the screensaver. You must enter the proper password before KDE will restore your desktop. This feature effectively denies unauthorized users access to your desktop while you're away from your computer. The Show Password As Stars option masks your password from view as you enter it into the dialog box to deactivate the screensaver. If you use the password option, it makes sense to use the Show Password As Stars option as well.

Leave the Priority slider at the Low end of the scale. This setting will allow background processes to continue running with minimal interference from the screensaver. Giving the screensaver higher priority may improve the screensaver's animation effects, but at the expense of your background processors and other users.

7. Click the Apply button to apply your new screensaver settings to KDE.

You won't see any immediate effect of applying the screensaver until your system remains idle for the specified wait time. Then the screensaver appears.

Changing the font

Colors aren't the only part of your desktop appearance that you can change. You can also control the fonts that KDE uses to display the text that appears in places such as menus, window titlebars, panel buttons, and icon labels. The fonts that appear on your desktop have a subtle, but surprisingly significant effect on the overall appearance of your desktop. You can choose simple fonts for maximum legibility or fancy, or specialty fonts for a bizarre visual effect. Or perhaps you want to take the conservative approach and select the fonts dictated by your corporate identity standard. (How boring!)

By default, KDE uses the Helvetica font for almost all desktop text. If you're looking for maximum legibility, beating the old standard, Helvetica, is hard. However, if you want to try something a bit more adventurous, you can select another font by following these steps:

1. Right-click the desktop and choose Display Properties from the pop-up menu that appears.

The Display Settings dialog box appears. (The step isn't necessary if the Display Settings dialog box is already open.)

2. Click the Fonts tab.

KDE displays the settings shown in Figure 6-7.

3. Select a font category from the large list box on the left side of the Fonts tab.

Most of the font categories are fairly self-explanatory.

- General Font is used for menus, icon labels, and most everything else that isn't listed separately.

- Fixed Font is used to display non-proportional text.

- Window Title Font is for the text appears in the titlebar of program windows.

- **Panel Button Font** is the font used to label the desktop buttons in the panel.

- **Panel Clock Font** is the font used to display the time and date in the panel.

4. **Select a font and font parameters from the settings on the right side of the Fonts tab.**

    Select a font from the Typeface drop-down list box. Then select the Bold and/or Italic options as appropriate. Adjust the type size by clicking the small plus or minus buttons at the right end of the Size box. Finally, select the appropriate character set in the Character Set drop-down list box.

    The text in the Sample Text box changes to show a preview of your font selection.

5. **Repeat Steps 2 and 3 for each of the font categories that you want to change.**

6. **Click the OK button.**

    KDE closes the Display Settings dialog box and redraws the desktop and panel to apply your new font settings.

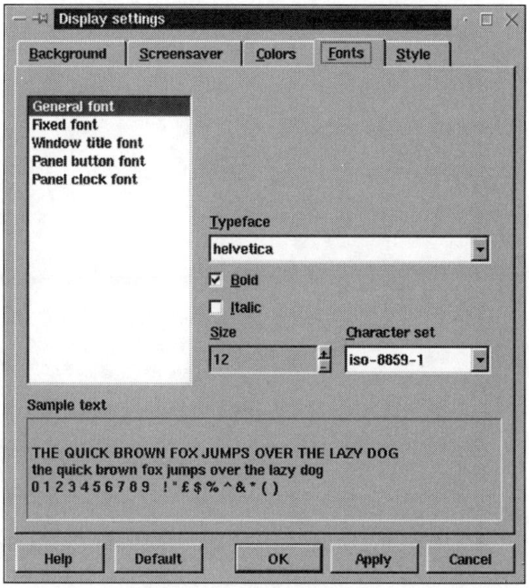

Figure 6-7:
You can change the fonts KDE uses to display menus, window titles, and more.

Detailing desktop icons

A good interior decorator is attentive to details, and KDE gives you the tools you need to be attentive to the details of decorating your desktop. In particular, KDE enables you to adjust some significant details that affect how desktop icons are displayed. To adjust the desktop icons settings, follow these steps:

1. **Choose KDE Menu⇨KDE Control Panel or click the KDE Control Panel button on the panel.**

   The KDE Control Panel window appears.

2. **Click the plus sign beside Desktop and then select Desktop Icons in the list box on the left side of the KDE Control Panel window.**

   The Desktop Icons tab appears too, as shown in Figure 6-8.

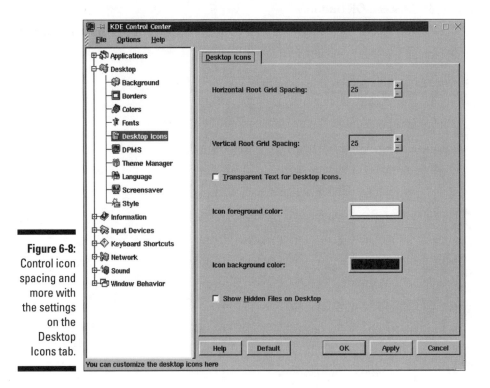

Figure 6-8:
Control icon spacing and more with the settings on the Desktop Icons tab.

3. **Adjust the settings in the Horizontal Root Grid Spacing and Vertical Root Grid Spacing boxes.**

   The numbers in these boxes determine the horizontal and vertical spacing between desktop icons. Actually, the settings adjust the size of an invisible grid on your desktop. KDE automatically places icons on the closest grid intersection. To adjust the grid spacing numbers, click the small plus or minus buttons at the right end of each box.

4. **Select or deselect the Transparent Text for Desktop Icons option.**

   If you deselect the Transparent Text for Desktop Icons option, the text label below each desktop icon appears with a rectangle or background box behind the text. If you select the Transparent Text option, the background box does not appear, thus allowing the desktop background to show around and behind the text.

   If your desktop background is a busy wallpaper pattern, you probably want to deselect the Transparent Text for Desktop Icons option. On such a desktop background, a contrasting background for the desktop icon text makes the labels easier to read. Otherwise, you probably want to select the option to reduce the visual clutter on your desktop by eliminating a separate background rectangle behind each desktop icon label.

5. **Click the Icon Foreground Color button, choose a color from the Select Color dialog box that appears, and then click the OK button.**

   This selection specifies the text color for the desktop icon labels. Refer back to Figure 6-3 and to Step 5 of the "Designing desktop color and wallpaper" section for instructions on using the Select Color dialog box.

   If you select the Transparent Text for Desktop Icons option, be sure to select an Icon Foreground Color that provides good contrast with your desktop background color.

6. **If you deselect the Transparent Text for Desktop Icons option in Step 4, click the Icon Background Color button, choose a color from the Select Color dialog box that appears, and then click the OK button.**

   This selection specifies the color for the optional background behind the desktop icon label text. It is grayed out if you select the Transparent Text for Desktop Icons option. Again, refer back to Figure 6-3 and to Step 5 of the "Designing desktop color and wallpaper" section for instructions on using the Select Color dialog box.

7. **Select or deselect the Show Hidden Files on Desktop option.**

   Remember that the icons on your desktop are really graphic representations of files contained in the Desktop subfolder of your home directory. The Show Hidden Files on Desktop option controls whether KDE shows or hides icons for any hidden files that may be contained in that directory. Normally, you leave this option deselected.

8. Click the OK button.

The Desktop Icons tab disappears from the KDE Control Center window and KDE redraws your desktop to apply any new settings.

Setting System Sounds

Using KDE does not have to be a silent experience. If you have a properly configured sound card and speakers, KDE gives you auditory feedback whenever system events occur. System events that trigger sounds include actions such as starting KDE, changing desktops, opening and closing windows, and logging out of KDE.

Like nearly everything else in KDE, you can customize the KDE sounds. You can choose what sound is associated with each of the many KDE system events. To adjust the sound settings, follow these steps:

1. Choose KDE Menu↷KDE Control Panel or click the KDE Control Panel button on the panel.

The KDE Control Panel window appears.

2. Click the plus sign beside Sound and then select System Sounds in the list box on the left side of the KDE Control Panel window.

The Sound tab appears, as shown in Figure 6-9.

3. Select the Enable System Sounds option.

You can use this option to enable (or silence) the KDE system sounds.

4. Select a system event from the Events list box.

5. Select a sound file from the Sounds list box.

KDE plays the selected sound whenever the system event you selected in the Events list occurs. If you don't want a sound associated with the selected system event, select (none) in the Sounds list.

If you have other sound files that you want to use, open a KFM window and navigate to the directory where those sound files are stored, and then drag the sound files from the KFM window and drop them on the Sounds list. KDE adds the sounds to the list where they are available for your selection.

6. Repeat Steps 4 and 5 as needed to define sounds for other system events.

7. Click the OK button.

The Sound tab disappears from the KDE Control Panel window and KDE updates your system sound settings. Whenever a system event occurs, KDE plays the associated sound file.

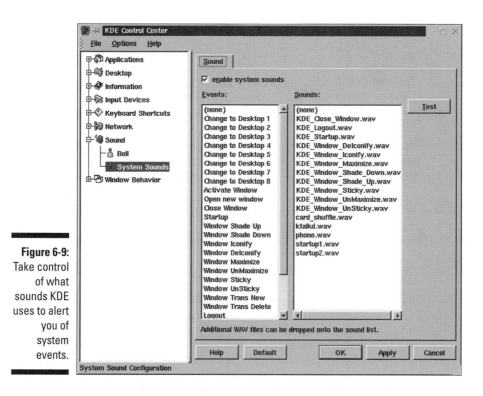

Figure 6-9:
Take control
of what
sounds KDE
uses to alert
you of
system
events.

KDE International — Languages and Keyboard Layout

KDE is truly an international product. Programmers from all over the globe contribute to the KDE project, so it's no surprise the KDE supports a variety of keyboard layouts for different languages. Not only can you select an individual keyboard layout for your native language, you can switch back and forth between different keyboard layouts with a keyboard shortcut or by clicking an on-screen button.

To configure the KDE international keyboard settings, follow these steps:

1. **Choose KDE Menu⇨KDE Control Panel or click the KDE Control Panel button on the panel.**

   The KDE Control Panel window appears.

2. **Click the plus sign beside Input Devices and then select International Keyboard in the list box on the left side of the KDE Control Panel window.**

   The three tabs of the international keyboard settings appear in the KDE Control Center window. By default, the General tab is selected as shown in Figure 6-10. The Keyboard Maps list box contains at least one keyboard layout.

3. **To add a keyboard map to the Keyboard Maps list, click the Add button, select a keyboard map from the drop-down list box in the Add Keyboard dialog box, and then click the OK button.**

   KDE adds the new keyboard layout to the Keyboard Maps list. You can rearrange the order of the list by selecting a keyboard map and clicking the Up or Down buttons. You can also delete a keyboard layout from the Keyboard Maps list by selecting a layout and clicking the Delete button.

4. **Select a key or key combination in each of the drop-down list boxes in the Switch and Alt Switch area.**

   The key combination you select in the left drop-down list box determines the keystroke you use to switch from one keyboard map to the next. The key you select in the right drop-down list box determines the key that you use to select alternate characters from the keyboard.

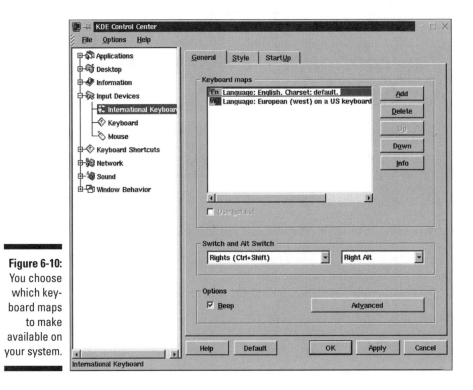

Figure 6-10: You choose which keyboard maps to make available on your system.

5. **Select or deselect the Beep option.**

   Select the Beep option to make KDE beep after you change keyboard layouts.

6. **Click the Style tab.**

   KDE displays the option shown in Figure 6-11.

7. **To change the appearance of the keyboard map button, click each of the four buttons (Foreground, Background, With Caps Lock, With Alternate). In turn, choose a color from the Select Color dialog box that appears and then click OK.**

8. **Click the StartUp tab.**

   KDE displays the settings available on the StartUp tab.

9. **Make sure to select both the Autostart and Docked options.**

10. **Click the OK button.**

    The three tabs of the International Keyboard settings disappear from the KDE Control Center window and KDE records the settings. However, if the keyboard switching utility is not already running, you won't be able to use it until you restart KDE.

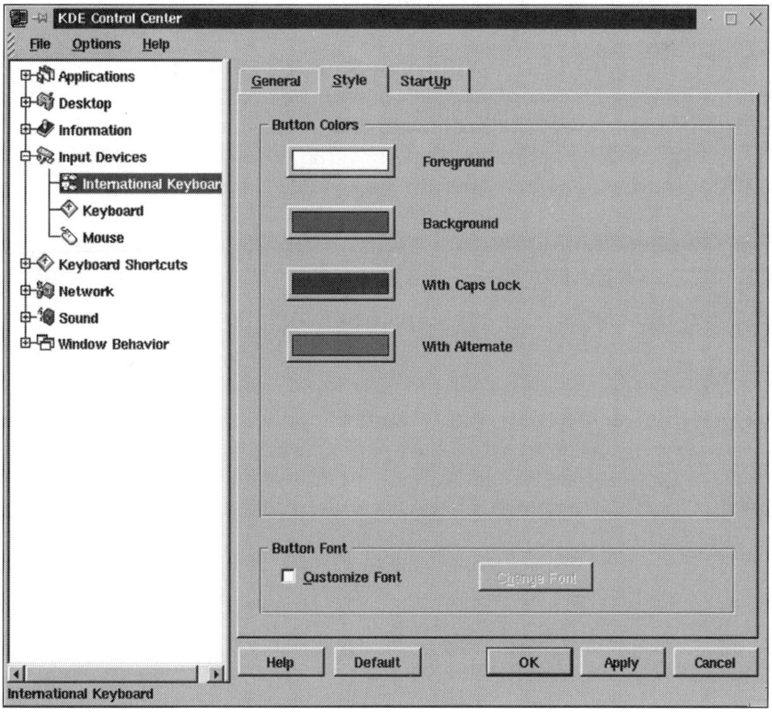

Figure 6-11: These settings control the appearance of the on-screen key map button.

After you configure the International Keyboard settings and restart KDE to activate the keyboard switching feature, notice a small box or button docked in the KDE panel or lodged in one of the four corners of your desktop. To switch from your default keyboard layout to another keyboard layout, click that button or press the Switch keys that you defined on the General tab.

More keyboard options

KDE enables you to configure a couple of other keyboard options. In the KDE Control Center window, select Keyboard under the Input Devices heading in the list on the left side of the window to display the Keyboard tab. The Keyboard tab offers the following options:

- **Keyboard Repeat:** Select On or Off to automatically enable or disable repeated keystrokes after you press and hold a key.
- **Key Click Volume:** Drag the slider to the right to increase the volume of a clicking sound KDE generates each time you press a key. To disable the key click sound, drag the slider all the way to the left.

Mouse maneuvers

KDE also supports a couple of options to control behavior of your mouse in the KDE environment. Like so many other configuration options, you edit the mouse settings in the KDE Control Center window. Select Mouse under the Input Devices heading in the list on the left side the window to display the Mouse tab. You can adjust the following settings:

- **Acceleration:** Drag the slider to the right to increase the speed and distance the pointer moves in response to a rapid movement of the mouse.
- **Threshold:** Drag the slider to the right to increase the zone in which you can make mouse movements without engaging the acceleration feature.
- **Button Mapping:** Select Right Handed or Left Handed. Right Handed button mapping is the standard configuration in which the left mouse button is designated for the main selection and dragging operations and the right button activates context menus and the like. Left Handed button mapping transposes those button assignments.

Chapter 7

Having a Theme Party

In This Chapter

▶ Defining a theme

▶ Managing multiple themes

▶ Finding famous themes online

▶ Exploring themes for former Windows wonks

▶ Creating themes for former Mac maniacs

▶ Devising themes for UNIX nerds

▶ Doing your own thing with themes

*H*ow would you like to be able to redecorate your office instantly, any- time you want? Wouldn't it be nice to change the wall color, carpet, and furniture to fit your mood? That may not be practical in real life, but you can certainly change the appearance of your KDE desktops with a few mouse clicks.

KDE is a highly customizable environment, and you can change almost every visible element of the user interface, if you're willing to work at it. But chang- ing one setting at a time can be tedious. Changing settings is not difficult, but just time-consuming to work through the many settings that affect the appear- ance of your desktop. That's why KDE includes a feature, called themes, which enables you to change the whole look of your desktop, all at once.

What's a Theme Anyway?

A KDE theme is a collection of desktop appearance settings that define a par- ticular look for your KDE desktop. A theme includes elements such as

✔ Desktop color and pattern

✔ Desktop icons

✔ Sounds associated with system actions

✔ Wallpaper

✔ Window border and buttons

✔ Window and title bar colors and background

For example, the Astronique theme, shown in Figure 7-1, is quite a departure from the appearance of the default KDE desktop.

Figure 7-1:
Applying a
theme often
results in
wholesale
changes to
your KDE
desktop.

Many of the settings contained in a KDE theme are the same settings you can change individually in the Display Settings dialog box, with the options available on the KDE Menu➪Settings menus, or in the KDE Control Center. (Refer to Chapters 5 and 6 for more information about changing colors and other desktop appearance settings.) A theme pulls all the different settings together into a single configuration file for easy organization and ready access. The advantage of using a theme is that you can select and apply a bunch of different settings all at once instead of having to work through several tabs and dialog boxes to access all the relevant settings.

In addition to the standard color and wallpaper settings that you can easily change with dialog box settings, a theme can also replace the standard KDE window borders and toolbar buttons with customized versions. The average user would have a hard time customizing borders and buttons this way without using themes. Manually locating and editing the files KDE uses to construct window borders and buttons isn't a simple task — such tinkering is best left to those who can afford to spend hours messing around with the innards of their computer system software. On the other hand, after some enterprising experimenter creates a set of custom window borders and buttons, and records them in a theme, anyone can use the theme to quickly and easily customize the look of their KDE windows.

A KDE theme is a compressed archive file containing the following component files:

✔ The theme configuration file — a text-based file containing a list of color settings and other configuration information

✔ A preview image — a screen shot of the KDE desktop with the theme applied

✔ Wallpaper image files

✔ Icon image files for toolbar buttons and desktop icons

✔ Other image files for window borders, titlebars, and panel backgrounds

✔ Sound files for system sounds

Required elements in a KDE theme are the theme configuration file and a preview image. The theme configuration file, with a name such as themename.themerc, is the heart of a KDE theme. The file contains all the color settings and other configuration settings that the theme can change. The preview image is what the KDE Theme Manager utility uses to show what the theme looks like. The various image files and sound files are optional — these files may, or may not, be included in a given theme, depending on whether the theme's configuration file needs to reference those files as custom alternatives for the standard KDE user interface elements.

Using the Theme Manager

Applying a theme to your KDE desktop used to require copying an assortment of files to various directories and then hand-editing several obscure configuration files to substitute the theme settings for the KDE defaults. That was quite a chore, which relegated themes to the realm of the GUI hackers. But no more! The KDE Theme Manager automates the process of applying themes so that you can change themes quickly and easily — a few mouse clicks is all you do.

The KDE Theme Manager is a new addition to KDE 1.1.2. The KDE Theme Manager is a special utility that is fully integrated into KDE and enables you to select a theme, see a preview of the selected theme, and apply all or part of the theme to your KDE desktop. The KDE Theme manager makes working with themes as simple and convenient as changing your desktop wallpaper. Now you can have fun customizing your KDE desktop — even if you're not a GUI geek.

Applying a complete theme with Theme Manager

To use KDE Theme Manager to apply a theme to your KDE desktop, follow these simple steps:

1. **Click the KDE Menu button and then choose Settings⇨Desktop⇨ Theme Manager.**

   KDE opens the KDE Theme Manager dialog box as shown in Figure 7-2. By default, the Theme Manager displays the Installer tab, with its list of available themes on the left and its preview box on the right. A short description of the selected theme appears below the preview box.

2. **Click a theme name in the list box on the left side of the Installer tab to select a theme.**

   A preview image of the selected theme appears in the large box in the center of the Theme Manager dialog box. Try clicking each theme name in succession and viewing the preview image until you find one you like.

3. **Click the Contents tab to make sure that *all* the checkboxes are checked.**

   A quick way to check all the checkboxes on the Contents tab of the Theme Manager dialog box is to click Clear and then click Invert.

4. **Click Apply or OK.**

   Clicking Apply applies the selected theme to your desktop without closing the Theme Manager dialog box. Clicking OK applies the theme and also closes the Theme Manager dialog box.

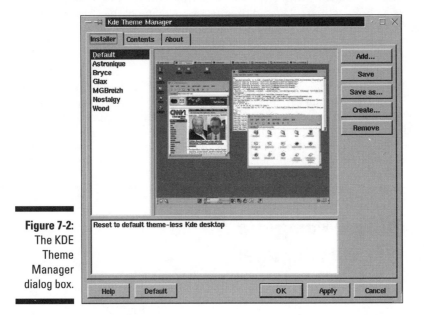

Figure 7-2: The KDE Theme Manager dialog box.

Picking and choosing theme elements

Just because a theme can give your desktop a complete makeover, complete with colors, wallpaper, window borders, titlebar buttons, and the lot, you don't have to adopt the entire theme for your desktop. Perhaps you really like the color scheme and window borders in a particular theme, but don't care for the titlebar buttons and wallpaper that are included in that theme. Perhaps you prefer the titlebar buttons from a different theme and the wallpaper from yet another theme.

Fortunately, using a theme is not an all-or-nothing deal. Theme Manager enables you to selectively apply parts of a theme to your desktop. As a result, you can pick and choose elements of several different themes to build your own custom desktop environment. To apply some parts of a theme (and not others) to your desktop, follow these steps:

1. **Click the KDE Menu button and then choose Settings⇨Desktop⇨Theme Manager.**

   KDE opens the KDE Theme Manager dialog box.

2. **Click a theme name in the list box on the Installer tab.**

   Select a theme that includes one or more elements that you want to apply to your desktop. Examine the preview image of the selected theme and note the theme elements, such as the colors, wallpaper, or window borders, that you want to use and those elements that you don't want to apply to your desktop.

3. **Click the Contents tab.**

   The Contents tab of the Theme Manager dialog box appears as shown in Figure 7-3. This tab of the dialog box lists all the components of a theme and shows which components are available in the selected theme.

   Not all themes include settings and source files for all the desktop elements. If the selected theme includes a given component (such as Wallpapers or Window Border), the status column on the right indicates that the option is *available*. If the selected theme doesn't include a component, the status column shows that the option is *empty*.

4. **Click the checkboxes to select the theme elements you want to apply to your desktop.**

   A check mark beside an option indicates that Theme Manager will install that part of the theme on your desktop (provided, of course, that the component is available in selected theme). Clicking a checkbox toggles the check mark on and off. You can select any combination of theme components you desire.

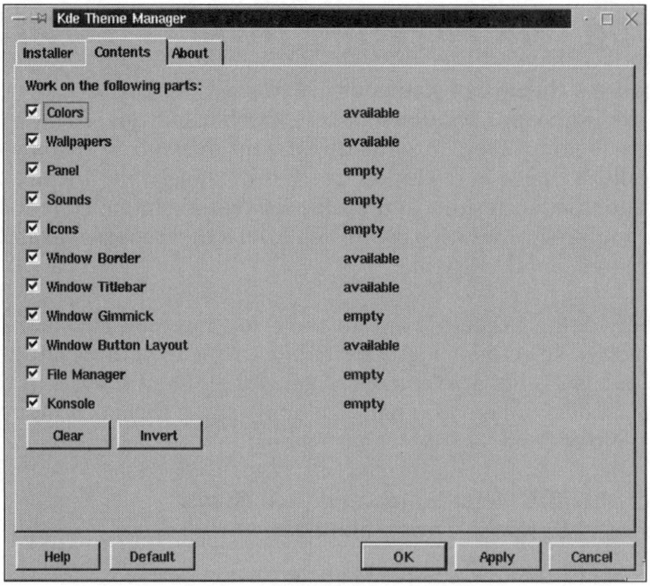

Kde Theme Manager

| Installer | Contents | About |

Work on the following parts:

☑ Colors	available
☑ Wallpapers	available
☑ Panel	empty
☑ Sounds	empty
☑ Icons	empty
☑ Window Border	available
☑ Window Titlebar	available
☑ Window Gimmick	empty
☑ Window Button Layout	available
☑ File Manager	empty
☑ Konsole	empty

| Clear | Invert |

| Help | Default | | OK | Apply | Cancel |

Figure 7-3:
The Contents tab enables you to customize a desktop theme.

To select just one or two options, first click the Clear button to remove the check marks from all the checkboxes and then click the individual checkboxes for the options you want. Clicking the Clear button avoids the need to click numerous checkboxes to un-select those options.

5. Click Apply.

Theme Manager applies the selected parts of the selected theme to your desktop. All other aspects of your desktop remain unchanged. For example, if you select just Colors and Wallpapers on the Contents tab, Theme Manager changes your desktop color scheme and wallpaper without affecting your window borders, sounds, titlebar buttons, and so on. The Theme Manager dialog box remains open.

6. To select and apply other theme elements, repeat Steps 2 through 5.

You can apply other elements from the same theme or select another theme and apply elements from a different theme. Continue the process until you achieve an effect you like.

7. Click OK.

KDE closes the Theme Manager dialog box.

If all your experiments with themes get out of hand, you can easily return to the KDE default desktop settings. The KDE Theme Manager includes a theme named Default and a special button to make selecting the Default theme easy. To restore your KDE desktop to the default settings, just use Theme Manager to apply the Default theme (be sure to select and apply all the options on the Contents tab of the Theme Manager dialog box).

Occasionally, remnants of an old theme stubbornly remain on your desktop, even after you apply a new theme or try to revert to the default desktop. The problem is usually caused by icon files in some of your local directories overriding the systemwide default icons stored elsewhere. To cure the problem, follow these steps:

1. **Use Theme Manager to apply the Default theme.**

2. **Use KFM to locate and delete any .xpm files you find in the following subdirectories of your home directory:**

   `~/.kde/share/icons`

   `~/.kde/share/icons/mini`

   `~/.kde/apps/kdeui`

   `~/.kde/apps/kfm`

   `~/.kde/apps/konsole`

   `~/.kde/apps/kpanel/pics`

   `~/.kde/apps/kpanel/pics/mini`

   `~/.kde/apps/kwm/pics`

3. **Restart the KDE panel by clicking the KDE Menu button and choosing Panel⇨Restart.**

4. **Redraw the desktop by right-clicking the desktop and choosing Refresh Desktop from the pop-up menu that appears.**

   KDE should redraw your panel and desktop with the default icons.

Adding themes to Theme Manager

The standard KDE installation includes a handful of themes that provide something for you to experiment with in Theme Manager. You find some nice themes in the standard assortment, but many more themes are available. KDE users around the world have been busy developing and sharing themes that can give your desktop dramatically different looks. You have a sizable collection of themes available for your use and new themes are being developed all the time. All you need is a copy of the theme file, which you can get by downloading it from the Internet. And you can easily add the new themes to Theme Manager to try on your own desktop.

Theme Manager works with two kinds of themes — global themes and local themes. Global themes are available to all KDE users on your system, while local themes are available only to an individual user ID.

The only real difference between global themes and local themes is the location of the theme files:

- ✔ **Global themes** are stored in the shared KDE directory tree that is accessible by all users.
- ✔ **Local themes** are stored in a subdirectory of the user's home directory, which is inaccessible by other users.

If a local and a global theme have exactly the same name, the local theme overrides the global theme in Theme Manager.

Adding a global theme to Theme Manager is a simple matter of copying the compressed archive file containing the theme to the main, shared Themes directory — usually: `/usr/share/apps/kthememgr/Themes` or `/opt/kde/share/apps/kthememgr/Themes`. (You need to be logged in as root to do this.) After you copy the theme file to the global Themes directory, the new theme appears in the theme list of all users the next time that they open Theme Manager.

Similarly, you can add local themes for an individual user by copying theme files to the Themes directory located under the user's home directory (`~/.kde/share/apps/kthememgr/Themes`). Or, you can add a local theme to Theme Manager by following these steps:

1. **Click the KDE Menu button and choose Settings⇨Desktop⇨ Theme Manager.**

   The Theme Manager dialog box appears.

2. **Click Add.**

   The Add Theme dialog box appears, as shown in Figure 7-4.

3. **Navigate to the directory where the new theme is stored and select the theme file you want to add to Theme Manager.**

   You can double-click folder icons in the Add Theme dialog box's list box to navigate the directory tree and then select a theme file by clicking it. Or you can type the path and filename of the desired theme file in the Location text box.

4. **Click OK.**

   Theme Manager closes the Add Theme dialog box and copies the theme file into the local Themes directory for the current user. The new theme appears on the list on the Installer page of the Theme Manager dialog box, where you can select and apply it to your desktop just like any other theme available in Theme Manager.

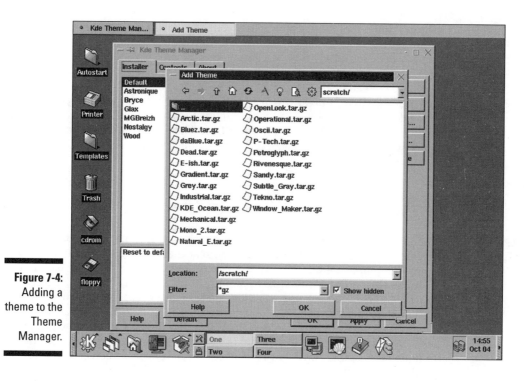

Figure 7-4:
Adding a
theme to the
Theme
Manager.

Themes that you add to Theme Manager using the Add Theme dialog box are local themes — available only to the user who added the theme. If you want to add a global theme to Theme Manager to be available to all users on your system, you need to log in as root and copy the theme to the master Themes directory.

Finding Themes Online

KDE comes with a small assortment of themes preinstalled. But you're not confined to that meager selection of themes. You have access to an active community of KDE users who are developing new themes and refining and updating the existing library of themes, and then making those themes available to other KDE users. In keeping with the open source spirit of the Linux and KDE projects, most themes are freely distributed and you can legally copy, use, and modify them.

The Themes.org Web site exists as a clearinghouse for the exchange of themes. Theme developers post new themes on the site and other users can view, download, and comment on the themes. You can search for themes by keyword or by several other criteria. After you find a theme you like, you can download the theme with a couple of mouse clicks. The Themes.org Web site supports themes for all the major X Window window managers. The KDE themes are located at `http://kde.themes.org`.

For your convenience, the CD that accompanies this book includes copies of many of the most popular themes from Themes.org. You can save yourself some download time by copying the theme files from the CD and adding them to your system. But don't forget to visit the Themes.org Web site to check out the new and updated themes that are available there.

Giving KDE a Familiar Face

Thanks to the versatility of the KDE user interface and the power of themes, you can easily give your desktop a makeover that emulates much of the look and feel of other popular operating systems and user interfaces. In fact, many users find that configuring KDE to mimic another, more familiar, operating system can help smooth the transition to KDE and make it easier to switch back and forth between KDE and another operating system. As a result, themes that seek to copy the look of other operating systems are very popular — or at least they were until those themes were withdrawn from circulation due to possible copyright issues and the actual or perceived threat of legal action.

Themes that copy the appearance of other operating systems too closely may not be available anymore, but you can still give your KDE desktop a familiar look. By combining elements from a couple of different themes with some other KDE settings, you can achieve the effect you want. The following recipes should yield a desktop stew with a familiar flavor.

If you're coming from Windows . . .

If you're a former Windows user who wants to retain some of the familiar appearance of the Windows environment on your Linux/KDE desktop, try this recipe for creating a Windows-style desktop:

1. **Open Theme Manager and use it to apply the Default theme to your desktop.**

2. **Select the Mono_2 theme and apply the Window Titlebar and Window Button Layout settings, and then close Theme Manager.**

3. **Open the Display Settings dialog box (right-click the desktop and choose Display Properties from the pop-up menu that appears) and click the Style tab. Select the Draw Widgets option and deselect the Menu Bar At Top option. Then click OK to close the Display Settings dialog box and apply the settings.**

4. **Open the KPanel Configuration dialog box (right-click the panel and choose Configure from the pop-up menu that appears) and, on the Panel tab, select Bottom as the location for both the panel and the taskbar.**

5. **Hide the panel (click the Collapse button at either end of the panel), leaving the taskbar occupying the bottom of the screen.**

The resulting desktop (shown in Figure 7-5) is sufficiently Windows-like to make most Windows users feel right at home. If you really want to make your desktop look like a Windows machine, you can rename the Trash icon Recycle Bin, and create some desktop icons to mimic the other standard Windows shortcuts. But please, try to come up with something more imaginative than My Computer for the label on the folder icon for the top-level directory.

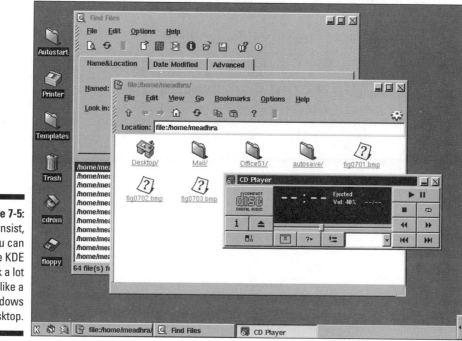

Figure 7-5:
If you insist, you can make KDE look a lot like a Windows desktop.

If you're coming from a Mac . . .

If you're a longtime Mac OS user, you may want to incorporate some of the familiar appearance and features of your old fruit-flavored friend in your new KDE desktop.

1. **Use Theme Manager to apply the Nostalgy theme. Use all the available components.**

2. **Open the Display Settings dialog box (right-click the desktop and choose Display Properties from the pop-up menu that appears), click the Style tab, select the Draw Widgets option and also select the Menu Bar At Top option. Click OK to close the dialog box and apply the settings.**

3. **Open the KPanel Configuration dialog box (right-click the panel and choose Configure from the pop-up menu that appears) and, on the Panel tab, select Bottom as the location for the panel and select Hide the taskbar area. Click OK to close the dialog box and apply the settings.**

4. **Hide the panel by clicking the Collapse button at either end of the panel.**

5. **Drag the Trash icon to the lower-right corner of your screen.**

A fan of the Mac OS would probably be comfortable working on a KDE desktop configured similar to the one shown in Figure 7-6. Notice the application menu bar positioned at the top of the screen instead of inside the application window. To make the desktop even more Mac-like, you can populate the desktop with icons for all the programs and folders you use frequently.

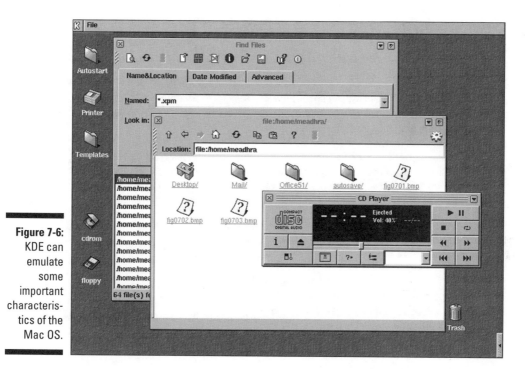

Figure 7-6:
KDE can
emulate
some
important
characteris-
tics of the
Mac OS.

If you're coming from command-line UNIX . . .

If you've spent a lot of time working at the UNIX command line, you've probably also worked with some of the other X Window System window managers.
You may even prefer the appearance of some of those other window managers. If so, try these themes and settings:

✔ If you like the Enlightenment window manager, try the E-ish theme.

✔ If you prefer the Window Maker window manager, check out its name-
sake theme.

✔ On the Style tab of the Display Settings dialog box, deselect the Draw
Widgets option and also deselect the Menu Bar At Top option.

✔ In the KPanel Configuration dialog box, select Left or Right as the location for the panel and hide the taskbar.

Creating your own themes

Creating a theme from scratch isn't exactly rocket science, but it isn't a simple process either. Designing window borders, buttons, and icons to use in a theme requires tedious work with the KDE Icon Editor program on numerous files. The only effective way to build a theme configuration file is by hand-editing a template. Then you need to gather all the components of the theme together and package them into a compressed archive file to create a theme you can use with Theme Manager.

The whole process is sufficiently complicated so that it's beyond the scope of this book. However, if you're really interested in creating themes and determined to give it a try, you can find some information on the Themes.org Web site that can get you started. Go to the http//:kde.themes.org site and follow the links to Documentation and the KDE Guide, and then peruse the section on creating themes.

Creating a theme by assembling components from other existing themes is somewhat simpler than building a new theme from scratch. However, as of this writing, creating a theme still requires hand-editing the theme configuration file and then assembling all the theme components into a compressed archive file with a utility such as Archiver. Again, this assembly is beyond the scope of this book. But the process should be getting easier soon. Plans are for Theme Manager to be able to create a new theme by saving your current desktop configuration. Who knows, by the time you read this, the feature may even be working in a new version of Theme Manager. One of the great things about KDE is that it's constantly being updated and enhanced by the army of developers working on the project.

Using a theme that emulates the look of another window manager is only a superficial change. For a UNIX command-line veteran, no GUI can completely replace the power of the command line. But never fear, KDE offers two command-line windows — Konsole and KVT — that give you instant access to the Linux command prompt. The default installation even includes a panel button for convenient one-click access to Konsole.

Part III
Getting Down to Business

The 5th Wave   By Rich Tennant

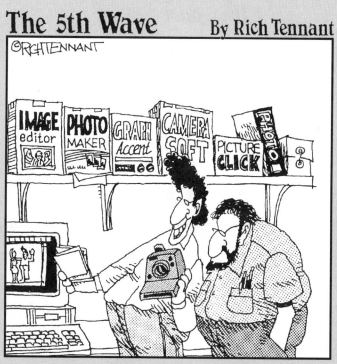

"...and here's me with Cindy Crawford. And this is me with Madonna and Celine Dion..."

In this part . . .

*W*hen you've had the guided tour of KDE's features and capabilities, the next item on the agenda is to take it for a spin on the Net. Before you lift off for cyberspace, this part gives you a preflight check-out. It walks you through getting connected, using KDE on the Internet, sampling the applications and utilities that are available for use with KDE, and playing (or working) with non-KDE applications in a socially acceptable manner. So work it on out . . . or have fun . . . whichever.

Chapter 8

Getting Connected

- -

In This Chapter

▶ Getting an account with a Linux-friendly ISP

▶ Configuring a Linux account

▶ Tinkering with your modem

▶ Hooking up with an Ethernet connection

▶ KDE's network utilities: quick troubleshooters

- -

*A*fter you have KDE set up and configured just the way you like it, you may want to start using your computer for things besides tinkering with the desktop. At the very least, you probably want to connect to the Internet, whether it's to download more neat KDE stuff or to share your joy about your new desktop with friends and strangers alike.

The KDE connection process is simple for Linux users who have already connected their machines to the Internet. If you are one of those already connected, skim through this chapter and confirm that your settings are correct. Unless you have some unexpected connection problems, though, feel free to jump off to the end of this chapter, where we cover Ethernet and some basic network diagnostic tools.

If you've never connected your Linux machine to the Internet, you have some work ahead of you. Luckily, it's a pretty straightforward process; just remember to complete all the steps. You also have to get in touch with your current *Internet Service Provider,* or *ISP,* to see if it supports Linux or other UNIX-based operating systems. Many don't, including America Online. You'll probably have better luck looking for a smaller regional or local ISP than for one of the HumongoISPs that are clearly targeted at Windows users.

Unlocking the Gateway

Connecting your computer to the Internet requires a couple of things.

- A *modem,* the piece of hardware that uses your phone line to transfer information between your computer and another computer.
- An account with an *Internet Service Provider (ISP).*
- A working installation of KDE.

Sure, you can get on the Internet without KDE, but one of the tools that KDE gives you is called Kppp, and it's a fast and flexible way to get all of those components talking with each other so you can get online. Kppp takes the information you give it about your ISP and your modem and sets up your computer to use that information so that you don't have to think about it.

Kppp is another way in which KDE makes your computing life easier and simpler. All you have to do is type some stuff in, and KDE does the rest of the work. Not bad!

Ready, Get Set...

What does it take to be Linux friendly? The most basic requirement is that the ISP permits its users to connect via UNIX-based operating systems and software. Beyond that, a Linux-friendly ISP should give its technical support staff some Linux training basic enough to answer those frantic "What do I do NOW?" calls. It's nice to have Linux-specific FAQs available on the company's Web site. Many ISPs use proprietary software (like AOL or MindSpring); make sure that it's not required, because it's almost always available only for Windows or MacintoshOS.

We assume that you already have an account with an ISP that is at least Linux aware, if not downright Linux friendly. If you haven't gotten that far, take a look at this chapter's "Do you speak Linux here?" sidebar. We've consolidated some of the basic questions you should ask an ISP about its Linux friendliness.

You really don't want to have the experience that we once had when calling a local ISP with a login problem. The tech support person said, "But you can't use Linux to connect to our system! We don't permit it!" (He was confused about the difference between *permitting* access from Linux users and *supporting* access from Linux users.) That was an odd response, given that probably half the ISP's user base was composed of hardcore UNIX sysadmins, and it's the sort of answer that sends chills down the spine of a newer Linux user with a question.

Do you speak Linux here?

Finding a Linux-friendly (or at least Linux-compatible) ISP can sometimes be a tricky process. Living near a major metropolitan area may or may not be helpful. Most of the major national (and international) ISPs are really slanted toward the Windows user; they use proprietary software that's released in Windows format and that may make it difficult for even Macintosh users to get a compatible copy of the software.

However, many of the mega ISPs — including EarthLink, , MindSpring, and WorldNet — claim to be open to Linux users. If you like the reliability of a major corporation and the freedom to move around the country without losing local dial-up numbers, you may want to look into accounts with the large ISPs. The major drawback is likely to be on the tech support end; if

you call WorldDomination.net's tech support line with a problem, the one person who knows Linux may be on break. In the worst-case scenario, the tech support person may even insist that the ISP doesn't support Linux. Because a massive majority of their customers use Windows, it's not a pressing need for the large ISPs to offer Linux-specific support.

Before you decide to go with a major corporate ISP, take a look at your local options. You may find happiness with a small ISP that's run out of an office park a few miles away and is based on Linux or another UNIX-based operating system. There, you may not compete with hundreds of thousands of other users for tech support. Check out some Linux-friendly ISPs at `http://howto.linuxberg.com/isp.html`.

You may not have very good luck convincing an ISP to be Linux friendly if it's running Windows NT. We aren't saying this just to Windows-bash; it's a serious philosophical difference that you need to consider when looking for an ISP. Companies that choose NT as their main operating system have deliberately chosen not to run UNIX or a UNIX-based operating system; you may be better off looking for a non–Windows NT ISP if one is available in your area.

When you've selected three or four possible ISPs, start making some phone calls or sending some e-mail. Ask each ISP the same questions, and then compare the answers when you're done phoning around. Here are some basic questions to ask:

- Do you support Linux?
- Do any of your users use Linux? How many?
- Do you have support materials written for Linux users?
- Are your technical support personnel trained to answer questions about your service from Linux users?
- Are your accounts normal PPP accounts? (That is, can I use any programs designed for use with a regular PPP connection?)
- Do you use any proprietary protocols or software? Are they required?

After you are hooked up with a good ISP, it's time to get your connection going. Get some basic information together in front of your computer, so that you don't have to search in the middle of the process. You need nine pieces of information:

✔ Your login ID, also known as your *username*.

✔ Your account password.

✔ The phone number your computer will dial to access the ISP.

✔ The authentication type used by your ISP, if it uses authentication.

✔ How your ISP assigns IP numbers: static or dynamic. If your ISP assigns static IP numbers, you need your IP number and the subnet mask.

✔ The IP numbers of the DNS servers.

✔ Gateway information. (You probably won't have specific numbers for this section, because ISPs often shift gateway functions from machine to machine. See the numbered steps in the next section for more information about gateways.)

✔ The device name of your modem. (This should look something like `/dev/modem` or `/dev/cua1`.)

✔ Whether you need to use hardware or software flow control.

Confused yet? Don't worry. Your ISP probably has most of this information typed up for you already; it's either in the sign-up material you received, or it's available on their Web page. (Obviously, it's kind of hard to go to a Web page if you're not connected to the Internet yet, but representatives can tell you this stuff over the phone or via fax as well.) All these terms are defined as configuring your connection is described.

Plugging in your information

Now that you have everything together, it's time to get started.

The configuration process is filled with acronyms and numbers. Make sure you type everything into the text boxes exactly as they're written on your information sheets. Use the same capitalization and dot placements. Otherwise, you'll have to do all of this again, and you have better things to do with your time!

1. **Open the KDE menu and select Internet⇨Kppp.**

   To open the KDE menu, click the button with the KDE logo in the panel. The KDE menu pops up, from which you can select your choices. For more information on using the KDE menu, see Chapter 1.

   The Kppp dialog box appears, as shown in Figure 8-1. Kppp is the handy KDE way to configure PPP connections. PPP (Point-to-Point

Protocol) is the most common way to connect to the Internet through your ISP.

2. Click the Setup button.

The Kppp configuration screen appears, with the Accounts tab already chosen.

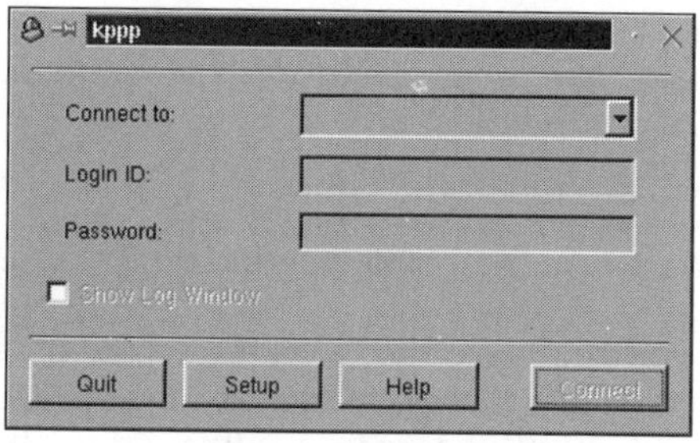

Figure 8-1:
The first step in setting up a new ISP account under KDE is to open Kppp.

3. Click the New button.

The New Account dialog box opens and the Dial tab is already chosen.

4. Enter or select the connection name, phone number, and authentication type.

- The connection name can be anything you want. It's probably easiest to use the ISP's name here, but if you have a burning desire to name your connection after your Aunt Ethelfrieda, go right ahead. (Then give her a call and tell her of the honor you've bestowed. She'd love to hear from you.)

- Your ISP may have multiple dial-in numbers for its modems. If you need to select a number based on your modem's speed, choose the one that matches your modem's highest speed. Dialing in to a higher-speed modem does not make your connection faster, and it blocks a line for someone who needs the faster modem.

- If your ISP says that its authentication type is None — and many do — choose Script Based as your authentication type. It won't hurt anything. You have to choose something.

5. Click the IP tab and then do one of these two things:

- **Select the Dynamic IP Address option.**

- **Select the Static IP Address option and enter your IP Address and Subnet Mask.**

Figure 8-2 shows the IP tab of the New Account dialog box. Unless you paid extra to get a static IP number, chances are overwhelming that you have dynamic IP allocation and don't need to change a single thing on this tab.

If your ISP assigned you a static IP number, select the Static IP Address option and enter your IP address and subnet mask into the appropriate text boxes.

6. Click the DNS tab and enter the DNS IP numbers you received from your ISP.

You should have two domain name server (DNS) IP numbers from your ISP. Enter the first one into the DNS IP Address box and click Add. The number drops down into the DNS Address List area, like the screen shown in Figure 8-3. Repeat the process with the second number. It, too, drops down into the DNS Address List area.

7. Click the Gateway tab at the top of the window.

You probably won't have to enter any information on this tab. The *gateway* is the computer that manages all the traffic between your ISP and the entire Internet. Usually there is only one gateway and it's set up as the *default gateway*. That means that your ISP can move gateway responsibilities to a different computer if necessary, but you don't have to change anything.

You are told if, for some rare reason, your ISP runs more than one gateway. In this case, your ISP gives you a static IP number to enter at this step.

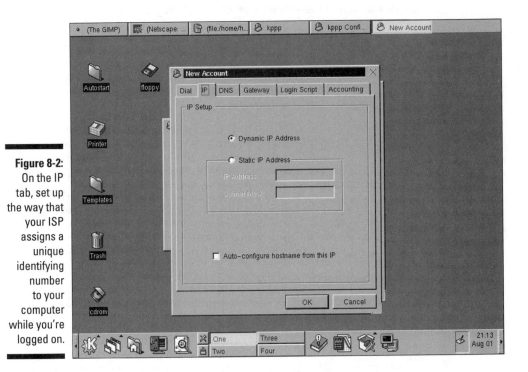

Figure 8-2:
On the IP tab, set up the way that your ISP assigns a unique identifying number to your computer while you're logged on.

TECHNICAL STUFF

Why the static?

What's the difference, right? Well, an *Internet Protocol address* (IP number) is a string of numbers that identifies a given computer on the Internet. Because most ISPs have many more customers than they have IP numbers to give out, the numbers are assigned *dynamically*. That is, when you log on, your computer gets the next available number; when you log off, someone else gets it. A *static IP number* means that you

have a specific string of numbers that identifies your computer all the time, whether or not you're logged on. This isn't necessary for most users, who do just fine with a dynamic IP. If you think you need a static IP, look into getting a cable modem or more advanced connection services like DSL or ISDN, which usually assign static IP numbers because the connection is always on.

Primary DNS server

Secondary DNS server

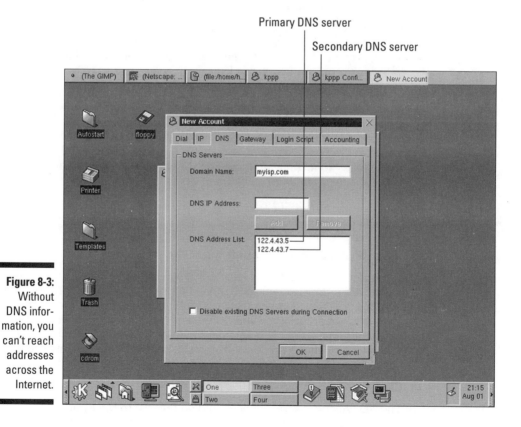

Figure 8-3:
Without DNS information, you can't reach addresses across the Internet.

Matching names and numbers

Another acronym? Yep. DNS stands for *Domain Name Server,* and it's the computer at your ISP that hooks up an individual computer with its IP number; every computer attached to the Internet (including yours) has a unique identifying number, and the DNS machines at the ISP do nothing but find those numbers for you. You have to tell your computer where to find the DNS machine so that you can do things like look up Web pages by using the *domain name* instead of the IP number. And you need two IP numbers because the ISP spreads the load across more than one machine.

8. Click the Login Script tab and edit the login script your system will use to pass your username and password to the ISP's computer.

Here, you set up the series of prompts and responses that enable your computer to automatically log onto your ISP's network. If your ISP doesn't require a *text-based login*, you can leave this page blank. (Many ISPs don't require a text-based login — they get your username and password automatically, as part of the connection protocol negotiations.)

A *text-based login* is exactly what it sounds like: The ISP prompts you for your username and password, and you type it in. The advantage of a text-based login is that you have to confirm that you want to log in (and prove you're you by remembering your password). The disadvantage is that it takes some time, and you have to be in front of your computer. Using a login script automates the process.

If your ISP does require you to use a login script, you need to create one from scratch. For help in writing a basic script, see the next section of this chapter, "The scriptwriting award goes to..."

9. Click the Accounting tab at the top of the screen.

KDE's Accounting feature tracks how much data you have uploaded or downloaded through your ISP connection. You'll probably only need this option if you have a metered-access account. This is fairly rare in the United States, where time limits on usage are much more common than bandwidth limits. Readers outside the United States may find this option useful for tracking costs; United States users will probably only use it for curiosity's sake.

10. Click the OK button.

The New Account screen closes, and you return to the Kppp Configuration dialog box. In the next section of this chapter, you continue to use Kppp Configuration to make sure that KDE and your modem are working together, so leave it open.

Huzzah! You are more than a third of the way through the ISP connection process. Next, you configure your modem and then test the setup. For now, though, take a break and stretch out. You should also take a minute or two to create a safe space for your ISP information, especially that sheet with all the IP numbers on it. Nothing is more irritating than needing to redo your configuration and not knowing where your IP information is.

Don't keep your password with your other ISP information. In fact, don't get in the bad habit of writing down passwords. An even worse habit is writing down your passwords and leaving them someplace convenient, like your top desk drawer or taped to the monitor. Passwords work because they're secret; making them public by writing them down defeats the purpose of requiring passworded access.

The scriptwriting award goes to...

If you need to use a login script in order to connect to your ISP, you have to spend a few minutes putting one together. Setting up a login script can be a little tricky; not all ISPs use the same sequence of events to handle logins. Following the steps given here produces a script that ought to work for most ISPs, but you may have to experiment and revise it a bit. (This is one of those times where it really helps you solve a problem if your ISP's tech support knows something about Linux.)

Begin creating a login script on the Login Script tab (as shown in Figure 8-4) of the Kppp Configuration screen. If you closed Kppp after the previous section or you need to add or adjust a script after you finished configuring Kppp, reopen Kppp. Open the KDE menu and select Internet➪Kppp.

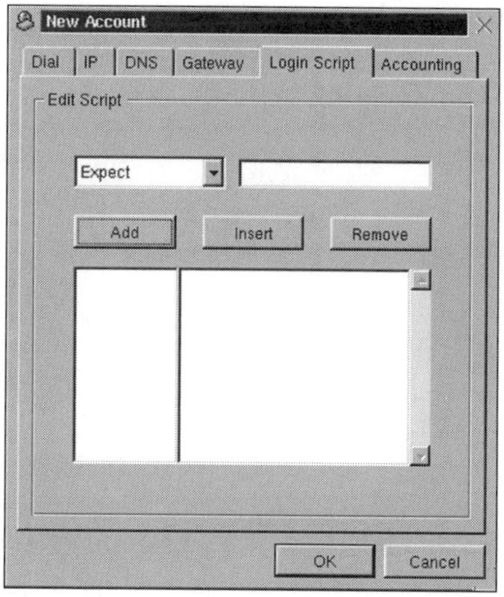

Figure 8-4:
Use the Login Script tab of the Kppp configuration dialog box to get your modem talking to your ISP.

1. **Type** `ogin:` **in the text box to the right of the word Expect; click Add.**

   Both words, `Expect` and `ogin:`, appear in the lower text area.

   Use `ogin:` — not `Login:` or `login:`. Some ISPs use the uppercase and some use the lowercase. If you leave out the L, you neatly avoid the entire problem. You'll need to drop the initial letter of each "Expect" entry in your script, as in Step 5. "Send" entries (your username and password) should be typed in full.

2. **Click the arrow to the right of the word Expect; select Send from the drop-down list box that appears.**

   Expect is replaced with Send.

3. **Type your username in the box immediately to the right of Send and click Add.**

   The word Send and your username appear in the lower text area.

4. **Click the arrow that accompanies the word Send in the upper-left box; select Expect from the drop-down box that appears.**

5. **Type password (without the p), plus a colon, in the box immediately to the right of Expect, as shown in Figure 8-5. Click Add.**

   You left out the P for the same reason you left out the L in login. Leaving it out avoids case confusion with your ISP.

6. **Click the arrow that accompanies the word Expect and select Send from the drop-down box that appears.**

7. **Type your password in the entry box to the right and then click Add.**

That completes a basic login script; you can see what it should look like in Figure 8-5. If this script doesn't work for you, ask your ISP what you need to do. The underlying principles of all login scripts are the same: Tell your computer what to expect from the ISP and what to send in response.

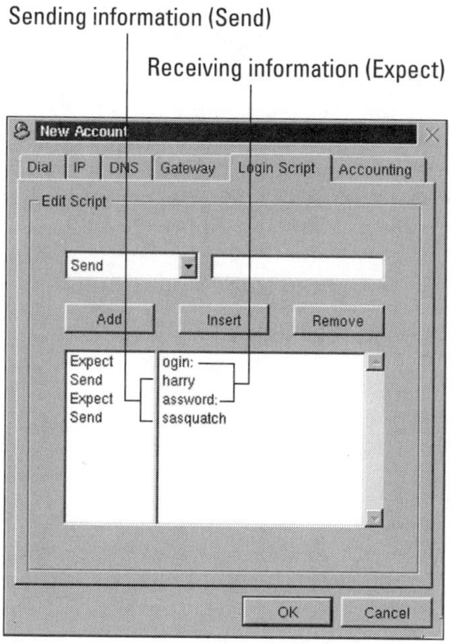

Sending information (Send)

Receiving information (Expect)

Figure 8-5:
A completed basic login script.

Feel that modem mania

Now that you have everything set so that your computer and your ISP are feeding each other the proper information, you have to do a bit of tinkering with your modem.

You work directly with your modem on a Linux machine two different times: when you set up the operating system and when you configure your PPP connection in KDE. This section assumes that you set up the modem correctly when you installed your operating system; if you didn't, or if you're just now installing a modem, finish that process first. This section is concerned with modem configuration only as part of setting up your Kppp connection.

If you need help setting up your modem at the operating system level, you may find *Linux For Dummies*, 2nd Edition by Jon "maddog" Hall, (IDG Books Worldwide, Inc.) a helpful resource.

Ready to go? Let's dive into the wacky and weird world of modems.

Modems are fragile little things. Those of us who live in lightning-heavy parts of the world know the sad sound of a modem fried by a lightning strike that traveled through the phone lines. (It sounds like the volume is turned way down and there's a lot of static when you pick up your regular phone. In worst cases, it can confuse incoming calls into thinking that the phone's off the hook.) The simplest protection is to unplug the modem from the jack when a storm is headed your way; you can also buy modem surge protectors to help protect the line when you're not home to unplug.

To configure your modem under KDE, you use a process that looks a lot like the New Account process. If you're continuing from the previous section, the Kppp Configuration dialog box is still open. If you exited Kppp, reopen it by opening the KDE menu and choosing Internet➪Kppp.

1. **Click the Device tab at the top of the Kppp dialog box.**

   The Device tab options appear, as shown in Figure 8-6.

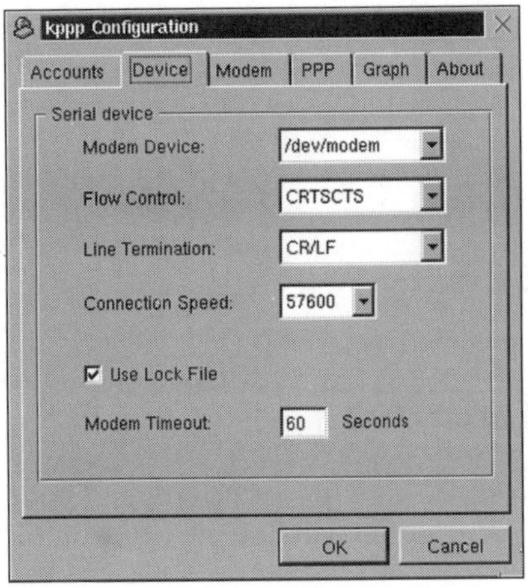

Figure 8-6:
Most of the modem configuration process takes place on the Device tab in Kppp.

2. **Click the Modem Device button and choose the device name of your modem from the drop-down list that appears.**

   If your modem was on COM1 under DOS or Windows, it's probably on /dev/cua0 under Linux. If it was on COM2 under DOS or Windows, it's probably on /dev/cua1 under Linux, and so forth. Some Linux systems make a link from /dev/modem to wherever the modem device is actually located. This is information you received when you installed your operating system or added a modem to your computer.

3. **Enter the required information about your modem in the remaining areas of the Device tab.**

   • In the Flow Control section of the screen, select the manner in which your modem exchanges information with your ISP's modem. You can choose between using hardware or software control. It's usually preferable to use hardware control, so select CRTSCTS.

   If you want or need to use software control instead, select XON/XOFF.

- Ignore the Line Termination option. If you're experiencing trouble with your modem connection, you can try toggling this option, but it's generally safe to leave it alone. Problems usually begin elsewhere.

- For the Connection Speed option, pick the highest speed your modem can handle. Don't go higher; it doesn't help.

  The speed on the modem box is the highest. Internet connections often proceed at a much slower speed, but nobody wants to market their modems as "Capable of 52K, but just try getting that speed on a regular basis!" Modem speed, like almost any other measure of speed on the Internet, is wholly relative.

4. **Click the Modem tab and enter a number in the Busy Wait text box, shown in Figure 8-7.**

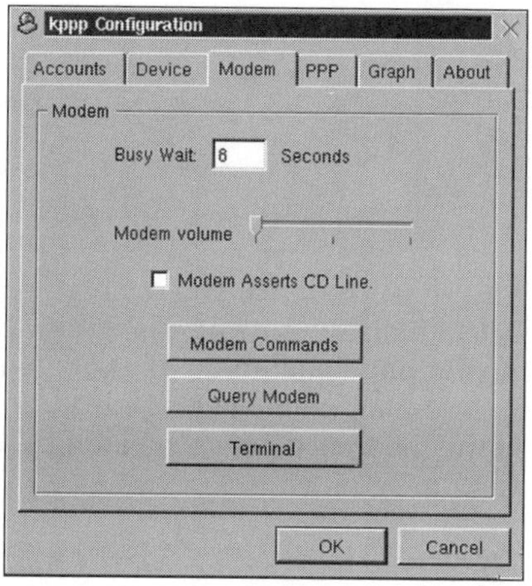

Figure 8-7:
Decide how long you want the computer to pause if it gets a busy signal from your ISP.

Figure 8-7 shows the Modem tab. The value you place in the Busy Wait text box sets the number of seconds your computer waits before redialing if it gets a busy signal from the ISP. Five or eight seconds is reasonable; more than twenty means you'll be waiting around a lot if your ISP is prone to busy signals.

5. **(Optional) Click the Modem Commands button and edit the settings in the Edit Modem Commands dialog box.**

If you have a regular Hayes or Hayes-compatible modem, you probably don't need to edit anything here. If you have another kind of modem, you may need to change the `init` string (the codes that tell the modem how to work). Consult your modem's manual to see the `init` string for your particular unit; if it's the same as the one displayed, just click the OK button. Look at a sample `init` string on the screen shown in Figure 8-8.

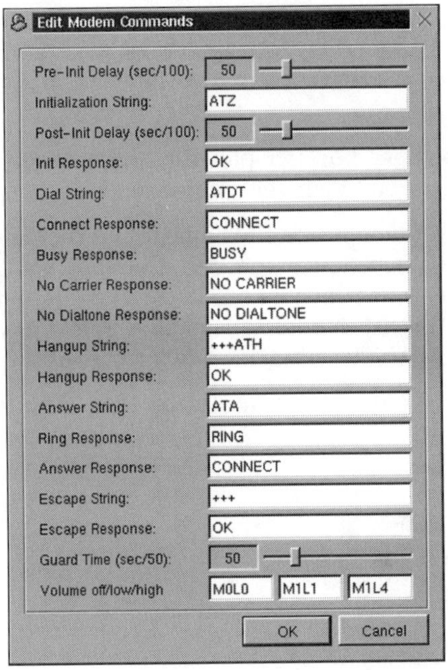

Figure 8-8:
The Edit
Modem
Commands
dialog box,
as it
appears
configured
for a Hayes-
compatible
modem.

Edit Modem Commands

Pre–Init Delay (sec/100):	50
Initialization String:	ATZ
Post–Init Delay (sec/100):	50
Init Response:	OK
Dial String:	ATDT
Connect Response:	CONNECT
Busy Response:	BUSY
No Carrier Response:	NO CARRIER
No Dialtone Response:	NO DIALTONE
Hangup String:	+++ATH
Hangup Response:	OK
Answer String:	ATA
Ring Response:	RING
Answer Response:	CONNECT
Escape String:	+++
Escape Response:	OK
Guard Time (sec/50):	50
Volume off/low/high	M0L0 M1L1 M1L4

OK   Cancel

Here's where you can get into some trouble if you're not careful. If you need to replace the modem's initialization string, make sure you type it in exactly as it is printed in your documentation. All those letters, numbers, and ampersands can get awfully confusing, but one transposed letter or skipped number is the difference between getting a dial tone and extreme frustration.

6. **Click the OK button.**

   The Edit Modem Commands dialog box closes, and the Kppp Configuration dialog box reappears on your screen.

7. **Click the OK button.**

   The Kppp Configuration dialog box closes, and the Kppp dialog box reappears.

Phew! That's done. Put your modem manual with your ISP configuration sheets and get ready to test.

Testing, testing, 1 2 3. . .

Have you done it right? Will it work? Just how close are you to being online? Time to find out.

If you just finished setting up your modem, the Kppp dialog box is still open; click the Connect button. (If you closed it, open the KDE menu and select Internet⇨Kppp to open the Kppp dialog box.) You should see (and hear, if you have modem volume turned on) a normal connection to the ISP. After you've established a normal connection, you can file away those information sheets and manuals. You won't need to redo this process unless you buy a new modem or something at your ISP changes (or, of course, if you change ISPs). High-five yourself and head to Chapter 9, where we describe the basic Internet utilities that KDE provides.

If you don't get a connection, move on to the "What's Troubling You?" section of this chapter for some simple ways to check your connection and see where the problem lies.

All-the-Time Online

Some lucky folks don't have to fuss with modems, `init` strings, or ISP busy signals. Instead, they have a direct connection to the Internet via a cable modem or DSL connection, or they are in a building that has full-time Internet access via Ethernet cabled throughout the walls (usually a school or office building, though some new homes are being built with full Ethernet wiring). Ethernet jacks look like oversized phone plugs. You'll know if you have this kind of access, and if your Ethernet system provides access to the Internet. If it doesn't, you'll need to use the regular ISP route to get online.

KDE doesn't have a particular set of protocols for handling constant access via Ethernet. The functions you need are best handled from the command line, and were probably done when you hooked up to that connection. If you're getting a new cable modem or DSL service or you want to attach your KDE machine to your company's network, consult your system or network administrator. The support person at your ISP, if you're connecting from home, also ought to be able to help. (Remember to determine whether they're Linux friendly!)

If you'd like to do your own research, start by consulting the *Linux Network Administrator's Guide* on the Web. You can find the guide at `http://metalab.unc.edu/LDP/LDP/nag/nag.html`.

What's Troubling You?

No matter how carefully you set up your connection, there will be times when you need to do some basic troubleshooting. Two kinds of problems exist: problems with your computer and problems with the Internet/your ISP. This section presents the most common problems of each type and shows you some easy ways to figure out what's wrong.

It's coming from inside the house

The simplest problems to fix are those that stem from a typo or a dangling wire in your computer room. If you configured Kppp and your modem according to the steps earlier in this chapter and yet you still don't get a connection, look through this list and try these solutions:

✔ Does the modem dial?

If you don't get a dial tone, you may have a modem configuration problem. Get out your modem manual and redo the modem steps, paying careful attention to the init string.

You should also check whether you have a phone line plugged into your modem. (It's one of those things that make you smack your head and say "D'oh!" just like Homer Simpson, but it's more common than you'd think.)

✔ Does the modem dial, but fail to make a connection?

Check to see if you entered the phone number for the ISP's modem bank correctly. If you have the right phone number, give your ISP a call. It may be a problem on their end, and you'll have to wait until it's fixed.

✔ Does the modem make a connection but refuse to let you sign on?

Did you enter your username and password correctly in the login script? Remember that usernames and passwords are case sensitive, so keep upper- and lowercase letters where they belong.

✔ Are you receiving strange messages from the ISP after you sign on, especially things about DNS lookup failures?

Make sure you entered all those IP numbers correctly. If that doesn't solve it, call your ISP. Be prepared to recite the error messages exactly as they appeared on your screen.

Knotted up in the Net

Sometimes you run into a problem that you simply don't know how to solve. It's not a problem with your own setup or with your ISP, but a problem with the great big beautiful world of the Internet. Because the Internet is a big old mess of networked computers, there are inevitably times that part of it won't work quite right.

When you're pretty sure you have an Internet connection problem, use KDE's basic network utilities to figure out what's wrong — or at least to get better information about what may be happening. The network utilities included with KDE are the same tools used by every network administrator and Internet expert. If you're having trouble, ping the problematic computer or run a quick traceroute before you ask for help. Having that data ready to go will make you look quite smart and speed up the search for a solution.

ping? ping!

Picture this: You're sitting at your home computer, trying to `telnet` to your work computer in order to get a file. No matter how hard you try or how long you wait, the computer you want is just not answering the phone.

If you're trying to connect to a specific computer on the Internet but you can't, you can use `ping` to see if that other computer is alive. `ping` is a utility that sends small bursts of data at regular intervals; if the receiving computer is running, it responds with identical bursts of data. If the computer is down, the packets of data aren't returned. Follow these steps to `ping` another computer:

1. **Open the KDE menu and select Internet⇨Network Utilities.**

   The Network Utilities dialog box appears.

2. **Click the Ping tab.**

3. **Enter the name of the computer that you're trying to reach into the Host box.**

   You can enter the IP number instead, if you know it.

4. **Click the Go! button.**

What do you get back? It will, frankly, look like gibberish. You don't have to pay attention to the details of the stuff that `ping` sends back, though. All you really need to know is whether the machine is functioning; if it doesn't respond to a `ping`, it's not working. Look at Figure 8-9 to see a sample `ping` of the KDE Web server.

Figure 8-9:
The results
of a `ping`
issued to
`www.kde.
org.`

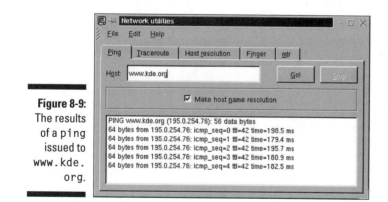

The top line shows the machine you're `ping`ing, with both its domain name and its IP number. It also shows you the packet size of the data being sent from your machine. The remaining lines show you the packets being returned from the machine being `ping`ed, and some information about the time it took for the `ping` to reach the other machine and return to you.

Driver, follow that route

ping isn't the solution for every problem, though. Take this situation: You know you're connected to your ISP, but you just can't connect to other machines on the Internet. Perhaps you can connect, but it's excruciatingly slow when you do. If it's not your ISP and it's not your computer, it may well be a traffic jam on the Net itself.

This is where traceroute comes in handy. traceroute is a utility that allows you to watch the path between your computer and any other computer on the net. Like ping, traceroute uses small packets of data. The results of traceroute show you the route that the packets followed between your computer and the computer you're tracing. (Traceroute may be in other directories, depending on your version of Linux.)

No matter how fast it may seem, there is almost never a direct connection between two computers on the Internet that aren't part of the same domain. Rather, information is relayed through many intermediate computers to get to its destination. When you run a traceroute, you see what those intermediate *hops* are. Often, they're multiple machines in the same domain, but with city names. Those are probably *backbone* machines, or computers that serve as the central nervous system of the Internet.

To use traceroute, follow these steps:

1. **Open the KDE menu and select Internet⇨Network Utilities.**

   The Network Utilities dialog box appears.

2. **Click the Traceroute tab.**

3. **Enter in the Host field the name of the machine you're trying to reach.**

   You can use the IP number instead, if you know it.

4. **Click the Go! button.**

Each computer between you and the target machine is listed, along with the time it took for the tracing packets to reach that machine. If there is a problem along the way and packets are lost, you see an asterisk instead of a time. Major problems are indicated by three asterisks on a line by themselves; this means that the next logical machine isn't operating and the packets have to be rerouted.

Chapter 9

Using Internet Applications

● ●

In This Chapter

▶ Sending and reading mail with KMail

▶ Mail call! — KBiff

▶ Spreading the news with KRN

▶ Browsing the Net with KFM

▶ Using KFM to download files from the Net

▶ Placing a call with KTalk

▶ Using the party line — Ksirc

● ●

*B*eing connected to the Internet isn't much fun, in and of itself. You could go around saying "Hey, I've got an ISP! And I'm online!" But you won't have much more to say than that — unless, of course, you start to explore the wonders of the Internet and all the great resources available there.

KDE has a bevy of fine programs that make your Internet activity easier. KMail and KBiff handle your e-mail, KRN gets you connected to the newsgroups of USENET, KFM is both a Web browser and a file transfer client, and KTalk and Ksirc help you to chat with friends and strangers around the world.

In this section, we assume that you have an account with a Linux-friendly ISP and that you've already configured Kppp and your modem to work together and make a reliable connection to the ISP. If you haven't done that yet, read Chapter 8 and get that set up; then, you can come back and configure all the Internet applications you want to use.

Get a Grip on Your E-Mail

Sure, the Internet is an interesting and crazy place. You find lots of stuff to do, Web pages to see, newsgroups to read. The function that's become almost indispensable, though, is e-mail. People use e-mail for everything these days, from telecommuting to checking in with Gramps about whether his lettuce seeds have sprouted yet this year. E-mail is a great way to get your communication revved up; an e-mail takes just a few seconds to travel around the world, and that's not something any postal service or overnight delivery company can do for you.

KDE makes getting your mail a simple procedure. Use two programs that come with KDE to manage your e-mail habits, and soon you'll have a slick process that will make you wonder how you ever handled your mail without the help of KDE.

Using KMail, your electronic post office

KMail is the KDE mail client, a program designed especially to handle e-mail. With KMail, you can organize your mail however you like, attach files from your hard drive, and compose or reply to e-mail in a straightforward fashion.

If you don't like KMail, you can find more information about other non-KDE mail clients (such as pine or elm) in Chapter 13. Take the lessons from this chapter and apply them to a program that works better for you.

Configuring KMail

Getting KMail set up is a lot like getting Kppp configured properly. You need a couple of items from your ISP, and you need to work through several dialog boxes to make sure that you've covered everything. Just as with Kppp, though, you can always go back and make changes if you need to or if something changes at your ISP.

If this is the first time you are using KMail, expect a bit of delay as KDE builds new file structures and creates the underlying organization needed for faster service later.

Ready to get going with e-mail? Use this procedure to configure KMail:

1. **Open the KDE menu and choose Internet⇨Mail Client to open KMail.**

   The KMail window appears. If this is the first time you have opened KMail, the Settings dialog box also appears (shown in Figure 9-1), opened to the Identity tab.

   If you've opened KMail before but haven't configured it, you need to use File⇨Settings to open the Settings dialog box.

2. **Type your personal information in the Settings dialog box fields.**

   What you type is the information that people see after they receive e-mail from you. Type your e-mail address in the Email Address field. You can leave Reply-To Address blank unless you want people to reply to a different address than the one in the Email Address field.

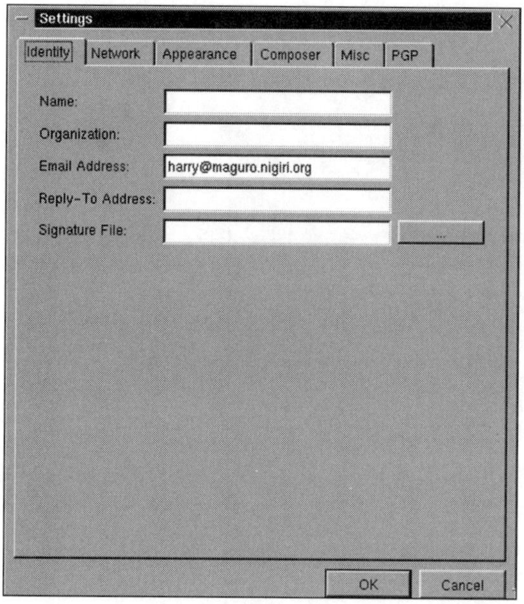

Figure 9-1:
Configuring
KMail
begins with
the Settings
dialog box.

In the Signature File field, you can enter information that appears at the bottom of every e-mail you send. Usually this file includes your name and e-mail address. If you're using KMail for business purposes, you may want to include your title and company name, or a business phone or fax number.

Don't ever put your home phone or address into your signature file. You have no way of knowing where that information will be forwarded or seen, and you're just asking for trouble to put personal information such as that randomly into public view. If you must put something, consider a post office box or a pager number.

3. Click the Network tab at the top of the Settings dialog box.

4. Click Add (located just under Incoming Mail, as shown in Figure 9-2) and select POP3.

Only select Local Mailbox if you've already arranged with your ISP to download your mail from the ISP directly to your local machine. You'll know if you've done this.

5. Click OK.

The Configure Account dialog box opens.

6. Enter the information you received from your ISP about its mail server.

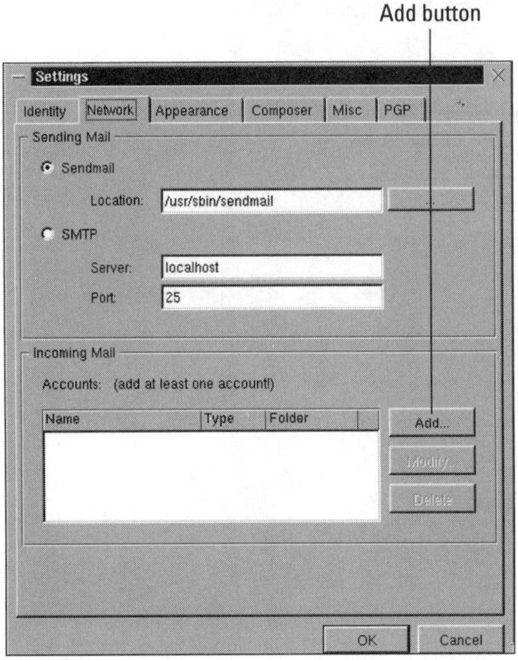

Add button

Figure 9-2:
Enter your
ISP's
specific
mailbox
information
on the
Network
tab.

In the Host field, enter the mail server's name, which usually looks
something like **mail.myisp.com** or **pop3.myisp.com**. Sometimes, the ISP
provides an IP number rather than a machine name; in that case, the
number looks like **127.1.1.1** or a similar string of numbers.

Unless you are told by your ISP to enter a specific number, leave the
Port field empty.

7. Click OK.

The Configure Account dialog box closes, and the Settings dialog box
reappears.

8. Click OK after you finish.

You can ignore the other tabs in Settings for now. If you need to change
something later, use File⇨Settings to reopen the Configure Account
dialog box.

Congratulations! You're ready to start working with your e-mail. In the other
parts of this section, we describe how to compose e-mail in KMail, how to get
your mail, and how to manage the mail you get. The next section covers
KBiff, a utility that tells you when you have e-mail to deal with.

Composing a new e-mail message

You won't be happy for long if all you can do is receive e-mail and never send any. Luckily, writing e-mail is a snap with KMail. Just follow these steps:

1. **Click the Compose New Message button, shown in Figure 9-3.**

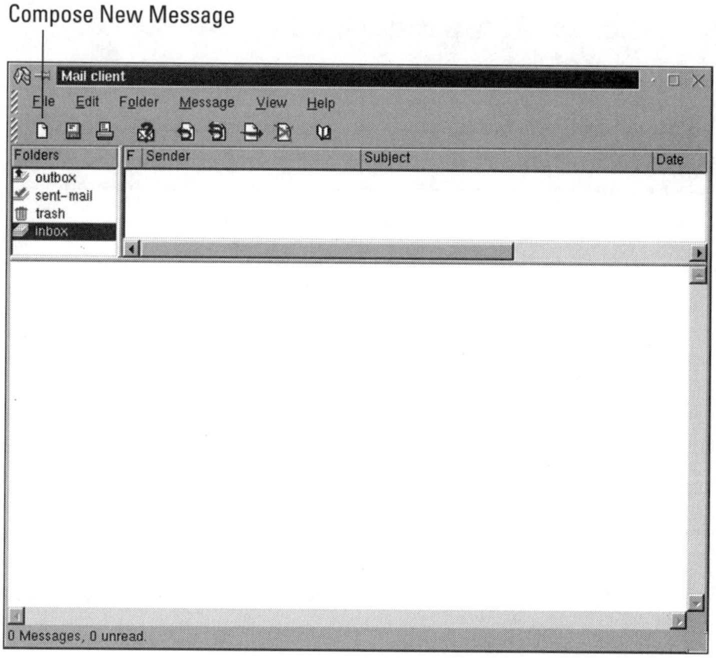

Compose New Message

Figure 9-3:
Writing an
e-mail is
easy with
KMail's
flexible
features.

The New Message screen appears (see Figure 9-4).

2. **Enter the recipient's e-mail address in the To: field. If you want to send carbon copies of the message, enter those e-mail addresses in the Cc: field.**

3. **Type your message in the large window at the bottom of the New Message screen.**

4. **Click the Send Message button after you've finished your e-mail.**

KMail automatically uploads your message to your ISP's mail server.

You can also use KMail to send files created in other programs, such as a word-processor document or an image file. To attach a file from your computer to an e-mail message you are composing in KMail, use the following procedure.

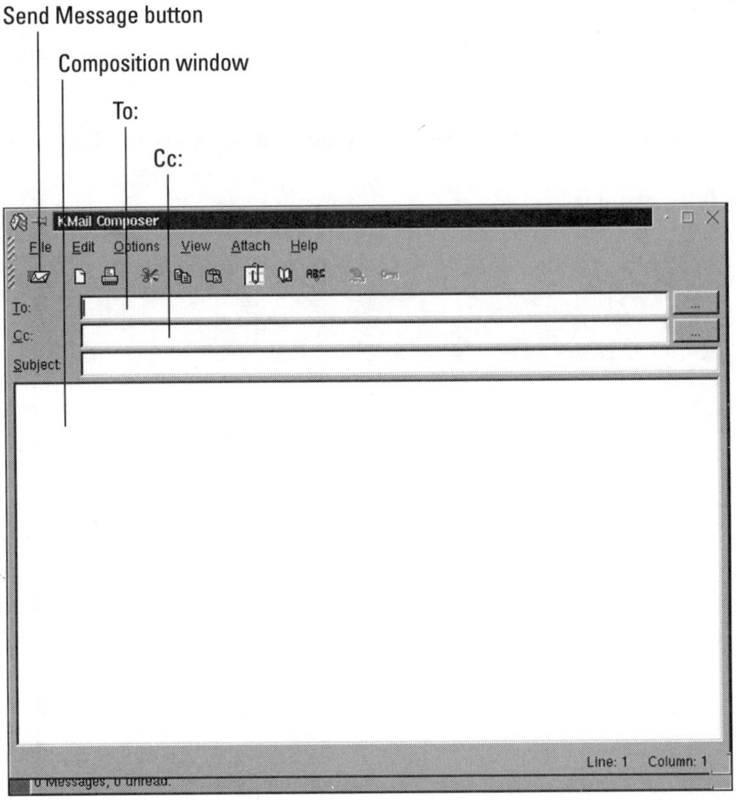

Send Message button

Composition window

To:

Cc:

Figure 9-4:
Use the
New
Message
Screen to
compose
a new
message, of
course!

1. **Choose Attach⇨Attach in the KMail composition window.**

   You can also click the paperclip button in the KMail toolbar.

   A file manager window appears.

2. **Select the file you want to attach to the e-mail message.**

   You may need to navigate through the file manager until you find the correct file.

3. **Click OK.**

   The file manager window closes, and the file attaches to the e-mail message. When you finish and send the message, the file will travel along to the recipient's mailbox.

Downloading new e-mail from your ISP

Getting your mail with KMail is also unbelievably easy. If you have KMail open, click the Get New Mail button (shown in Figure 9-5)! KMail then contacts your ISP to get any new mail that's been sent.

Inbox

Get New Mail

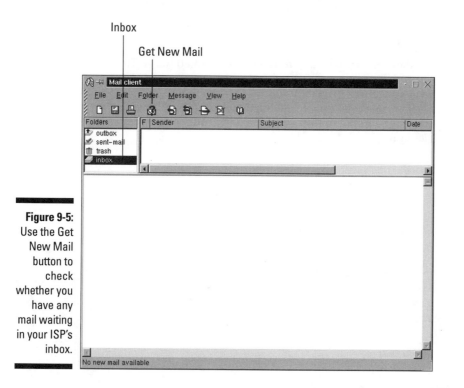

Figure 9-5:
Use the Get New Mail button to check whether you have any mail waiting in your ISP's inbox.

After you send KMail to go get your e-mail, click the name of your inbox in the upper-left corner of the KMail screen. If you have new mail, the subject lines and senders' names appear in the upper-right window of the screen. Click any of these messages to display the e-mail message in the large window at the bottom of the screen.

Replying to e-mail

More often than not, you want to reply to a message you've just read. KMail gives you several options for e-mail replies, including individual reply and group reply. You can also choose to attach files to your replies. To reply to an e-mail that's currently open, use this procedure:

1. **Click the Reply to Author button (see Figure 9-6).**

   The KMail composition window appears. You see that the text of the e-mail to which you're replying is already quoted in the message, and the e-mail address of the sender is already in the To: field.

2. **Delete the parts of the quoted message that you don't want to answer directly and compose your reply.**

3. **Click Send Message after you're finished.**

   KMail sends your reply to the person named in the To: field.

If the message was originally sent to several people and you want to reply to all of them, use the Reply to All Recipients button (shown in Figure 9-6) instead of the Reply to Author button, and proceed as you would with a single reply.

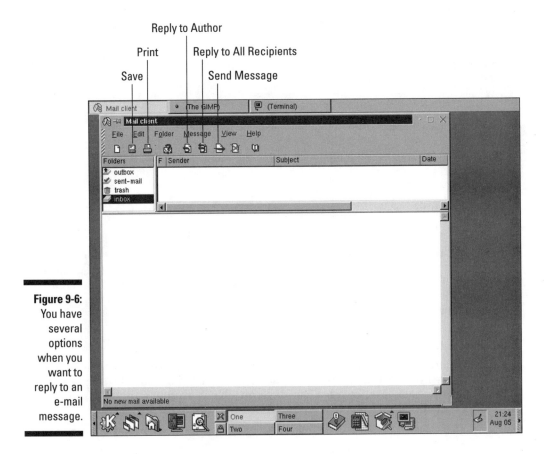

Figure 9-6:
You have several options when you want to reply to an e-mail message.

Be aware to whom you're sending e-mail! If you receive a message that was sent to several people, but you want to make a snide comment to the author alone, be very sure that you click Reply to Author and not Reply to All Recipients. You can get into a really embarrassing jam if you don't pay attention.

If you want to attach a file to your reply, follow the process described in the "Composing a new e-mail message" section of this chapter.

Saving and printing e-mail

You'll want to keep some of the e-mail you receive, whether by saving your e-mail to your hard drive or printing it out.

✔ To save an e-mail message, click the Save button above the message (refer to Figure 9-6). The Save dialog box opens; select the location where you want to save the message.

✔ To print an e-mail message, click the Print button above the message (refer to Figure 9-6).

Automating mail call with KBiff

If you have better things to do with your time than clicking the Get New Mail button repeatedly, you'll probably like having KBiff on your side. KBiff is a small utility that runs in the background, sitting quietly on your toolbar until mail arrives. KBiff constantly checks your ISP for incoming mail, and lets you know when mail has appeared. If you've seen one of those America Online television ads in the last five years or so (and really, who hasn't?), you know that cheerful "You've Got Mail!" voice, which is the AOL version of KBiff.

Here's a nerdy piece of folklore for you: It's said that the KBiff program is named for a friendly pup called Biff, who would bark insanely when the mailman arrived. The dog's owner created a little program that'd do the same for e-mail, and thus the biff program was born.

Here's how to set up KBiff:

1. **Open the KDE menu and choose Internet⇨KBiff.**

   The KBiff Setup dialog box appears, as shown in Figure 9-7, with the General tab selected.

2. **Select the default icon or choose one that you like better.**

   The default icons are shown on the buttons at the bottom of the dialog box; they are file trays that are either full or empty, depending on whether or not you have mail. If you want a different icon, click the button and select the new icon from the file manager window that appears.

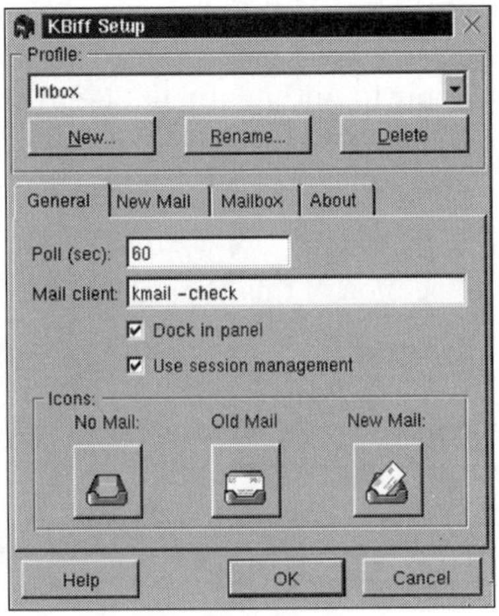

Figure 9-7:
Setting up
KBiff is a
quick
process.

3. **Click the New Mail tab and select the default sound file (a beep) or choose one that you like better.**

   Pick something you like hearing; if you get a lot of e-mail, you'll hear the sound file a lot. Shorter is better. Do you really want to hear the entire theme from *2001: A Space Odyssey* every time you get e-mail from your boss?

   The "System beep" box is selected by default. If you want another sound file, enter the file path in the text box above "System beep."

4. **Set your Poll time, the interval at which KBiff checks for e-mail.**

   If you get a lot of mail, you may want to set this at two or three minutes. If you don't get much mail, every 30 minutes may be enough.

5. **Click the Mailbox tab at the top of the dialog box.**

   Fill in the same information you provided when you configured KMail. You need your ISP's mail server name and your e-mail address.

6. **Click OK.**

   The KBiff icon appears in your toolbar. After new mail appears, you hear a beep (or the sound file you selected), and the icon changes.

Spread the News with KRN

While e-mail is a great way to carry on conversations with one or a few people, newsgroups (also referred to as USENET) are a fantastic way to participate in conversations about a single topic with thousands of other people.

A newsgroup has a name that denotes its topic, such as `alt.collecting.beanie-babies` or `rec.sport.pro-wrestling`. In that group, you find anywhere from 10 to 800 or more messages loosely centered on that topic. You can find a newsgroup for almost any concept under the sun.

The KDE news client is KRN, which is a specialized KDE version of the tried-and-true newsreader `rn`.

Reading newsgroups

You can spend a very happy life on USENET just reading what other people post. KRN helps you out by sorting the articles into *threads,* by using the Subject line of each article to arrange the various threads within a particular group. To read your favorite newsgroups with KRN, use this procedure:

1. Open the KDE menu and choose Internet⇨News Client to open KRN.

The KRN screen opens with the list of newsgroups you read in a collapsed tree format (see Figure 9-8). Your list is blank if you're reading USENET for the first time on this machine.

Otherwise, KRN looks for a file called `.newsrc` in your home directory and shows you groups based on the contents of that file. KRN automatically generates `.newsrc`; you don't have to do anything.

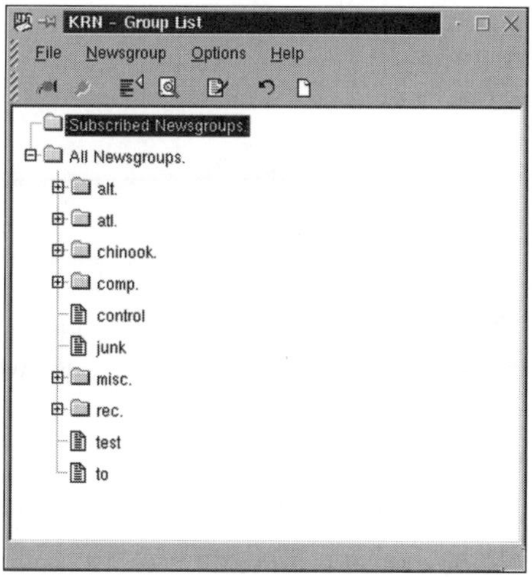

Figure 9-8:
Finding
news
to read
depends on
what news-
groups your
ISP carries.

2. **Click on the small plus sign to expand the tree one level.**

   If you haven't already downloaded the newsgroups list from your server, KRN asks if you want to do this now. Click Yes. Depending on the speed of your connection and the number of groups your ISP carries, downloading may take a while.

   You can only read newsgroups that your ISP carries. For some people, this means that they have a relatively small selection of groups to read. Many ISPs will add newsgroups at the request of their subscribers; others won't. If your ISP won't carry the groups you want to read, consider subscribing to a third-party service such as the ones offered at www.newsguy.com or www.deja.com.

3. **Continue clicking the plus sign to expand the tree until you see newsgroup names.**

4. **Double-click the name of a newsgroup you want to read.**

   The KRN reader window appears, as does a KRN Confirmation dialog box.

5. **Enter the number of articles you want to download and the order in which you want them downloaded into the KRN Confirmation dialog box (shown in Figure 9-9).**

Figure 9-9:
Use the KRN Confirmation dialog box to tell KRN which messages you want to read.

KRN connects to your ISP's news server and downloads the articles you select. The articles appear in the upper portion of the KRN window, as shown in Figure 9-10.

6. **Click the article you want to read.**

   KRN displays the article in the lower portion of the KRN window.

7. **Repeat this process with each group that you want to read.**

8. **Choose File⇨Exit after you have finish reading news.**

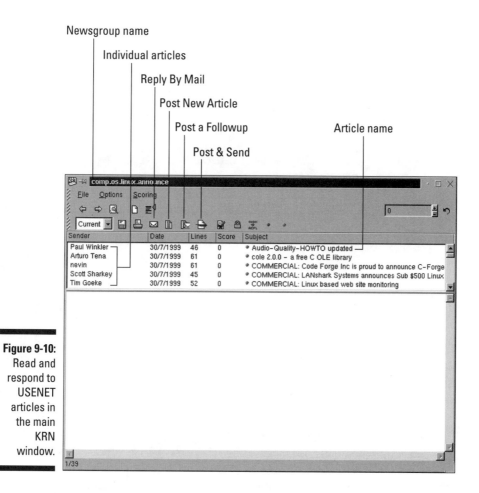

Newsgroup name

Individual articles

Reply By Mail

Post New Article

Post a Followup

Post & Send

Article name

Figure 9-10:
Read and
respond to
USENET
articles in
the main
KRN
window.

Posting a new article

You may not find an article or thread discussing the subtopic you really want to talk about in a particular group. If you're ready to post a new article to a USENET group, use this simple process:

1. **Click the Post New Article button (shown in Figure 9-10).**

   The KRN composition window appears, as shown in Figure 9-11.

2. **Fill in the Subject line and type the message.**

   Make sure your Subject line is clear and descriptive. "Seeking Harley Softail Engine Specs" is more descriptive than "Help me with my Harley!!!" Most people skim Subject lines and don't read every single message.

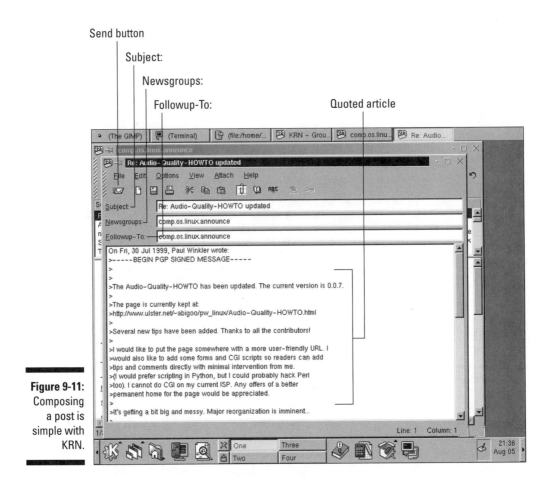

Send button
Subject:
Newsgroups:
Followup-To:
Quoted article

Figure 9-11:
Composing
a post is
simple with
KRN.

3. **Click Send after you finish your post.**

KRN uploads your message to your ISP's news server, and your message is distributed around the world.

Responding to an article via USENET

Sooner or later, you see an article that makes you want to respond immediately. You may agree wholeheartedly, or you may think the article's author is an unmitigated moron. The most common way of responding to an article that you see in a newsgroup is to "follow it up." To post a follow-up to a USENET post, use this process:

1. **Click the Post a Followup button (refer to Figure 9-10).**

   The KRN Composition window opens (refer to Figure 9-11). The title of the article is in the titlebar of the composition window, and the Subject, Newsgroup, and Followup To: fields are already filled in. The article to which you're responding is quoted in the text area for your convenience.

2. **Edit the article to which you're responding.**

   Make sure you delete material that you don't want to address in your reply, which makes downloading much faster.

   Add your response after the quoted material. Interspersing your comments with the quoted material is okay.

3. **Click the Send button after you finish.**

   KRN uploads your article to your ISP's news server. Depending on propagation times, your article begins to appear on news servers around the world.

Responding to an article via e-mail

If you prefer to respond to a particular article via e-mail, use this process:

1. **Click the Reply By Mail button (refer to Figure 9-10).**

   The KRN Composition window opens. The title of the article to which you're responding is in the titlebar, and the To and Subject lines are filled in. The article is quoted in the lower text area.

2. **Edit the article to which you're responding.**

3. **Click the Send button after you finish.**

   KRN uploads your message to your ISP's mail server, and then is delivered to the recipient.

If the person you're replying to has a *munged* e-mail address, your reply may be returned to you as undeliverable. A munged e-mail address is one that's been altered in an attempt to avoid getting unsolicited commercial e-mail by foiling address-harvesting robots that roam USENET. The problem is that munging doesn't work very well; many spammers employ people to write programs that remove the munges and put your address in a file anyway. Munging is impolite because it requires extra work on the part of someone who wants to mail you; munging can even cause serious and expensive problems for real companies. You're better off signing up with an ISP that has a vigorous anti-spam policy than munging ineffectively.

Responding both on USENET and via e-mail

Sometimes, you may want to post and e-mail a reply at the same time. Generally responding both ways is not a good idea, unless the poster has explicitly requested it; otherwise, the recipient may not know whether or not you've sent private e-mail. If you're going to post and mail the same message, put a note at the top saying "Posted and e-mailed." Use this process:

1. **Click the Post & Send button (refer to Figure 9-10).**

   The KRN Composition window opens. Headers for both mail and news are filled in already.

2. **Edit your message with a note that you've both posted and e-mailed the response.**

3. **Click the Send button.**

   KRN sends a copy of your message to the mail server, where the message is sent via e-mail and to the news server, where your message is posted to the newsgroup.

Netiquette: The rules of the road

News has existed since the early days of the Internet. Like anything that's been around for a long time, a set of behavior rules has grown up. On USENET, these rules are referred to as *netiquette,* or Internet etiquette. You can find several documents dealing with appropriate USENET behavior on the wonderful newsgroup news.newusers.questions, which we recommend as one of the groups you read regularly.

The basic tenets of netiquette are

- ✔ Read a group for a while before you post. The old rule used to be six months; these days, a couple of weeks is usually sufficient.

- ✔ Read the FAQ, so that you don't jump onto a group you never posted to before and ask a bunch of questions that are answered in a single document.

- ✔ If you ask a question on a newsgroup, stick around for the answers.

   To ask a question and say, "Please e-mail me the answer as I don't read this group" is considered extremely rude.

- ✔ Don't get into flame wars. Keep violent arguments in e-mail. The general tone of USENET can be somewhat abrasive and rude; do your part to elevate the tone by thinking before you send a post that's insulting and mean.

Hunting and Gathering with KFM

What's KFM doing way over here in Chapter 9? Yes, we know we cover KFM pretty thoroughly in Chapter 4, but KFM isn't just for managing your machine more efficiently — KFM is also useful for Internet projects! You can use KFM as a Web browser, or you can use it to download files from FTP archives.

Browsing the Web with KFM

To use KFM as a Web browser, just use File⇨Open Location. The Open Location dialog box appears; type the URL of the page you want to visit into the box, and click OK. After the page loads, you see it in the right-hand side of the KFM window, while your machine's file tree remains visible on the left. See Figure 9-12 for an example.

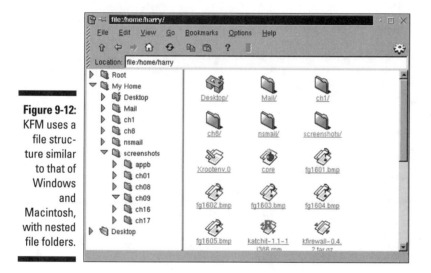

Figure 9-12:
KFM uses a file struc-ture similar to that of Windows and Macintosh, with nested file folders.

KFM is not as advanced a Web browser as Netscape, but it serves as a quick way to check a site without firing up another program. For serious recre-ational surfing, you want to use Netscape. See Chapter 12 for more informa-tion on using Netscape with KDE.

The major downside to using KFM as your Web browser is that KFM uses up a lot of your available memory. If you're running anything else at the same time, you may see your machine's swap partition going nuts.

Downloading files with KFM

Even though KFM isn't the greatest browser for purely fun purposes, it does have a very strong advantage over Netscape in one particular function. KFM is stellar for downloading files from the Internet. If you have an FTP (File Transfer Protocol) program that you like, you can use that just as easily, but KFM's file transfer capabilities are simple and graphical.

To use KFM as an FTP client, use this method:

1. **Open KFM by clicking its button in the panel.**

2. **Choose File⇨Open Location.**

   The Open Location dialog box appears.

3. **Type the FTP site address in the text area and click OK.**

   FTP URLs begin with `ftp://` instead of `http://`. In Figure 9-13, you see an open FTP session with `ftp://sunsite.unc.edu/pub/linux/X11/kde`, which has a lot of KDE programs available for download.

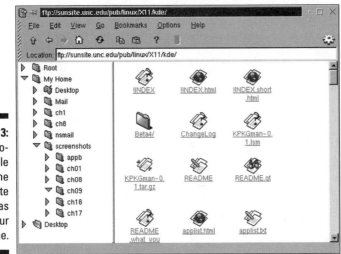

Figure 9-13: KFM provides a file tree for the archive site as well as for your machine.

4. **Find the file you want to download by clicking through the directory tree in the right-hand window.**

   Your computer's file tree is in the left window and the FTP site's in the right window.

5. **Click and drag the filename to the appropriate directory in your computer's file tree in the left-hand window.**

6. **Release the mouse button. In the dialog box that appears, select the Copy option.**

KFM copies the file from the FTP site to the location you select on your computer. A progress bar shows how much of the file has been copied; if the file is small, the bar may zip away rapidly. If the file is huge and you have a slow modem, go have a cup of coffee or order a pizza.

Make a Quick Call with KTalk

Want to have a real-time conversation with a friend without waiting for e-mail to pass back and forth? Try KTalk (the KDE version of an old UNIX warhorse, talk). Talk is the Neanderthal predecessor to today's instant message software for Windows and Macintosh, such as ICQ or AOL Instant Messenger. In KTalk, your typing goes instantly across the Net and appears on your friend's screen; KTalk is personal and quick, but not particularly pretty (see Figure 9-14 if you don't believe us).

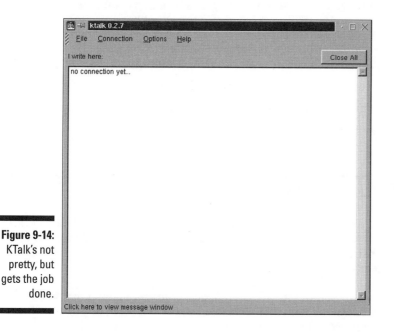

Figure 9-14: KTalk's not pretty, but gets the job done.

You have three requirements to use KTalk successfully. Your friend must be logged on, using a UNIX-based operating system, and accepting talk connections. For security reasons, some systems administrators do not allow talk connections. Check with your ISP if you're not sure.

If you can say "Yes, indeedy!" to those conditions, you're ready to use KTalk.

1. **Open the KDE menu and choose Internet⇨KTalk.**

   The main KTalk screen opens.

2. **Choose Connection⇨Talk To.**

   The KTalk Connection dialog box appears.

3. **Type the e-mail address of the person you want to talk to and click the Talk button.**

   The Connection dialog box closes, and the KTalk screen reappears.

   Notice a difference? While you're KTalking, the screen is split into two by a horizontal line. The text you type shows in the top area, and your friend's responses appear in the bottom area. Getting used to following a conversation that is split in two takes a few minutes, but you get used to the split screen the more you use KTalk.

   When you're using KTalk, whatever you type goes instantly to your friend's screen, and we do mean instantly. Each letter gets sent as soon as you lift your finger from the key. Your friend will find out just what a lousy typist you really are . . . and, in the worst case, you may find out exactly what your friend thinks before he has a chance to backspace and rephrase something more politely. For this reason alone, try not to get into KTalk sessions with your boss if you're really cheesed off at her!

4. **After you finish your session, click Disconnect.**

   The connection closes. You can now make another connection if you like.

5. **Choose File⇨Exit to leave KTalk.**

Getting Gabby with Ksirc

IRC, or Internet Relay Chat, is to talk what USENET is to e-mail. That is, with talk you can talk to one other person, but with IRC, you can talk to dozens at one time. Ksirc is KDE's IRC client, a program that makes it easier to participate in the IRC channels.

IRC is a real subculture. Before you plunge in, we recommend that you look at the various FAQs and help files available at www.irchelp.org to get a better idea of what you can find online.

Chatting away

Unlike KMail and KRN, you don't have to do any special configuring of Ksirc before you use it. You just have to find a server and be ready to chat! (If you don't know any IRC servers, look at the next section, "Finding places to chat," which gives some good references.)

Here's how you chat with Ksirc:

1. **Open the KDE menu and choose Internet⇨Chat Client (Ksirc).**

   The Server Control screen appears.

2. **Choose Connections⇨New Server from the drop-down menu.**

   The Connect to Server dialog box appears.

3. **Click the arrow next to Recent, under Group (see Figure 9-15).**

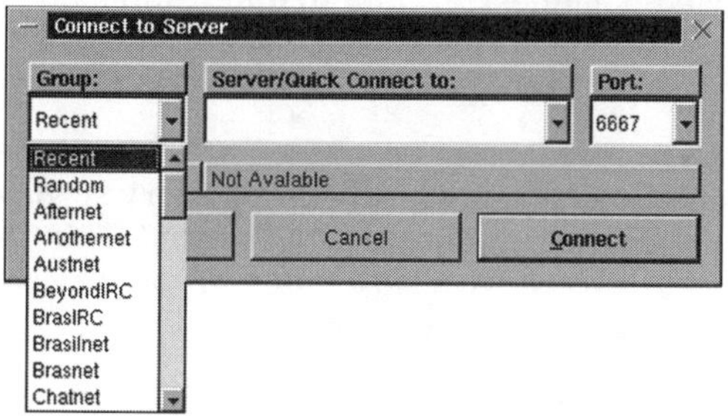

Figure 9-15: Get ready to chat by selecting a network.

Connect to Server			✕
Group:	**Server/Quick Connect to:**		**Port:**
Recent ▾	▾		6667 ▾
Recent ▲	Not Available		
Random			
Afternet	Cancel	**Connect**	
Anothernet			
Austnet			
BeyondIRC			
BrasIRC			
Brasilnet			
Brasnet			
Chatnet ▾			

The drop-down list that appears contains a list of major server networks. Pick one.

Unlike the Web, IRC servers are not all connected together. Several main networks house most IRC channels. These include EFnet, DalNet, and Undernet. However, as you get more involved with IRC, you may find that more specialized networks carry the sorts of channels you want to use. See the next section for information on these nets.

4. **Under Server/Quick Connect to:, select an IRC server for the network you choose.**

   You can often tell from a server's name where it is located. Choosing a server geographically close to you helps reduce lag, a major problem on IRC.

5. **Click Connect.**

   The Ksirc screen appears. A batch of text scrolls by (don't try to read it frantically; you can always scroll back).

If all goes well (meaning the IRC network is stable and you can have access to the server you chose), the Pick A Nick dialog box appears.

6. **Type the nickname you want to use into the Pick A Nick dialog box.**

   If somebody else is already using that nickname, or nick, for short, somewhere on the network, you are asked to choose again. (Yes, this means that if you're named Dave, you probably won't be able to use the nick Dave. You're competing for your own name with all the other Daves on that network. Try SuperDave or MagnifiDave or DaveTheRed. Obscene nicks, though, are never a good idea.)

   After you manage to select a unique nick, more text scrolls past, which means you're connected to the server you selected.

7. **Type the name of the channel you wish to join on the text entry line, using the format** `/join #channelname`.

   Channel names are always preceded by the pound sign, # (known as a hashmark to geeks and programmers).

   You should know what channel you want to join before you connect. You find hundreds of open channels in existence at any given time. If you really have no idea what channel you want, type `/list` on the text entry line.

   WARNING!

   Typing `/list` is an action of last resort because every single channel in existence on that server at that point in time is listed. This can be longer than a thousand lines. If you have a slow modem, you may actually be disconnected by your ISP before the list is finished.

   If you see text scrolling across the screen, you've been connected to the channel you selected. You can tell who else is on the channel by looking at the right window of the Ksirc screen, shown in Figure 9-16; the window lists the nicks of everyone joined to that channel. Comments being typed by these people fill the main text window.

8. **Send a message to the channel by typing your remark into the text entry box and press Enter.**

   Unlike KTalk, you can edit your remark in Ksirc before you send it, as long as you don't press Enter.

   If you want to portray an action, type `/me performs action`. For example, if you wanted to show that you were drinking milk, you would type

   `/me chugs an icy-cold glass of moo juice.`

9. **After you finish, type** `/quit` **in the text entry box.**

   The Ksirc window closes, and the Server Control dialog box reappears.

10. **Choose File⇨Quit to exit Ksirc.**

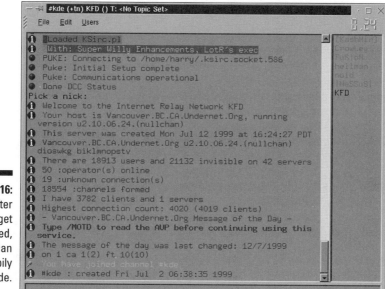

Figure 9-16:
After
you get
connected,
you can
chat happily
on #kde.

Finding places to chat

As we note in the previous section, IRC is an Internet subculture that is like no other. Before you jump into IRC, you probably can benefit from a bit of research. At the very least, knowing how IRC works is good, where the channels you want may be found, and some basic "chatiquette."

You can find all of this information, and much more, at these sites:

✔ www.irchelp.org is the main source for FAQs, channel lists, network information, and even scarier stuff such as how to defend yourself against viruses and worms that transmit via IRC.

✔ www.ircliszt.com is the IRC arm of www.liszt.com, a site that tries to catalog every mailing list on the Internet. At the ircliszt site, it does the same with IRC channels. You can even jump on IRC via its Web interface if you find yourself away from Ksirc.

✔ www.netway.com/~marci/songs/ is a collection of, well, songs about IRC. If you, too, come to find IRC one of the most entertaining aspects in your life, hum one of these songs to let your friends know how far over the edge you've gone.

Chapter 10

Applications and Utilities, Part 1 — Work

*W*hen you start work at a new job, you are usually assigned an office (or cubicle) equipped with a desk, chair, file drawer, phone, and other obvious workstation components. Despite that, your new office usually starts out as a pretty barren space. To work efficiently, you need additional tools such as pencils and pads of paper, letter trays to organize those papers, a calculator, pads of yellow sticky notes, and a long list of other supplies and accessories. Often, your first task when you start a new job or move into a new office is to make a trip to the supply room or office supply store to procure all the miscellaneous stuff you need.

The KDE desktop provides a working environment that is analogous to your physical office or cubicle. In addition, KDE includes an assortment of accessories and utilities that provide the computer equivalent of accessories such as a calculator, pads of paper, and even those ubiquitous yellow sticky notes. After you install KDE, you may not need to run to the virtual supply room. Using KDE is like moving into a new office that is already supplied with well-stocked drawers and shelves containing most of the tools and supplies you need.

Together, this chapter and Chapter 11 provide an overview of the accessory programs and utilities that are included as part of a typical KDE installation. The utility programs mentioned here may not be essential components of the core KDE system, but they go a long way toward making your experience using KDE more productive and enjoyable. All the KDE utility programs are designed specifically for the KDE environment to ensure compatibility with KDE and other KDE programs.

A lot of utility programs are packaged with KDE — that's why it takes two chapters to cover them all. This chapter covers the serious side of the KDE accessory programs, such as productivity tools and miscellaneous utility programs. Chapter 11 covers the fun stuff, such as games and multimedia accessories.

Getting It Down — Using KDE's Text Editors

KDE includes not one, but two, text editors among its assortment of standard accessory programs. Of course, a *text editor program* does exactly what its name implies — it enables you to create and edit text files. And both KEdit and KWrite can perform that basic task with aplomb.

KEdit and KWrite are similar, but not quite identical. Both provide a basic text editor window where you can edit text files by using the same time-tested techniques for selecting and editing text with mouse or keyboard that you use in virtually every modern word processor program. Both programs offer easy-to-use alternatives to working with traditional command-line text editors (such as vi or emacs) in a terminal emulation window. You can use either KEdit or KWrite to create and edit your KDE and Linux configuration files, shell scripts, HTML documents, and other text files and to view `readme` files and other online documentation stored as plain text files.

- **Opening KEdit:** Click the KDE Menu button and choose Applications⇨Text Editor. Figure 10-1 shows KEdit at work with an e-mail message.

- **Opening a text file for viewing or editing in KEdit:** Right-click the file's icon in a KFM window and choose Text Editor from the pop-up menu that appears.

- **Opening KWrite:** Click the KDE Menu button on the panel and choose Applications⇨Advanced Editor. Figure 10-2 shows a KWrite window displaying a configuration file for editing.

Despite their similarities, KEdit and KWrite are two separate and distinct programs. Although the basic purpose of both programs is the same and the basic functions are remarkably similar, each program includes a slightly different set of supporting features. For example, KEdit can open and save to a URL, and the program also has a link to the KDE e-mail client to facilitate using KEdit to compose e-mail messages. KWrite, on the other hand, includes an Undo and Redo feature, plus indents, bookmarks, and more extensive configuration and formatting options.

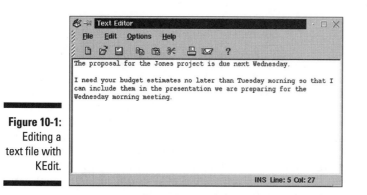

Figure 10-1:
Editing a
text file with
KEdit.

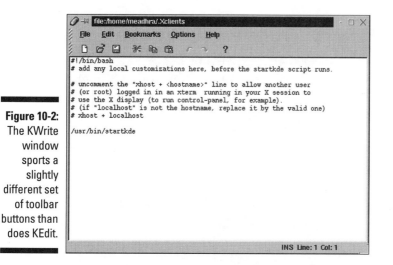

Figure 10-2:
The KWrite
window
sports a
slightly
different set
of toolbar
buttons than
does KEdit.

Scheduling Events and Appointments with KOrganizer

In today's busy world, nearly everyone needs an appointment calendar of some kind. If you are spoiled by the convenience of using a computer-based personal information manager (PIM) in another computing environment, you may be concerned about how you will do without your favorite PIM when you're using KDE. Never fear: KOrganizer is here and it delivers all the essential features you've come to expect from a Personal Information Manager.

KOrganizer is a multipurpose program that includes an appointment calendar, appointment and event scheduling, reminder alarms, and a prioritized to-do list. The program can set up recurring appointments with very flexible scheduling options. For advanced users, KOrganizer supports group scheduling features, vCalendar data interchange with other programs, and synchronizing your KOrganizer data with your 3Com PalmPilot. (The KPilot utility is required for PalmPilot synchronization.)

To start KOrganizer, click the KDE Menu button and choose Applications⇨ Organizer. The KOrganizer window opens and displays the appointments and to-do items in your most recently used calendar file. (If you're opening KOrganizer for the first time, the program displays a blank New Calendar file.) KOrganizer can put on a number of faces with which to display your calendar information. The Day view, as shown in Figure 10-3, shows a small calendar display for the current month, a to-do list, and an appointment calendar for the current date with one-hour time blocks.

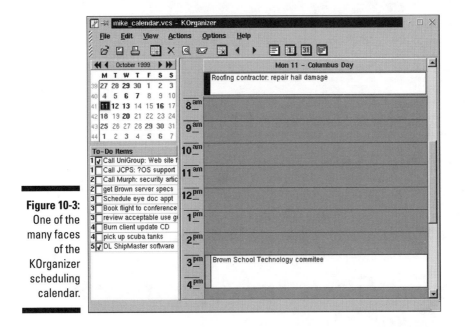

Figure 10-3:
One of the many faces of the KOrganizer scheduling calendar.

When you start KOrganizer, the program also launches a control applet that is docked into the KDE panel. The KOrganizer applet enables you to close the main KOrganizer program and still get reminder alarms for your scheduled appointments. You can double-click the KOrganizer applet icon to quickly reopen KOrganizer without going through the KDE menu.

Creating an appointment or event

KOrganizer enables you to schedule two kinds of date-dependent activities: appointments and events. An *appointment* is an activity that you schedule to occur at a specific date and time — for example, a meeting, an interview, or a doctor's appointment. An *event*, on the other hand, occurs on a specific date but does not involve a set time. You use events to track all-day occurrences — such as holidays, vacation days, and birthdays — and to note project deadlines.

To add an appointment or event to your KOrganizer calendar file, follow these steps:

1. **Click the New Appointment button on the KOrganizer toolbar or choose Actions⇨New Appointment.**

   KOrganizer opens the New Appointment dialog box with the General tab selected, as shown in Figure 10-4.

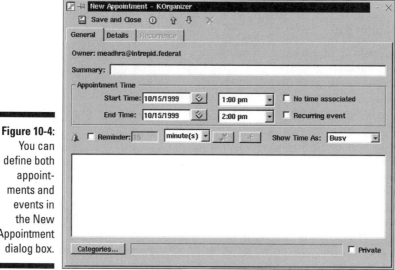

Figure 10-4:
You can define both appointments and events in the New Appointment dialog box.

You can also open the New Appointment dialog box by right-clicking anywhere in the appointment calendar portion of the KOrganizer window and choosing New Appointment from the pop-up menu that appears.

2. **Enter a short description of the appointment or event in the Summary text box.**

   The text you enter here is what appears in the appointment calendar display in KOrganizer. A very brief entry, such as "Staff Meeting," usually works best. If you need to record more detailed information about the appointment, click the large unlabeled text box in the lower half of the New Appointment dialog box and type the supplemental information there.

3. **For an appointment, enter or select the date and time in the Start Time and End Time text boxes. For an event, click the No Time Associated option.**

   By default, KOrganizer enters the currently selected date in the date portion of the Start Time and End Time boxes. You can change those dates by typing a new date or by clicking the button at the right end of the text boxes to display a date picker calendar and selecting the date by using the arrow to scroll to the correct month and then clicking the desired date. Similarly, you can enter starting and ending times for the appointment by typing the time in the appropriate text box or by clicking the button in the time box and selecting a time from the drop-down list.

   To create an event instead of an appointment, click the No Time Associated option. When you do, the Start Time and End Time boxes disappear from the New Appointment dialog box.

4. **(Optional) Click the Reminder option; then enter a number and select a unit of time.**

   This sets an alarm to go off in advance of your appointment, at the time you've indicated here. If you select the Reminder option, KOrganizer automatically displays a message on-screen (and optionally plays a sound and/or runs a program) before the appointment's start time. If you don't want a reminder alarm associated with this appointment, just leave the Reminder checkbox unselected.

   When you set up a reminder alarm, you set it to go off a specified length of time before the appointment's start time. For example, the reminder for a 3:00 appointment appears at 2:45 if you keep the default setting of 15 minutes before the appointment. You can enter a different number in the text box beside the Reminder option and select minutes, hours, or days from the adjacent drop-down list box to change how far in advance of the appointment the alarm is set. You can also change the sound KOrganizer plays by clicking the button that looks like a musical note and selecting a sound file from the Open dialog box that appears. Similarly, you can select a program or script for KOrganizer to run; click the button with a running stick figure on it and select a file from the Open dialog box.

5. **Select Busy or Free in the Show Time As drop-down list box.**

   Select Free to instruct KOrganizer to accept without complaint other appointments and meeting requests that conflict with this appointment. Typically, you select Busy for most appointments and Free is most often for events.

6. **(Optional) Click Categories and either select or enter a category in the KOrganizer Categories dialog box that appears; then click the OK button.**

Categories are a convenient way to classify appointments and events by the kind of activity they represent or to associate them with a project.

When you click the Categories button in the New Appointment dialog box, KOrganizer opens the KOrganizer Categories dialog box, as shown in Figure 10-5. To select an existing category, simply click the category name in the Available Categories list box and then click Add. To create a new category, type the category name into the New Category text box and then click Add. In either case, clicking Add adds the category to the Selected Categories list. You can select multiple categories for an appointment or event. Clicking OK closes the KOrganizer Categories dialog box and adds the selected categories to the text box beside the Categories button at the bottom of the New Appointment dialog box.

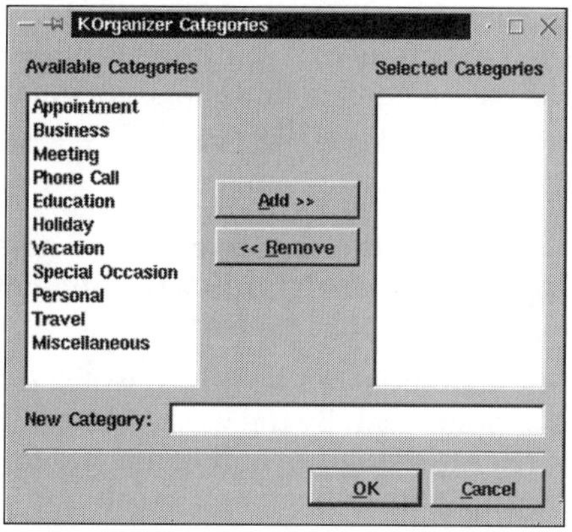

Figure 10-5:
You can
assign each
appointment
to one or
more
categories.

KOrganizer Categories
Available Categories	**Selected Categories**
Appointment	
Business	
Meeting	
Phone Call	
Education	Add >>
Holiday	
Vacation	<< Remove
Special Occasion	
Personal	
Travel	
Miscellaneous	
New Category:	
OK	Cancel

7. Click Save and Close.

KOrganizer closes the New Appointment dialog box and adds the appointment or event to the schedule calendar display. A new appointment appears in the appointment calendar portion of the KOrganizer window and occupies the block of time corresponding to its scheduled start and end times. An event appears at the top of the appointment calendar with no time beside it. Refer to Figure 10-3 to see examples of both appointments and an event displayed on the appointment calendar.

The Details tab of the New Appointment dialog box enables you to create a list of attendees at a meeting, complete with their e-mail addresses and meeting roles. If you're part of a network that includes compatible e-mail and group scheduling services, KOrganizer can invite attendees to your meeting and track their acceptance.

Scheduling a recurring appointment

If you're like most people, many of your appointments and activities are on a recurring schedule. Whether it's for the Monday morning staff meeting at work or the Saturday afternoon soccer game with the kids, you need a convenient way to enter a series of appointments without having to create each appointment individually.

KOrganizer makes it easy to define recurring appointments and events. You can create an appointment just once and make it a recurring appointment by defining how often it repeats. KOrganizer automatically creates additional appointments and adds them to your calendar at the interval you specify.

The easiest way to create a recurring appointment is to start by creating a regular appointment for the first occurrence. (See the steps outlined in the "Creating an appointment or event" section of this chapter.) You transform the regular appointment or event into a recurring appointment by following these steps:

1. **Select an appointment or event in the appointment calendar and then choose Actions⇨Edit Appointment or right-click the appointment and choose Edit from the pop-up menu that appears.**

   KOrganizer opens the Edit Appointment dialog box, which displays the settings for the selected appointment. By the way: Although the commands and dialog boxes refer to editing an appointment, you use exactly the same commands and dialog boxes to edit an event.

2. **Click the Recurring Event option on the General tab.**

   A check mark appears in the Recurring Event checkbox and the date portion of the Start Time and End Time options disappear from the General tab. The Recurrence tab, which was previously grayed out, becomes active.

3. **Click the Recurrence tab.**

   KOrganizer displays the recurrence scheduling options, as shown in Figure 10-6.

4. **Select Daily, Weekly, Monthly, or Yearly in the Recurrence Rule area.**

   When you select a basic recurrence rule type, the options on the right side of the Recurrence Rule area change to reflect the settings appropriate to the selected rule.

5. **Adjust the detail settings in the right side of the Recurrence Rule area to define the frequency of the recurrence.**

   For example, if you select Daily in Step 4, you can specify the number of days between appointments. If you select Weekly in Step 4, you can specify how many weeks should pass between appointments and on what days of the week the appointments occur.

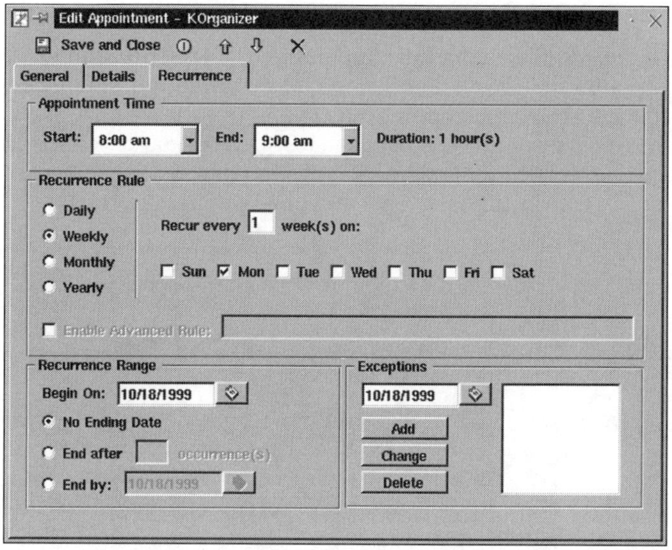

Figure 10-6:
Settings on
the
Recurrence
tab enable
you to
define the
rules for
recurring
appoint-
ments.

6. **Adjust the settings in the Recurrence Range area to define the beginning and ending dates for the series of recurring appointments or
   events.**

   By default, the Begin On setting shows the original start date for the
   appointment. Normally, you can just accept that date, but you can
   change it if necessary by clicking the button at the right end of the text
   box and selecting a new date from the pop-up date picker calendar that
   appears.

   To continue your series of recurring appointments indefinitely, click the
   No Ending Date option. If you want to define an ending date for your
   series of appointments, you can click End After and enter a number of
   occurrences in the adjacent text box, or you can click End By and specify the date for the final appointment in the series.

7. **(Optional) Select a date and click Add, which is in the Exceptions
   area.**

   This step defines exceptions to the Recurrence Rule. When you select a
   date and click Add, the selected date appears in the list box in the
   Exceptions area. Use this list to specify dates on which the recurring
   appointment should *not* occur even though the dates meet the recurrence rule. For example, that weekly staff meeting that normally occurs
   on Monday mornings shouldn't be scheduled for Monday holidays such
   as Memorial Day and Labor Day. Adding those dates to the Exceptions
   list prevents Organizer from creating recurring appointments on those
   days. Of course, that means you need to manually enter appointments
   that are rescheduled rather than canceled.

8. After defining the recurrence pattern, click Save and Close.

KOrganizer closes the Edit Appointment dialog box and enters the series of appointments you just defined into your appointment calendar. You can easily tell which appointments and events are part of a series or recurring appointments because KOrganizer marks recurring appointments with a symbol composed of two curved arrows. Figure 10-7 shows both recurring appointments and one-time appointments.

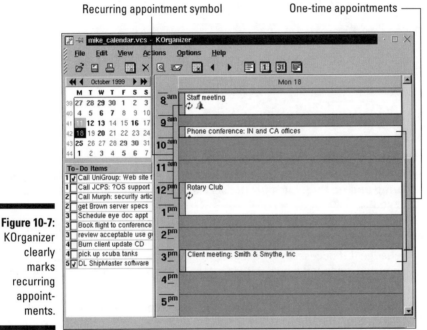

Figure 10-7: KOrganizer clearly marks recurring appointments.

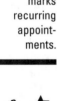
Never forget a birthday or anniversary again! Enter those important dates into KOrganizer as events, with a reminder alarm set to alert you a few days ahead of the special day (so you have time to go shopping or make reservations). Make them recurring events with a recurrence rule set for Yearly, On This Date to get the same reminder again next year, and the year after, and so on. Use the same technique to remind yourself of due dates for things such as quarterly tax payments and annual insurance premiums.

Working with the to-do list

In addition to date-related occurrences such as appointments and events, you probably need to keep track of tasks — things you need to do but that aren't tied to a specific date or time. Instead of jotting down a list of tasks on a scrap of paper and then misplacing it, let KOrganizer help you maintain your to-do list.

- **Adding details to a to-do list task:** Right-click the task in the to-do list and choose Edit To Do from the pop-up menu that appears. KOrganizer opens the Edit To Do dialog box. Edit the settings, add a detailed description, and assign categories as needed; click Save and Close to record your changes and close the dialog box.

- **Adding a new task to the to-do list:** Right-click the to-do list and choose New To Do from the pop-up menu that appears. KOrganizer adds a line to the to-do list and selects it for editing. Type a short description of your task and press Enter.

- **Arranging the to-do list by priority:** Right-click anywhere on the to-do list and choose Sort by Priority from the pop-up menu that appears. KOrganizer rearranges the list with the priority 1 items on top and other tasks arranged in decreasing priority order.

- **Marking a task as completed:** Simply click the item's checkbox in the to-do list.

- **Prioritizing a to-do list item:** Click once on the item in the to-do list to select it and then click the number to the left of the checkbox. A drop-down list of numbers appears. Click a number on the list to assign that priority level to the task.

- **Removing completed tasks from the To Do list:** Right-click anywhere on the to-do list and choose Purge Completed from the pop-up menu that appears.

Changing views in KOrganizer

The standard KOrganizer window presents the appointment calendar for one day on the right side of the window and your to-do list and a small monthly calendar on the other. Click a date in the calendar to display appointments for that day. Use the arrow buttons at the top of the calendar to display other months.

The Day view is only one of six different ways to view your calendar data in KOrganizer. Here's a summary of the views that are available:

- **List:** Replaces the appointment calendar with a simple list, one appointment or event per line.

- **Day:** The standard view (refer to Figures 10-3 and 10-7).

- **Work Week:** The appointment calendar portion of the standard view is divided into five columns — one for each day of a typical work week (Monday through Friday).

✔ **Week:** Like the Work Week view except that the appointment calendar section displays an entire week in seven columns.

✔ **Month:** The entire KOrganizer window is devoted to a monthly calendar in the traditional block or grid style as shown in Figure 10-8.

✔ **To-Do List:** This view expands the to-do list to fill the whole KOrganizer window.

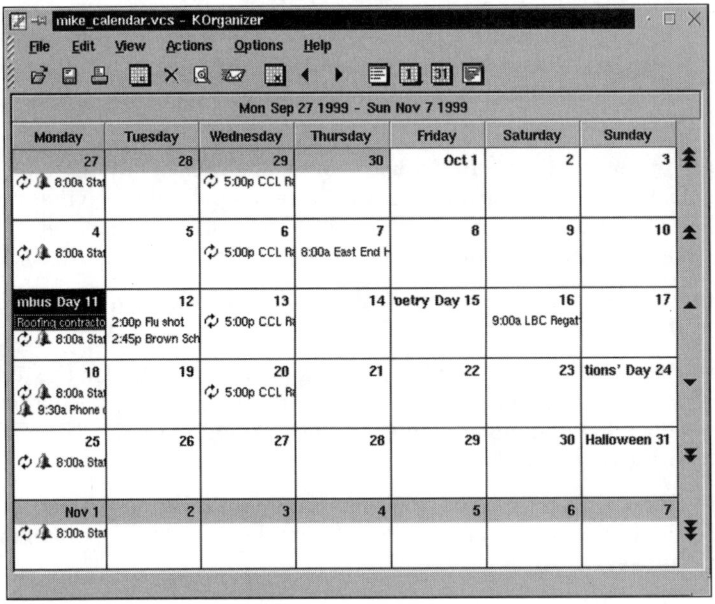

Figure 10-8:
The Month view gives you an overview of your schedule.

Making Your Life a Little Easier — KDE Utilities

In addition to the text editors and organizer programs on the Applications menu, KDE comes with an assortment of utility programs that perform a variety of specialty functions. You can find all the programs covered in this section on KDE's Utilities menu. (To start any of these programs, click the KDE Menu button on the panel, choose Utilities, and then select the program name.) The KDE utilities are a mixed bag. They range from serious system maintenance tools to frivolous amusements.

Address Book

With a name like KDE Address Book, you can probably guess what this utility does — it's a small database for storing names and associated contact information such as street addresses, e-mail addresses, and phone numbers.

✔ **Adding an entry to the Address Book:** Choose Edit⇨Add Entry. The Edit Current Entry dialog box appears. Fill in the information on the various tabs of the dialog box. (*Tip:* The contents of the Formatted Name box is what appears in the list of Address Book names.) Click OK to close the Edit Current Entry dialog box and add the entry to the Address Book database.

✔ **Opening the Address Book:** Click the KDE Menu button and choose Utilities⇨Address Book. The KAB window appears.

✔ **Viewing information about an entry in the KAB window:** Select the desired entry from the drop-down list box at the top of the window. Address Book displays the entry's data in the window as shown in Figure 10-9.

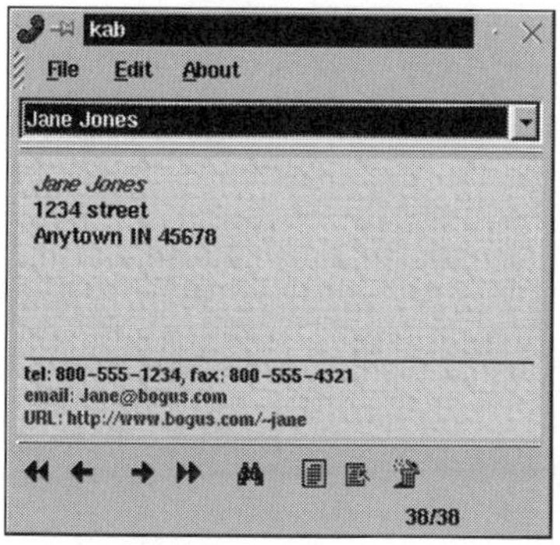

Figure 10-9:
The KDE
Address
Book is your
on-screen
Rolodex.

Archiver

The Archiver utility (also called Ark) enables you to create and maintain compressed archive files (*.tar.gz).

✔ **Adding files to the archive:** Drag file icons from a KFM window and drop them on the Archiver window.

✔ **Creating a new archive file:** Choose File⇨New, enter a filename in the Save As dialog box, and then click OK.

✔ **Opening the Ark utility:** Click the KDE Menu button and choose Utilities➪Archiver.

✔ **Viewing the contents of an existing archive file:** Choose File➪Open and click OK. The contents of the archive file appear in the Archiver window. Right-click a filename in the Archiver window and then make a selection from the pop-up menu that appears to extract, view, or delete the selected file from the archive.

Calculator

If you need to do some number crunching on a scientific calculator, just open KCalc (KDE Menu➪Utilities➪Calculator). When the KCalc utility appears on-screen (as shown in Figure 10-10), just use your mouse pointer to click on-screen calculator buttons instead of using your finger to press the buttons of a handheld calculator. Clicking the large KCalc button beside the answer opens the KCalc Configuration dialog box, where you can adjust settings that change the precision and switch between trigonometry or statistical modes or select a different font to display the results.

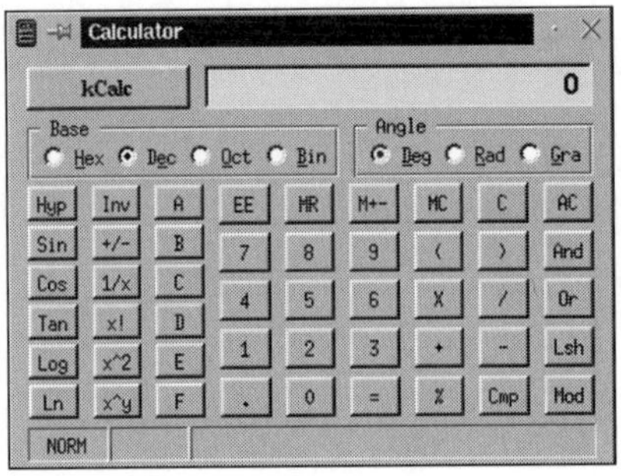

Figure 10-10: KCalc provides a handy on-screen version of your trusty scientific calculator.

Cut & Paste History

If you do a lot of cutting and pasting, you'll love the Klipper utility. When you launch the Klipper utility, the program docks a small icon into the panel and begins tracking your cut, copy, and paste activities. Klipper expands the standard KDE Clipboard to make room for multiple items. As a result, you can cut or copy multiple text passages before stopping to paste any of them to a new location.

✔ **Launching Klipper:** Click the KDE Menu button and choose Utilities➪Cut & Paste History.

✔ **Using the text stored on the Klipper Clipboard:** Click the Klipper icon docked in the panel and select the clipped text you want to use from the pop-up menu that appears. Press Ctrl+V or choose Edit➪Paste to paste the selected text into your application.

Find Files

Clicking the KDE Menu button and choosing Utilities➪Find Files is another way to launch the KDE Find Files utility — the same one you can launch by clicking the Find Files button on the panel (as explained in Chapter 4).

Hex Editor

If you need a hexadecimal editor to view and edit the contents of binary files, KHexdit is ready to oblige. But remember, unless you know what you're doing, binary files are strictly "look, don't touch."

✔ To launch the hex editor utility, click the KDE Menu button and choose Utilities➪Hex Editor.

✔ To use the utility to view a binary file, choose File➪Open and select the file you want to view in the Open dialog box; then click OK. The contents of the file appear in the Hex Editor window.

HP LaserJet Control Panel

The HP LaserJet Control Panel is a simple little utility that enables you to send configuration commands to your HP LaserJet printer. Choose KDE Menu➪Utilities➪HP LaserJet Control Panel to open the LJet Tool dialog box where you can select options, such as the paper size, printer resolution, end-of-line mode, font, and more. Select the settings you want and click OK to send the appropriate configurations to the printer. It's simple, convenient, and works with most of the popular HP LaserJet series of printers.

KFloppy

The KFloppy utility makes formatting floppy disks a simple task. Choose KDE Menu➪Utilities➪KFloppy to open the KDE Floppy Formatter dialog box as shown in Figure 10-11. You can then select the floppy drive, the disk density, and the file system (DOS or ext2fs), and choose between a quick erase and a full format. After you click OK, KFloppy formats the floppy disk and even displays a progress bar for constant status updates during the process. Hey, it's more convenient than typing a long command at the command line. With KFloppy, you don't need to pop open the man page to check on some hard-to-remember parameters before you can issue the command.

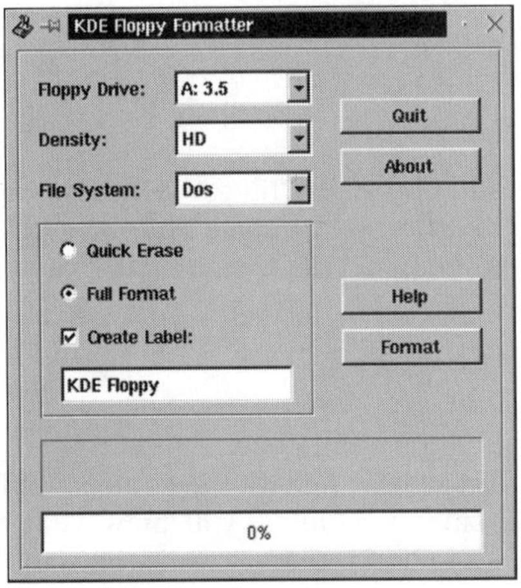

Figure 10-11:
Formatting
floppy disks
is easy with
KFloppy.

KJots

KJots is an interesting utility that enables you to jot down notes and scraps of text and keep them organized for future reference or reuse. You can create multiple "books" of notes with multiple "pages" in each book even though the KJots window displays only one page of notes at a time.

- ✔ **Adding a book to the hotlist:** Select the book and then choose Hotlist➪Add Current Book to Hotlist. A *hotlist* is the row of buttons just above the status bar at the bottom of the KJots window.

- ✔ **Adding a new page to a book:** Choose Edit➪New Page or click the New Page button on the toolbar.

- ✔ **Adding text to a page:** Type in the large text box in the middle of the KJots window.

- ✔ **Creating a new book of notes:** Choose File➪New Book. KJots prompts you to supply a name for the book. After you enter the book name, the name appears in the status bar at the bottom of the KJots window. This indicates that it is the active book.

- ✔ **Naming a page of notes:** Type a name in the text box beside the book name at the bottom of the KJots window.

- ✔ **Opening KJots:** Choose KDE Menu➪Utilities➪KJots. The KJots window appears, as shown in Figure 10-12.

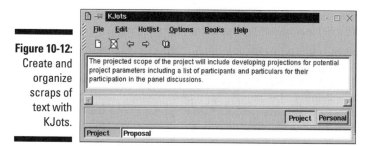

Figure 10-12:
Create and
organize
scraps of
text with
KJots.

✔ **Selecting a different book:** Choose Book⇨Bookname, where Bookname is the name you assigned to the book you want to open. If the book is on the hotlist, you can just click the Hotlist button for the book.

✔ **Selecting a different page in the current book:** Use the horizontal scroll bar below the text box to scroll from page to page.

KNotes

Those little yellow sticky notes are everywhere! There's even an on-screen version of them in KDE — KNotes. When you choose KDE Menu⇨Utilities⇨ KNotes, a little yellow KNote window materializes on the screen (as shown in Figure 10-13) and the KNotes Control Applet icon appears docked in the panel. Just start typing to create a note.

Figure 10-13:
KNotes
creates an
on-screen
version of
those yellow
sticky notes
that are
so handy
on your
physical
desk.

The KNotes window isn't a standard KDE window — it lacks a window border, menu bar, and the usual inventory of titlebar buttons. However, there is a titlebar that you can drag to move the note to a different location and a Close button that you can click to close the note. Closing the note doesn't remove the KNotes Control Applet that is docked in the panel.

✔ **Creating a new note:** Click the KNotes Control Applet icon and choose New KNote from the pop-up menu that appears.

✔ **Renaming a note:** Right-click the note and choose Operations⇨Rename Note from the pop-up menu that appears; then type a new name in the dialog box that appears and click Rename. (You can use a similar technique to perform most operations, such as saving and deleting notes. The commands and options that normally appear on a program's menus are available on the pop-up menus in KNotes.)

✔ **Reopening a note:** Click the KNotes Control Applet icon and choose the note name from the pop-up menu that appears.

✔ **Shutting down the KNotes utility:** Right-click the KNotes Control Applet and choose Exit KNotes from the pop-up menu that appears.

Konsole and Terminal

For fans of the command line, KDE offers not one, but two terminal emulation utilities. Both Konsole and KVT create terminal windows where you can use the Linux command line in text mode. Konsole offers a few more options and is intended to be a replacement for KVT, but KVT remains in the KDE utility inventory — at least for now. See Chapter 12 for more information on using a terminal window to work with the Linux command line.

✔ To launch Konsole, choose KDE Menu⇨Utilities⇨Konsole.

✔ To launch KVT, choose KDE Menu⇨Utilities⇨Terminal.

KPackage

One of the innovations that has made installing and updating system components and applications much simpler and more convenient is the use of binary packages instead of the traditional `tar`ball of source code that you must compile and install manually. The Red Hat, Debian, Slackware, and BSD Linux distributions all include package-management software to facilitate software installations. The KPackage utility provides a graphical front end for these package-management programs that makes them even easier to use. To launch KPackage, choose KDE Menu⇨Utilities⇨KPackage. Refer to Chapter 13 for detailed information about installing software using KPackage and the package-management programs.

Menu Editor

The KDE Menu Editor utility is available from the Utilities menu (KDE Menu⇨Utilities⇨Menu Editor), as well as from the Panel menu. As its name implies, this is the utility that you use to edit and add to the menus that appear when you click the KDE Menu button on the panel. We cover this utility in detail in Chapter 5.

MoonPhase

MoonPhase is a novel application of computer technology. When you choose KDE Menu⇨Utilities⇨MoonPhase, the MoonPhase icon appears docked in the KDE panel. Naturally, the icon looks like a full moon. When you point to the MoonPhase icon with your mouse, a pop-up tip box displays the current phase of the moon. It's a handy reference for those times when you're stuck inside or are disoriented because the moon isn't visible in the sky.

If you see a very bright celestial object when you venture outside and your first thought is that the moon is on fire, you may want to consider a short vacation to reacquaint yourself with sunlight.

Mouspedometa

Do you ever wonder how far you move your mouse in a day? Sure, you're moving it around in the same 8-inch square all the time, but going back and forth so much must add up to lots of feet, yards, and even miles. The Mouspedometa utility seeks to answer this burning question by monitoring mouse movement and displaying the results on-screen.

- ✔ **Closing Mouspedometa:** Right-click the counter display and choose Quit from the pop-up menu that appears.
- ✔ **Resetting the counter:** Right-click the counter display and choose Reset Odometer from the pop-up menu that appears.
- ✔ **Starting Mouspedometa:** Choose KDE Menu⇨Utilities⇨Mouspedometa. A pair of counters appear on-screen, looking much like the odometer in an automobile dashboard. One counter tracks the mouse position relative to its starting point. The other tracks cumulative distance traveled.

Personal Time Tracker

If you need to keep track of time spent working on various computer projects, you'll really like the Personal Time Tracker utility (also known as

Karm). It enables you to create a list of tasks and then track the time you spend on each task with a built-in stopwatch that you can start, stop, and restart as needed. The Personal Time Tracker always shows the cumulative time recorded for each task, no matter how many times you start and stop the clock.

✔ **Creating a new task:** Choose Task⇨New, enter a name into the Task Name text box in the dialog box that appears, and then click OK. The task appears on the task list in the Personal Time Tracker window.

✔ **Recording time spent on a task:** Select the task and then choose Clock⇨Start or click the Start Clock button on the toolbar. Personal Time Tracker begins timing the task. When you finish working on the task, choose Clock⇨Stop or click the Stop Clock button in the toolbar. You can stop and restart the clock and switch tasks as often as needed.

✔ **Selecting a task:** Click the task name in the Personal Time Tracker window.

✔ **Starting Personal Time Tracker:** Choose KDE Menu⇨Utilities⇨Personal Time Tracker. The Personal Time Tracker window appears, as shown in Figure 10-14, displaying a list of tasks and the cumulative time spent on each one. (When you first open Personal Time Tracker, the window is empty until you create a task.)

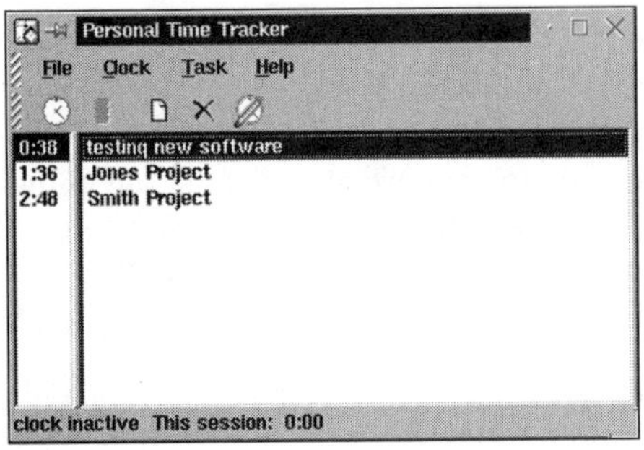

Figure 10-14:
Track time
spent on
several
tasks with
Personal
Time
Tracker.

Printer Queue

The KDE Printer Queue provides a graphical interface for your Linux print spooler, which makes it easy to manage print jobs waiting in the queue to be printed.

✔ **Moving a print job to the top of the list in the printer queue:** Select the print job by clicking it; then click Move to Top.

✔ **Selecting a different printer queue:** Select the print spool from the Printer drop-down list box.

> ✔ **Starting the Printer Queue utility:** Choose KDE Menu⇨Utilities⇨Printer
> Queue. The Printer Queue window shows the status of the print jobs in
> the selected printer queue.
>
> ✔ **Updating the status of the print queue display:** Click Update.

Your printer must be set up to work properly in the Linux operating system
before the KDE Printer Queue can do its job. That usually means running a
separate printer configuration utility to install drivers and set up print spool
directories before you attempt to use Printer Queue for the first time.

Process Management

The KDE Process Management utility enables you to view and manage the
processes running on your system. It's a powerful tool for experienced
system administrators, but it's not something the average user should mess
with. Choose KDE Menu⇨Utilities⇨Process Management to open the KPM
window (as shown in Figure 10-15). The window displays a graphical representation of CPU load, memory, and swap space usage, plus a complete list of
the running processes and their status. Right-click a process and choose from
the commands on the pop-up menu to do things such as kill, terminate, or
hang up the selected process. Be careful and make sure you know what effect
your actions will have.

Figure 10-15:
The Process
Management
utility shows
system
performance
statistics
and much
more.

	kpm@intrepid									· □ ×
Window	**Process**	**Signal**	**View**	**Options**	**Help**					

cpu [   ]   mem [████████]   swap [   ]
■ user ■ nice □ sys □ idle   ■ used ■ buff □ cach □ free   up 12 days, 17:25

PID	USER	PRI	NICE	SIZE	RSS	SHARE	STAT	%CPU	%MEM	TIME	CMDLINE
14783	meadhra	8	0	3888	3888	2664	R	1.19	6.15	0.41s	kpm
9623	meadhra*	11	0	9384	9384	1616	R	0.79	8.26	3:04	/etc/X11/X :0 –auth /h
9630	meadhra	2	0	3980	3980	2932	S	0.40	6.29	0:19	kwm –nosession
14718	meadhra	1	0	4996	4996	2936	S	0.59	7.90	4.77s	ksnapshot
519	xfs	0	0	1552	1492	488	S	0.00	2.36	0:29	xfs –droppriv –daemon
9667	meadhra	1	0	6480	6480	4336	S	0.00	10.25	0:12	kfm
9631	meadhra	0	0	3672	3672	2740	S	0.00	5.80	2.40s	kbandwm

Tape Backup Tool

If you have a tape drive installed on your system, you'll want to investigate the
KDE Tape Backup Tool, also known as KDAT. The program provides a single
graphical interface where you can mount, unmount, and format tapes, back up
files to tape by using the `tar` tape archive format, verify archived files against
local files, and restore files from tape. KDAT supports multiple archives on the
same tape, selectively restoring files from tape, and creating backup profiles
to simplify the process of selecting and creating backups. In short, KDAT

includes all the features you expect to find in a backup utility program. KDAT is too complex to cover in detail here, but the following steps should give you a general idea of how you may use KDAT to create a simple backup:

1. **Choose KDE Menu⇨Utilities⇨Tape Backup Tool.**

   The KDAT window appears.

2. **Choose File⇨Mount Tape; follow the prompts to format the tape if necessary.**

3. **Select the files to back up by expanding the directory tree display on the left side of the KDAT window and clicking a file or directory to highlight it.**

   You can also select files for backup by clicking the checkbox beside file or directory names in the directory tree. KDAT backs up only the selected files.

4. **Choose File⇨Backup.**

   KDAT displays the Backup Options dialog box, where you can review and edit file selections and backup options.

5. **Edit or accept the backup options and click OK.**

   KDAT starts backing up the selected files to tape. The program displays a progress report in the Backup dialog box to show throughput and estimated time remaining.

World Watch

The World Watch utility is a simple little program that shows the current time and also displays an approximation of the current daylight and dark areas projected onto a world map. To start the program, choose KDE Menu⇨ Utilities⇨World Watch. The world map in the KDE World Wide Watch window says it all (see Figure 10-16). Let's see, if it's 8 p.m. in Texas, what time is it in Sydney, Australia?

Figure 10-16: World Watch helps you visualize the march of time across the globe.

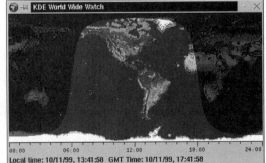

Previewing KOffice

KOffice is the collective name for a group of office productivity programs currently under development. The goal of the KOffice project is to create a complete office suite that is built on the same foundations as KDE and has capabilities comparable to the popular office suites for other platforms.

KOffice is a work in progress. As this book goes to press, KOffice is under intensive development, but it's still in the *alpha stage* (a sort of programmer's equivalent of a rough draft). Although preliminary versions of some of the KOffice component programs are available for preview, none of the KOffice components are ready for serious *beta testing* (like the final editing and proof-reading of a manuscript), much less complete and ready for general use. Consequently, it's too early to tell exactly what features the various KOffice components will have. The plans for KOffice call for the office suite to include the following components:

- ✔ **Katabase** — The KOffice database component — it's similar to Paradox or Microsoft Access.

- ✔ **KChart** — A program for drawing charts and graphs.

- ✔ **KFormula** — A program for drawing properly formatted scientific formulas (see Figure 10-17), which you can then incorporate into presentations and documents you create with other KOffice programs.

- ✔ **KIllustrator** — A vector drawing program (along the lines of Adobe Illustrator or CorelDraw) for creating diagrams, illustrations, logos, and such.

- ✔ **KImage** — An image viewer application.

- ✔ **KImageShop** — An image editor for creating and manipulating bit-mapped images, such as digital camera pictures, scanned images, and screen captures. See Figure 10-18 for a sample.

- ✔ **KPresenter** — A presentation graphics application with capabilities roughly comparable to Microsoft PowerPoint or Lotus Freelance Graphics. See Figure 10-19 for a preview.

- ✔ **KWord** — A word-processing program with FrameMaker-like desktop-publishing capabilities. See Figure 10-20 for a sneak peak at what Kword looks like at the alpha stage of the process.

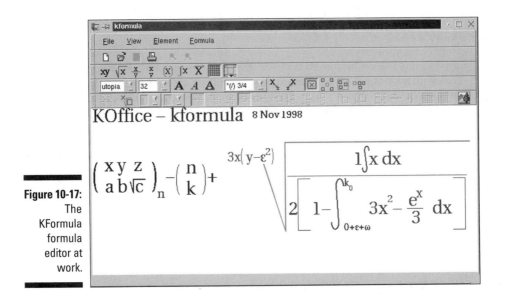

Figure 10-17:
The
KFormula
formula
editor at
work.

Figure 10-18:
The
KImageShop
image
editor.

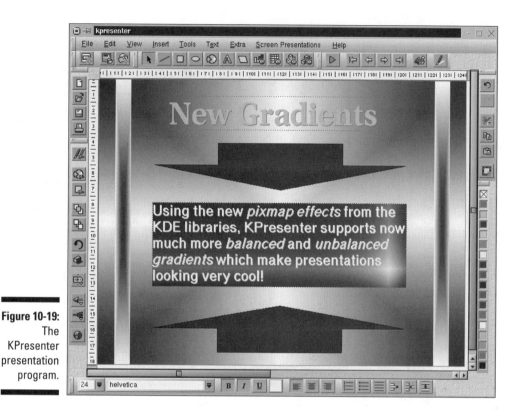

Figure 10-19:
The
KPresenter
presentation
program.

When you compare KOffice to some of the popular commercial office suites, certain component applications seem conspicuous by their absence. For example, KOffice doesn't include a Web browser component. But then, KOffice doesn't need a separate Web browser because KFM fills that niche in KDE. Similarly, there's no need for e-mail and news clients in KOffice because KMail and KRN are already part of KDE; KOrganizer handles appointment scheduling and to-do lists, so you won't find that function duplicated in KOffice, either. So, when all is said and done, KOffice, combined with other utilities already available in KDE, will provide a comprehensive office productivity solution that is a completely free and open source.

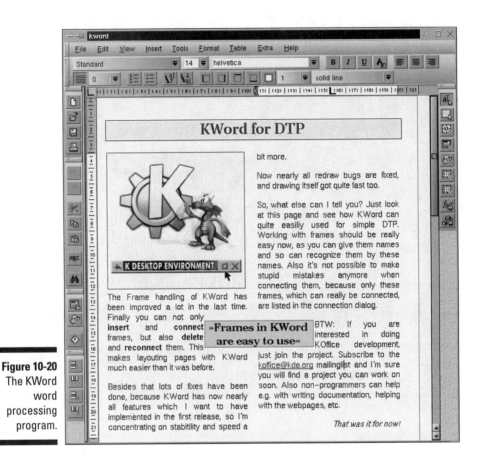

Figure 10-20
The KWord word processing program.

Chapter 11

Applications and Utilities, Part 2 — Play

In This Chapter

▶ Getting the picture with graphics utilities

▶ Viewing and editing graphics

▶ Taking screenshots

▶ Playing some tunes with sound utilities

▶ Having some fun with KDE games

*Y*ou work on your computer every day — you need a little time to relax and play! KDE offers several ways to bring that fun into your computing life — who knows, you may even find handy ways to use these great programs to enhance your work productivity!

Some of the most popular software programs are those that allow you to edit images, like photographs or drawings, and those that let you play music through your computer speakers. (Of course, games are the *real* reason we all buy computers, aren't they?) KDE has all of these things for you — yes, even the games — as part of the basic distribution. If you're longing for a little more, search through the various Web sites described in Appendix B; you'll find new games and programs designed to make your leisure time more electronically enhanced.

This chapter discusses various programs that work with image and sound files. In all cases, it's assumed that you'll use these programs in conjunction with your own creative efforts or with files you've obtained legally. Copyright law applies to digital media as much as it does to print or broadcast media; you really don't want to get into trouble for altering a copyrighted image and claiming it as your own, or for obtaining a copyrighted file illegally. Trust us and the fine lawyers at IDG Books.

Getting the Picture

You've definitely seen the TV ads. You know, the ones for spiffy new computers and fast Internet access? The ones that say, "Our computer is perfect for sending pictures of little Leroy to Grandma and Grandpa"? Well, you don't need a special kind of computer to play with graphics; you simply need good software. Luckily for you, KDE has some good basic graphics software built right in to its basic distribution.

You should remember, though, that working with graphics is a memory-intensive thing. The more you ask of your computer, the slower it works. If you find working with graphics to be an indescribably boring task because you have to wait five minutes for every single action, you definitely need more memory. You'll also benefit from a larger hard drive, because graphics files are big, with some formats (like .tif) producing astonishingly huge file sizes.

The KDE graphics software is competent and useful for daily graphic fun. If you're a professional, you'll probably already have specific products that you use to generate the files that pay your bills, such as Adobe PhotoShop, Macromedia Fireworks, or the freeware program The GIMP. Some of us, though, are hopelessly unartistic, and are really, really happy to figure out how to get an overexposed photo's contrast back to decent levels. It is for us that the KDE graphics programs exist.

Have a lot of time to play with? Want to let your inner graphic artist out to play for a while? Check out The GIMP. You can find it, along with FAQs and tutorials, at www.gimp.org. GIMP stands for Graphic Image Manipulation Program; it's basically a freeware version of Adobe PhotoShop. Be aware, though, that The GIMP and programs like it take a while to learn.

Viewing graphics

Most of the time, all you want to do is view a graphics file. Maybe you got that photo of Leroy in your e-mail and you'd like to see what the little squirt is planning for Halloween, or perhaps your boss handed you a disk with the company's new logo. No matter what format the file is saved in, you need to view the image with an image viewer.

The KDE image viewer is called, imaginatively enough, KView. It's a simple program; it opens images from your computer and shows them to you in a new window, as shown in Figure 11-1. It's different from something like a Web browser in that you just see the image. Even if there's something that looks like a hyperlink, you can't click it. KView is the electronic version of the slide projector.

Figure 11-1:
Sneak a peek with the KDE image viewer.

To use KView, make sure you know the location of the graphics file you want to view, whether it's on your hard drive or on a mounted CD or floppy. Follow these steps from there:

1. **Open the KDE menu and choose Graphics⇨Image Viewer.**

   The KView window appears.

2. **Choose File⇨Open.**

   Specify the file you want to open. (This is where you need to know the location of the image file.)

3. **KView displays the file.**

4. **Choose either File⇨Open to view another image file or File⇨Exit to leave KView.**

Editing graphics

KView is a fantastic way to see image files. It also has some basic graphic editing functions, including crop, zoom, orientation, and a few filters. These are all the tools most people need to clean up their pictures. If you need more, or you feel constrained and limited by the range of KView's offerings, you should definitely check out The GIMP or similar programs.

This section talks about KView's graphic editing tools as they apply to snapshots. Most people who use their computers for photographs are trying to get a finished product that will work on the Web or one that is good enough to send to family. Even the junkiest photograph can often be improved a great deal with some judicious editing. Who knows? You may be so impressed by your skills at graphic editing that you'll finally be able to share all those ugly vacation snaps that live in the shoebox in the hall closet.

You can't use your computer to work on a photo if it's still on paper. In order to edit the image, you must have a digital version of the photograph. There are three ways to get digitized image files of your pictures:

✔ Go out and buy a digital camera.

✔ Have the photo shop put your images on a CD. (Kodak is interested in advancing this technology, so any Kodak affiliate will be able to get your photos put onto a CD.)

✔ Scan the printed photo with a scanner. If you don't want to buy a scanner yourself, ask local photocopy stores if they'll scan your images to a floppy disk.

Resizing your photo

There are two ways to resize an image: make it smaller or make it bigger. KView offers crop tools to cut an image's size and zoom tools to enlarge it.

Cropping an image

Cropping is the most effective way to fix an uninspiring photograph. Who hasn't taken a shot that needed cropping? Perhaps the classic example is the "child at a famous place" shot, where little Tanya fits neatly into the lower-right corner of the picture while the Disneyland Matterhorn looms overhead. You have two choices with a picture like this: leave it as it is to prove that you actually were at Disneyland or crop it so you have a picture of Tanya on the happiest day of her four-year-old life. (Here's a hint: There are millions of pictures of the Matterhorn, but only one of that grinning little girl.)

Figure 11-2 is a photograph of a metal fish because we don't actually know any four-year-olds named Tanya. Here's how to crop an image with KView:

1. **Open the image file in KView, as described in the "Viewing graphics" section of this chapter.**

   See Figure 11-2 for the original photo.

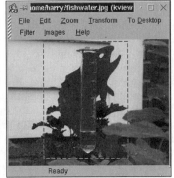

Figure 11-2:
The fish is surrounded by a lot of extra space that makes the photo seem out of balance.

2. **Click one corner of the image and simultaneously drag the mouse diagonally.**

   A rectangular box follows your mouse's path; the area contained in the box will be saved when you crop, and everything else will disappear.

3. **Release the mouse button when you've selected the portion you want to save.**

   A shimmering line surrounds the selected area.

4. **Choose Edit⇨Crop.**

   The selected portion of the image moves to the upper-left corner of the KView window and everything else disappears, as shown in Figure 11-3.

Figure 11-3:
The cropped
picture
puts all the
emphasis
on the fish.

5. **To undo your crop, choose Edit⇨Reset.**

   The original image is restored.

6. **Choose File⇨Save As after you have an image you're happy with.**

7. **Choose either File⇨Open to open another image file or choose File⇨Exit to leave KView.**

Before you start working with an image file, be sure to save a copy of it and work from the copy. If you make an irreparable mistake, you can make another copy from the original. If you work from the original and make an error, you have to rescan the image. (If you are using a digital camera, the photo opportunity may be long over.)

Zooming an image

You can also change the size of an image by *zooming,* or expanding, certain portions of the image to a larger size. You should experiment with both crop and zoom to see which technique works best for your particular photograph or image. There are six types of zoom available in KView, which are described in Table 11-1.

Table 11-1	Zoom Types in KView
Zoom Type	**Effect**
Zoom in 10%	Increases the size of the image by 10 percent. Makes items in the photo appear larger.
Zoom out 10%	Reduces the size of the image by 10 percent. Makes items in the photo appear smaller.
Double Size	Doubles the size of the image.
Half Size	Cuts the image size in half.
Max Size	Enlarges the size of the image to the size of the KView window. May stretch or squash the image, depending on the size of the Kview window.
Max Aspect	Enlarges the image to the size of the Kview window, while retaining the height-to-width ratio of the original image.

To use the KView zoom feature, follow this procedure:

1. **Open the image in KView.**

2. **Choose Zoom⇨Zoom in 10%.**

   The photograph enlarges by 10 percent, making the objects in the image appear larger, as seen in Figure 11-4.

3. **Choose Edit⇨Reset if you don't like the result.**

   Your original image reappears.

Figure 11-4:
The fish appears larger when zoomed, but some white space is still there.

4. **Choose File⇨Save As when you've zoomed the image to your liking.**

5. **Choose either File⇨Open to open another image file or File⇨Exit to leave KView.**

Crop or zoom? You make the call

Sometimes it's not clear whether you would be better off cropping an image or zooming in on part of it. Keep in mind that both kinds of edits change the size of the image, but neither changes the picture quality. If you zoom in at a tremendous rate, eventually your picture will blur — due either to the quality of the original photo or the way it was scanned. Low-resolution scans, like 72 dpi (which is a good resolution for photos destined for the Web), appear blurry and pixelated when zoomed too far.

A good alternative is to crop the image judiciously and then zoom or resize it. That way, you can keep precisely what you want, delete the rest, and then decide how to handle the remaining image.

Transforming your photo

Despite the menu's neat name, KView's Transform menu controls the image's orientation. (Wouldn't it be neat if it really did transform the images? It would bring a whole new level of swimsuit satisfaction to summer beach pictures.) You may not use this type of photo edit a lot, but it's very useful when you do need it. See Figures 11-5, 11-6, and 11-7 for an idea of what the Transform menu does.

Figure 11-5:
The original image is a picture of the KDE mascot, Konqi.

Figure 11-6:
The original
image of
Konqi has
been flipped
vertically.

Figure 11-7:
The original
image of
Konqi
has been
rotated one
quarter-turn
clockwise.

The Transform menu has four options, described in Table 11-2. Regardless of how you choose to alter the image's orientation, we suggest that you work from a saved copy rather than the original.

Table 11-2	Transform Options in KView
Menu Selection	*Effect*
Flip Horizontal	The image flips from right to left: for example, the right side of the picture flips to the left.
Flip Vertical	The image flips from top to bottom: for example, the top of the image is now the bottom. See Figure 11-6 for an example.

Menu Selection	Effect
Rotate Clockwise	The image rotates one quarter-turn clockwise (to the right). Select this option again to continue rotating in quarter turns. See Figure 11-7 for an example.
Rotate Counter-Clockwise	The image rotates one quarter-turn counterclockwise (to the left). Select this option again to continue rotating in quarter turns.

Using filters to adjust your photo

If you've ever used a fancy 35mm single-lens reflex camera or watched someone use one, you've probably seen the wide variety of *lens filters* — small round circles of colored glass or film — that photographers use to manipulate the way the image imprints on the film. Lens filters can adjust brightness, color, intensity, and so on.

KView's filter options can do many of the same things lens filters can, and some things that lens filters can't. With KView's filters, you can make many alterations to your photo that improve its appearance or make it seem like something completely other than it is. The basic uses of each of the KView filters are covered here, but spend some time experimenting with this fun option! You'll find some strange and odd effects that may make your photo even more fun than the original.

All of these options are located in KView's Filter menu:

✔ **Filter⇨Intensity⇨Brightness**

This filter is a brightness control. The base level of brightness is 100 percent. If you enter a number smaller than 100, the image dims. If you enter a number larger than 100, the image brightens. Too much on either side results in a flat black or white image.

✔ **Filter⇨Intensity⇨Gamma Correction**

This filter is a contrast control. (That's not technically what gamma correction is, but it's what most people use the filter to do.) The base level is 1. Enter a number larger than 1, and the image appears *washed out,* without much contrast. Enter a number smaller than 1 (you can use negative numbers), and the image looks darker, less colorful, and more "contrasty."

✔ **Filter⇨Greyscale**

This filter removes color from the image. If you have a scanned color photo that you'd like to have as a black and white image, use this filter to strip the color. Colors change into shades of grey. For obvious reasons, you won't see any effect if you apply this filter to an image that is already in greyscale.

✔ **Filter⇨Smooth**

This filter removes minute variations from the image. It's great to make surfaces look more uniform, but be careful if there are a lot of edges in the image. Smooth tends to make edges blurry. Give it a try to see if you can live with the blurriness in order to make the rest of the image smoother.

The filters provided in KView are basic ones, though you can have a great deal of fun using them to transform your original picture to something quite different. They help you make a regular photo looking a bit better, so that you can e-mail it to a friend or put it on your Web page for the whole world to view. Think of KView's image-editing options as basic cable; you can get by just fine with the offerings included, but there may be some extra channels that would make you happy to have.

If you really want to upgrade to the expanded cable of image-editing software for KDE, we suggest that you try The GIMP or another professional image-editing program. The filters and options available to you in such programs permit much more exact and specialized work with your images than does a basic viewer/editor like KView.

However, for most of us, doing photo editing in The GIMP is like putting a pig in a dress; no matter how much silk you drape over the pig, you still have a pig. The kind of photos that we want to share with friends and family are the pictures that we take at family events or on our vacations; they're an amateur record of our lives, not a professionally designed portrait shot. Be proud of your pictures: Use KView's filters to fix the most glaring problems (over- and underexposure, lack of contrast, and so on) and get those photos to people who want to see them.

Finishing up

After you have a version of your image just the way you want it, save it by using File⇨Save As. You can save multiple versions of the same image as long as you select a different name for each saved version. Try using the original image's name with a version number: grandpa1, grandpa2, and so on.

A quick word about image file formats: No matter how many options your image scanning software gives you, it's best to save photos as JPG or GIF files. These are the two most popular image formats and those most likely to be readable in any given image viewer. You may be perfectly capable of viewing TIFF (an uncompressed format) or PNG (a newer format) in your browser, but your Aunt Maylene may be using a very old version of Netscape that can only handle GIF or JPG. It's always safe to use these formats when you're sharing an electronic version of your images, whether as e-mail attachments or on Web pages.

Posing for a Screenshot

There's an urban legend that's popular among techie-types: the help-desk guy who asked the customer on the phone to take a screenshot and send it to him so he could help her diagnose a computer problem. A week later, a 3-x-5 photograph arrived for him in the morning mail. Like most urban legends, though, it's easy to see where the confusion comes in.

Screenshot sounds a lot like snapshot, and it's really much the same thing. A *screenshot* is an image file created when specialized software "takes a picture" of whatever's on your monitor — no cameras needed. You may not need to use screenshots much, if at all, in your daily life. There may come a time, though, when you need to provide a screenshot to someone trying to solve a software problem. You may even find yourself writing a computer book in a popular line of black and yellow books — all the pictures in this book are screenshots from our computers.

For the screenshots in this book, we used a special little program that's built directly into KDE, called KSnapshot. (Yes, this does keep that confusion about the difference between screenshots and snapshots. Rest assured that *you* know the difference.)

To use KSnapshot, first get your desktop looking the way you want it to look. Perhaps you want to take a shot of a new theme you built, or you have a particular problem you want to document. After you have your desktop in order, use the following procedure to take a screenshot:

1. **Open the KDE menu and select Graphics⇨Snapshot.**

    The KSnapshot window appears, as shown in Figure 11-8.

2. **Enter a name for the snapshot in the Filename field.**

    As always, be as descriptive as you can. "goldberg-theme" is better than "wrestling-theme," which is better than "theme4."

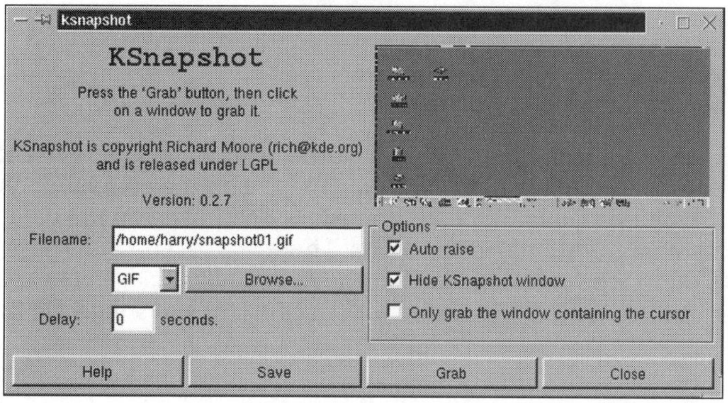

Figure 11-8:
The KSnapshot window offers several options.

3. **Click the Grab button.**

   Your hard drive whirs as KSnapshot records the image of your desktop. Depending on the amount of memory in your computer, this may be a nearly instantaneous process or it may take a few seconds.

4. **Click the Save button.**

   Your screenshot is saved under the filename you selected in Step 2. If you'd like to look at it, open KView and view it as you would any other image file.

5. **Click the Close button to leave KSnapshot.**

Want to take a screenshot but don't want to take a picture of your entire desktop? You can take a screenshot of a single window on your desktop. Just open KSnapshot, and select the Only Grab the Window Containing the Cursor option; move the cursor onto the window that you want to grab. This works best when you set a delay between the time you click Grab and the time the computer actually takes the screenshot. Set a delay by entering a number in the Delay field; if you enter a 2, KSnapshot waits two seconds before grabbing, and so on. You can see the KSnapshot window set up for a single-window grab in Figure 11-9.

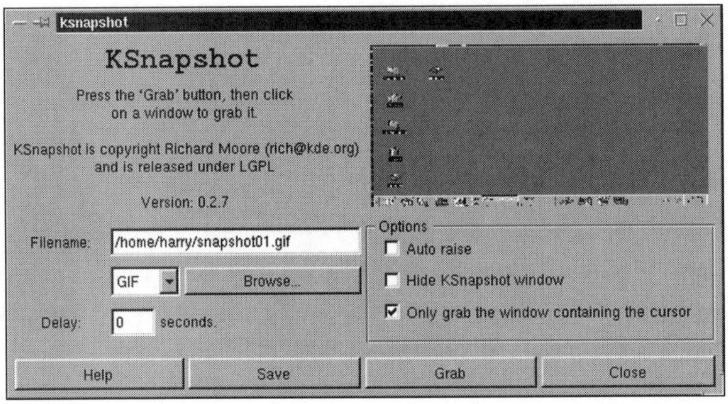

Figure 11-9:
Use
KSnapshot
to make a
screen grab
of a single
window.

Grooving to the Music

If you like to type and tap your toes at the same time, you're not alone. Lots of people love to listen to music while they're on the computer. As you've probably noticed, a lot of popular music is composed on the computer instead of on traditional instruments! There are several types of sound files, just as there are several kinds of image files. Unlike image viewers, though, sound utilities tend to be written for specific kinds of sound file formats.

KDE sound utilities include Kscd, which allows you to play an audio CD in your computer's CD-ROM drive; Kmedia, which plays files saved in the .wav format; and KMIDI Player, which plays MIDI files (as the alert reader probably guessed).

Just like you can't use mouse shortcuts if you don't have a mouse, you won't be able to listen to music via your computer if you don't have both a sound card and a set of speakers. Sound cards range from low-priced basic cards to high-powered cards with their own on-board memory, designed for composers and audiophiles. It's the same with speakers. Do some comparison shopping and see what best fits your desire and budget.

Kscd: For your massive music collection

Wouldn't it be convenient to plop your favorite CDs right into your computer to accompany your computing, without having to get up and slog across the living room to your stereo? KDE programmers thought so, and the result is Kscd, the KDE CD player. Use the following procedure to add a soundtrack to your hours in front of the monitor:

1. **Open your CD-ROM drive and insert an audio CD.**

2. **Close the CD drive.**

   You don't need to mount the CD-ROM drive, as you would if you were using files on the disk. Kscd merely sends the audio data directly to your sound card, rather than interpreting it as a file structure.

3. **Open the KDE menu and choose Multimedia⇨CD-Player.**

   The Kscd CD Player window opens, as shown in Figure 11-10.

Figure 11-10:
Kscd lets you play audio CDs directly from your CD-ROM drive.

4. **Use the familiar CD player buttons to manage the music.**

5. **Click the X in the upper-right corner when you're done to close Kscd.**

Kmedia: For system sounds and riding the .wav

The traditional sound file format for system sounds is .wav. *System sounds* are those little sound files that accompany various actions or results: e-mail arrival, closing a window, and so on. You can associate .wav files with actions on your computer or you can turn them off. If you want to listen to some .wav files to see if you want to use them, use Kmedia to check them out.

1. **Open the KDE menu and choose Multimedia⇨Media Player.**

   The Kmedia Media Player screen resembles a plain old tape deck, with Play, Stop, Rewind, Fast Forward, Beginning, and End buttons; see it in Figure 11-11.

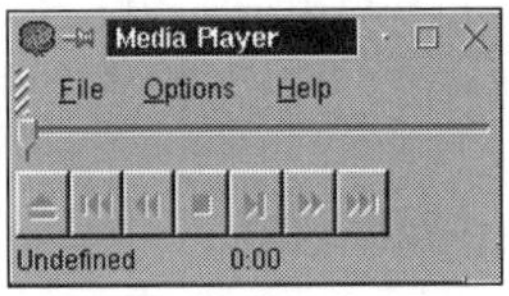

Figure 11-11:
Use Kmedia
to listen to
sound files
in the .wav
format.

2. **Choose File⇨Open to select the .wav file you want to hear.**

3. **Use the Kmedia buttons to control how the file plays.**

4. **Choose File⇨Exit to leave Kmedia.**

KMIDI Player: For the composer in you

If you're involved at all in musical composition on your computer, you likely have hardware that allows you to record MIDI files (Musical Instrument Digital Interface). If you are an aficionado of computer-composed music, you may have a source of MIDI files that contain the sounds you love.

The KMIDI Player handles the MIDI sound file format with ease. Open the KDE menu and select Multimedia⇨MIDI Player to open it; the program operates much like Kscd, with standard CD-player buttons and functions. See Figure 11-12 for a glimpse of the KMIDI Player screen.

Figure 11-12:
Play sophisticated compositions with the KMIDI Player.

Chances are that if you've been hanging around the Internet long enough, you're interested in *.mp3 files,* which is a new compact file format that reproduces sound faithfully and is easy to create from prerecorded compact discs. The KDE .mp3 player utility is called Kmp3, and you can get it at http://area51.mfh-iserlohn.de/kmp3/ or via one of the file archives described in Appendix B. Kmp3 is not covered here because it's still a fairly young program, and it's single-use. Chapter 12 discusses RealPlayer, a multipurpose non-KDE program that handles .mp3 files with ease. If you're determined to use a KDE program, Kmp3 is the one you want; if you also want to handle streaming audio and video from the Web, you want RealPlayer.

Fun and Games

Whether it's a quick five-minute break from your work, or a multihour war against the computer, games are the secret friend of almost every computer user. The most effective games are often the simplest. Although it's fun to blast through dungeons in a rousing game of Quake, it's kind of hard to mask your bloodthirsty glee under a spreadsheet when your boss (or spouse) walks by — and that doesn't even take the blaring game sound into consideration!

The KDE installation that's included on this book's CD-ROM includes the KDE games package. This package houses 15 small games, ranging from the traditional computer game, Solitaire, to more complex games of logic and multiplayer strategy games. Give each a try; you're likely to find both old favorites and new obsessions in the basic games package.

If these 15 games aren't enough for you, remember to check out the file archives described in Appendix B. New KDE games are released frequently, at various levels of stability, and come in all flavors of entertainment.

Here's a quick introduction to the games included in the KDE games package:

- **Abalone**

    Abalone is a computer version of a popular German board game. It's based on Chinese Checkers and involves the strategic positioning of colored marbles on a hexagonal board.

- **Asteroids**

    If you're in your 30s, you lost part of your youth playing Asteroids in the video arcade. (Yes, you did. Confession is good for the soul.) This is pretty much the same game, although adapted for the mouse rather than the huge trackball of the arcade version.

- **KBlackBox**

    Those of you coming to KDE from more traditional UNIX backgrounds may recognize a new interpretation of the traditional emacs game BlackBox. It's kind of like Minesweeper: There are hidden objects in black boxes and you must use the minimum number of laser shots to locate them.

- **Konquest**

    Konquest is a multiplayer strategy game. The plot is that you and your buddies are all trying to gain control of the galaxy and build an interstellar empire.

- **Mah-jongg**

    A computer version of the traditional Chinese tabletop tile game. Match identical tiles to remove them from the pile. If you remove all the tiles, you win.

- **Minesweeper**

    A classic Windows game, redesigned for KDE. Bombs hide under the tiles; use the hints to defuse the bombs and clear large tiled areas. The difficulty level determines the number of tiles and bombs.

- **Patience**

    Basic Solitaire, with the remaining cards in a turn-up pack at the side. This version has several levels of difficulty.

- **Poker**

    KDE Poker is the same five-card game that you find in a casino or tavern video Poker game. It's sneakily addictive; watch the time when you play this one.

- **Reversi**

    Another strategy game, this one involving reversible discs and a gridded board. Take control of as much of the board as you can in order to win.

✔ **SameGame**

SameGame is a popular Macintosh game, redone here for KDE. It's like a reverse form of Tetris; start with a full screen of colored balls and remove them systematically, attempting to clear the screen entirely.

✔ **Shisen-Sho**

A Japanese contribution to the KDE games library, Shisen-Sho is another Mah-jongg variant. Click matching tiles to remove them from the screen; the fewer tiles left at the end of the game, the closer you are to winning.

✔ **Sirtet**

A KDE version of the old war-horse game, Tetris. Sirtet is a faithful interpretation of the original, with square, colored blocks forming various shapes that drop from the top of the screen. Match three or more of the same color to remove the blocks; you're still playing as long as the blocks don't reach the top.

✔ **SmileTris**

The other Tetris version in the basic KDE package, SmileTris has a funkier appearance than Sirtet. Choose between the two or play both!

✔ **SnakeRace**

In SnakeRace, you're a snake. You need to eat all the apples you can find and navigate your way out of the screen to the next level. It has a strong Pac-Man feel.

✔ **Sokoban**

Chapter 12

Working with Non-KDE Applications

• •

In This Chapter

▶ KDE versus non-KDE: What's the difference?

▶ Utililizing the top four non-KDE applications

▶ Running programs that aren't on the KDE menu

▶ Running text-based programs

▶ Adding non-KDE programs to the panel

▶ Keeping KDE from muscling in on other programs

• •

*A*lthough you can find tons of programs written specifically for KDE, you're being happy running nothing but KDE-specific programs from now until the end of time is unlikely. Two major types of non-KDE programs are covered in this chapter — graphical programs written for the general Linux platform and text-based programs written for the original nongraphical UNIX and Linux environments.

Many of the programs mentioned in this chapter have been covered more closely in other chapters of the book (peek at the Index to see exactly where). We're not planning to give you the absolute rundown on Netscape, StarOffice, or pico here. Rather, we want to give you an understanding of the difference between programs that are written specifically for KDE and programs that are not, and when that distinction may matter.

So, What's the Difference?

Here's the difference between using a KDE program versus a non-KDE, in a nutshell. (Almond, if you were wondering.) KDE applications are programs that were written with KDE specifically in mind. That is, some programmer sat down and said, "You know, the KDE world needs a program that calculates the mileage you've put on your mouse," and thus Mouspedometa was born.

(Don't believe us? Look on the KDE menu, under Utilities⇨Mouspedometa.) More practically, developers may think that they have a better idea for an office suite of applications than what's available already. That's how KOffice, a KDE application, got started (you can learn more about KOffice in Chapter 10).

KDE applications have a unique look and feel. After you open a series of KDE applications on your desktop, the windows all look similar: same titlebar, same kind of menu bar, and so on. Even the help pages are standardized across most KDE applications. KDE developers stay pretty close to the accepted visual standards for their programs, so that you get a consistent "feel" as you use multiple KDE programs.

Non-KDE programs, however, don't share that feel. A non-KDE program is simply one that wasn't originally written to run under KDE. The program can be a Linux version of a popular program, such as Netscape. If you download and install Netscape, you won't find a special KDE version. You just grab the latest Linux version and get going. The program can also be a standard UNIX application, such as the text editor, emacs. Emacs looks pretty much the same no matter what platform it runs on; emacs is not a graphical program, so it doesn't need to be reworked for the KDE platform.

To reiterate, the distinction between KDE programs and non-KDE programs is small. The biggest difference is in the look of the program window. Non-KDE programs don't automatically get an icon in the panel, although you can easily make one. Don't let the lack of a K stop you from installing non-KDE software, though. If the program runs on Linux, it runs on your KDE box.

This seems like a good time for a reminder that KDE is a graphical interface to a regular Linux environment. You're not running a special distribution of Linux called KLinux, you're running Red Hat, Debian, Yellow Dog, or Corel distributions of the Linux operating system, and then using KDE as your desktop. If you find a Linux program that you want to run, installation is easier if you can find a package tailored to your distribution, but it doesn't matter whether you plan to run the program with KDE or in text mode. The Linux operating system doesn't care.

Our Four Faves

You probably notice that, throughout this book, we mention several non-KDE programs. In some cases — The GIMP and Netscape, in particular — we go a little overboard and talk about them a lot. Because this chapter is concerned with programs written for a general Linux environment, this is a good place to showcase those programs, let you know where to get the programs, and explain why we love them so. The next section of this chapter explains how to run these non-KDE programs and how to install the programs into your panel.

Netscape

Netscape is, hands down, the best Web browser for Linux. Sure, you have
times where you want to use KFM over Netscape, especially if you're down-
loading files. Still, Netscape is the way to go for general Web browsing needs.
As you see in Figure 12-1, Netscape looks the same in KDE as it does on
Windows or on a Macintosh. Just as KDE programs have a consistent feel,
Netscape feels the same across platforms.

We figure that, if you've used the Web in the last three or four years, you
know about Netscape. If you've managed to live this long without it (either
because you've been running Microsoft Explorer or you've been browsing in
text-mode with Lynx), you can find out more about Netscape, or download
Linux versions, at www.netscape.com.

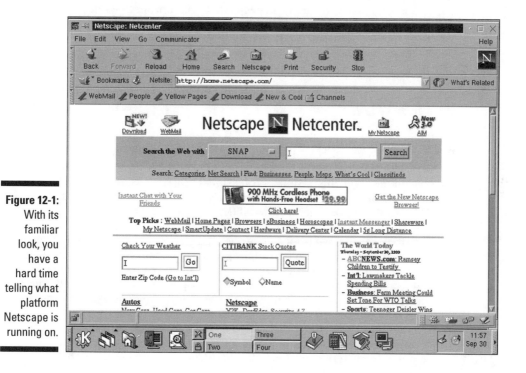

Figure 12-1:
With its
familiar
look, you
have a
hard time
telling what
platform
Netscape is
running on.

If you don't want to run Netscape for some reason, you have two other alternatives besides KFM.

- ✔ **Lynx** is the text-based UNIX Web browser; you won't see the pretty pictures or the advanced graphics, but Lynx is fast, and you get the information you need. Not all Web pages are Lynx-compatible, unfortunately. You still need to have a graphical browser available for those cases. Most Linux distributions include a package for Lynx; check your directories to see if you have it installed already. If not, you can certainly obtain Lynx from just about any UNIX file archive on the Internet.

- ✔ **Opera** is a newer browser from Scandinavia. Opera is not free (the license fee is $35), and it's not yet available for Linux (although a development team is working busily to get it to your desktop), but it has an interesting slant on the Web. Opera only displays pages that are wholly compliant with the HTML standards set by the WWW3 Consortium. This means that you won't see pages that are improperly coded. (The drawback, of course, is that your favorite site may code badly — it's a trade-off you have to be ready to make.) Find out more at www.operasoftware.com.

The GIMP

If you read Chapter 11, you know we're high on The GIMP. A full-featured graphics program, The GIMP gives high-quality results and is free. You can use The GIMP for everything from touching up photographs to creating your own anime-style illustrations. Professional graphic designers use The GIMP, as do ordinary schlubs like us. The basic GIMP window is shown in Figure 12-2, but it's impossible to show all the program's features in one look.

The GIMP's Web page is located at www.gimp.org; you find FAQs, downloads, and much more. You also find an art gallery of unbelievably complex images created with The GIMP. If you're interested in Linux-specific art, you can even find a link to the how to draw Tux, the Linux penguin page. (Useful if you ever want to get a Tux tattoo. Don't laugh — we know someone who has one.)

Mystified by The GIMP? Don't worry — most folks are, at first glance. We strongly recommend that you pick up a good reference guide if you plan to do much work in this program. *The GIMP for Linux Bible*, by Stephanie Cottrell Bryant from IDG Books Worldwide, is a good place to start.

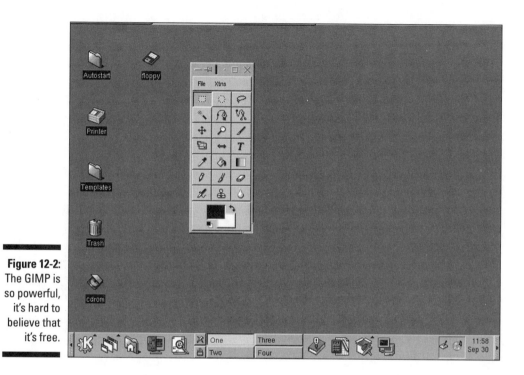

Figure 12-2:
The GIMP is
so powerful,
it's hard to
believe that
it's free.

StarOffice

KOffice, the KDE office suite, is covered in Chapter 10. KOffice is a great suite of office applications with lots of options; however, KOffice is still very young, and not all the bells and whistles are fully functional yet. (The developers even warn you not to use some of the applications for critical materials yet, given their stage of development.) So, what's a Linux-lover to do for an office suite if you need something stable and integrated? We suggest giving StarOffice a try.

StarOffice is an integrated office suite, originally developed by StarDivision GmBH of Germany and now owned by Sun. The suite includes a word processor, a database program, a spreadsheet, a presentation/slideshow program (shown in Figure 12-3), an organizer and calendar, and an e-mail client. StarOffice was originally written for Linux, but recently expanded to the Windows platform (isn't it nice to see platform expansions going in the other direction for once?).

We admit that we're biased — all three of us as authors have written about StarOffice, and naturally we think our books are pretty darn good references on the subject. If you're curious about running this office suite, we humbly suggest *StarOffice 5.1 for Linux Bible* or *StarOffice For Linux For Dummies*, both published by IDG Books Worldwide.

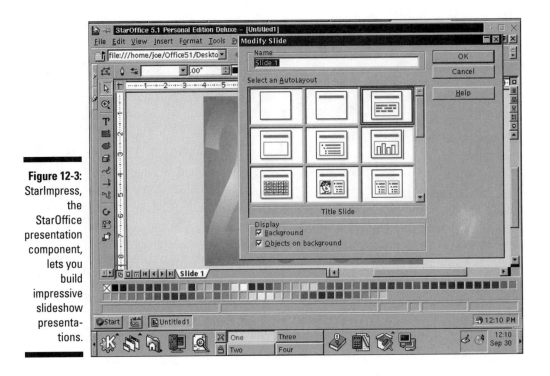

Figure 12-3:
StarImpress,
the
StarOffice
presentation
component,
lets you
build
impressive
slideshow
presenta-
tions.

Okay, so maybe you're not interested in StarOffice. You need an office suite that includes programs your boss has heard of in order to convince her that you can run Linux at work and still coexist happily with the Microsoft and Mac users. By the time this book is published, the WordPerfect Suite 2000 for Linux should be available from Corel. This suite is the Linux version of the wildly popular WordPerfect Suite 2000 for those other operating systems, and will include WordPerfect, QuattroPro, Presentations, and Paradox.

RealPlayer

As recently as two or three years ago, thinking that someday local radio and TV stations would be able to broadcast worldwide via the Internet was a nice fantasy. With the advent of streaming technology, that fantasy has come true in an explosive way. (In fact, the soundtrack to this chapter is WFMT, the Chicago classical radio station that Kate listened to in college; even though she's 2,000 miles away, the magic of streaming audio brings Chicago traffic reports to her desktop.)

RealPlayer is a wonderful program that handles all sorts of input. You can use it to listen to streamed audio (as in Figure 12-4), watch video clips, or just listen to sound files stored in the .mp3 format. Visit the RealPlayer Web site at www.real.com to learn more.

Figure 12-4:
Use
RealPlayer
to listen to
your college
radio station
at your
desk.

You need a sound card and speakers in order to process audio files properly. For streamed audio and video, you also need a fast and reliable connection to the Internet. A 56K modem is considered somewhat slow for streamed files; you need a larger buffer if you're listening over a dial-up 56K link. Far better is a cable modem, DSL, or ISDN connection. These full-time connections over a separate cable make streaming files a pleasure.

Waiter, Where's the Program I Ordered?

If you're new to Linux, you may be befuddled by the KDE menu system. Even if you have installed all the programs in the previous section of this chapter, the programs won't automatically appear in the KDE menu. This can be a shock for folks used to the Windows 95 or 98 installation process, which almost always includes the query "Include program icon in Start Menu?" But fear not — you can easily get to all the other great programs that you've installed. You even have a couple of choices for starting the programs or a way to avoid the choice altogether.

File manager launches

You can always start your programs from KFM, whether programs are KDE or not. If you know the location of the file in the directory structure, open KFM and navigate to the file. After you find the file, start the program by simply double-clicking on the filename. Figure 12-5 shows the KFM method of starting StarOffice.

If you don't know where the program lives on your hard drive, use the handy Find utility to locate it.

1. **Click the Find icon in the panel.**

   The Find window appears.

2. **Enter the program's name in the text entry box of the Find window.**

   You only have to enter the program's name, not a specific filename. Figure 12-6 shows a search for RealPlayer.

3. **Click Find.**

   The utility searches the hard drive and reports the file's location.

4. **Click the X at the right end of the titlebar to close Find.**

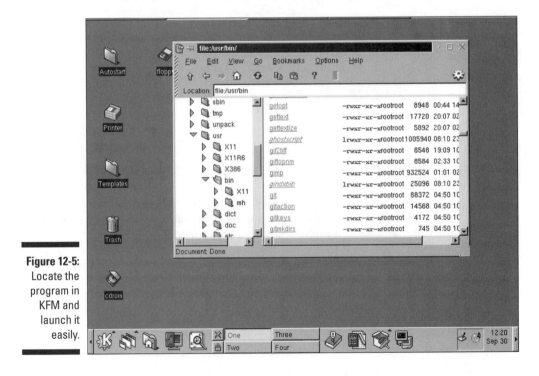

Figure 12-5: Locate the program in KFM and launch it easily.

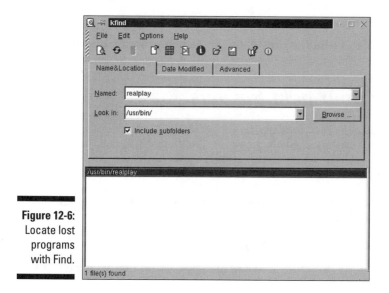

Figure 12-6:
Locate lost
programs
with Find.

5. **Open KFM and navigate to the file's location.**

6. **Double-click the filename to launch the program.**

Command-line launches

An even simpler way to launch non-KDE programs is to use the built-in command-line interface, which doesn't require you to launch a terminal window; KDE offers a single-line window sufficient to get a program going.

1. **Right-click the desktop.**

   The desktop context menu pops up.

2. **Choose Execute Command from the context menu.**

   The Command window appears, as seen in Figure 12-7.

Figure 12-7:
Launch
programs
directly from
the desktop
with a single
right-click.

Command: netscape

3. **Type the program's name at the text prompt and press the Enter key.**

4. **The Command window closes and the named program launches.**

Pushing your own buttons

Both of the methods described above are perfectly fine for launching non-KDE programs. However, if you have a program that you use all the time, putting its icon into the panel is worthwhile. That way, you're never more than a mouse-click away from the programs you rely on.

Panel configuration is covered in detail in Chapter 5, but here's a quick reminder of how to add icons.

1. **Open KFM, the KDE File Manager.**

2. **Navigate to the directory housing the application that you want to add to the panel.**

3. **Click the application name and drag it to the panel.**

   A new icon, dedicated to that application, appears in the panel. The icon is the generic KDE gear icon, so you may want to change the icon to something more memorable.

4. **Right-click the icon.**

5. **Choose Properties from the pop-up menu.**

   The Properties screen appears.

6. **Click the Execute tab.**

7. **Check the Execute field to make sure that it contains the correct name of the application you want to add.**

8. **Click the gear icon.**

   The icon window appears, as in Figure 12-8, with a variety of icons shown.

9. **Select the icon you want to use to represent this application in the panel.**

   If possible, select an icon that reminds you of the application: a page for a word processor, a picture for a graphics program, and so forth.

10. **Click OK.**

11. **Click the Application tab of the Properties window.**

12. **In the Comment field, type the name of the program.**

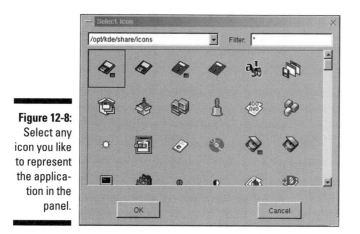

Entering the program's name in this field means that, if you hold your
mouse over the icon, a small window with the application's name pops
up. Entering a name in the Comment field is a good way to remind yourself what the button stands for, especially if you didn't choose a very
memorable icon.

13. Open the KDE menu and choose Panel⇨Restart.

The Panel program restarts. Your application icon is now visible. Use it
to start the program quickly.

Sticking to the Text

Way back in the days when graphical interfaces were just experimental toys,
most applications were text based. If you're in your early 30s or older, your
first computer may very well have been a plain old DOS box, in which case
you remember text-based programs just fine.

UNIX and UNIX-based operating systems have always relied on text-based
programs, both for system maintenance and for actual applications. Having a
constant graphical interface, such as KDE, is a fairly recent phenomenon, and
many Linux people still prefer to run text-based programs where possible.
Text-based applications are improved and developed as frequently as graphical applications, so that you don't find a a big quality trade-off. Some of these
applications are very good and have maintained a following even in the face
of graphical applications with many bells and whistles, while other text programs are so specialized that no graphical alternative has been wanted.

If you've used UNIX or Linux before, even if it wasn't a machine you adminis-
tered, you may be familiar with a few of these programs. Lynx, as mentioned
above, is a text-based Web browser. Pine is a multifunction e-mail program,

while trn and strn are designed especially for USENET newsgroup reading. Pico, emacs, and vi are text editors; we talk more about text editors in Chapter 10. Give some of these old warhorses a try; you may find them more suitable to your habits than some of the newer graphical programs.

Where do you find them? You probably already have these programs loaded. Most Linux distributions include the basic text programs as part of the standard installation. Check through your file directories, or look at the listing of contents for your installation CD to see what you have available to you that's text-based.

Text-based programs take up a lot less memory when they're running. If you have a chronic memory shortage and can't afford to add a few megabytes to boost productivity, consider using text-based applications to minimize the load. You still need graphic applications for some things, but you will be amazed at what you can get accomplished with a simple text editor and an e-mail program, such as Pine.

So what do you do if you want (or need) to run one of these text-based programs? Simple: You run the program in a terminal window. Terminal windows are launched with the K Virtual Terminal program, or KVT. KVT's icon in the panel looks like a window plugged into a computer, and it's usually located near the Pager buttons.

A *terminal window* is simply a KDE window opened to a text prompt. The window lets you do things directly with Linux, without having to log out of KDE to a text prompt and then restart KDE after you're done. A terminal window also permits you to run regular text programs within the graphical environment. (If you've got true geekish tendencies such as one of us — we won't say who — you may run KDE simply to have access to Netscape and RealPlayer, but do all your work in old-fashioned text programs running in terminal windows.)

1. **Click the KVT button in the panel.**

   A terminal window appears, as shown in Figure 12-9. Note that it looks exactly like your screen if you're using a text log-in, except that it has a titlebar and a toolbar like any other KDE window.

   You can do anything in this terminal window that you would do with the computer in text mode, whether it's system maintenance or application work.

2. **At the text prompt, type the name of the program you want to run.**

   The program launches within the terminal window. Text-based programs do not spawn new windows as graphical applications do, so that you need to open a new terminal window for each text-based application you want to run simultaneously.

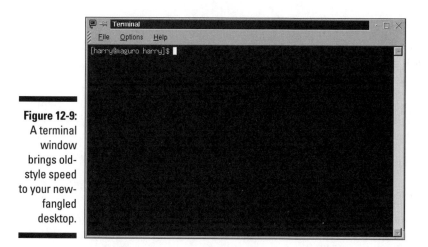

Figure 12-9:
A terminal
window
brings old-
style speed
to your new-
fangled
desktop.

3. **After you're finished with the text-based program, click the X in the titlebar to close the terminal window.**

   Unlike the text mode, if you're not logged into KDE, you can't log yourself out of your user account by typing **logout** at the system prompt. You need to close the terminal window and exit KDE in order to do that.

Making KDE Play Nice with Others

Sometimes, through no fault of yours or anyone else's, a non-KDE program doesn't work quite right after you run it under KDE. The usual manifestation of a problem is an oddly sized window or very strange font appearances.

What's happening here is that KDE is trying to muscle in on the other program's territory. KDE is trying to apply its own font and window rules to the non-KDE program, whether or not the non-KDE program is set up to accept the KDE rules. Sometimes you never notice a thing and the program works fine; other times, the program looks nasty and may give you a headache.

Fortunately, you have a couple of options you can try in such a situation.

1. **Open the KDE menu and choose Settings⇨Desktop⇨Style config panel.**

   The Style Config Panel (Display settings) screen appears.

2. **Click the checkbox next to Apply KDE Settings to non-KDE Apps to remove the checkmark.**

3. Click OK.

Do not click Apply. If the new setting doesn't seem to work, redo this procedure and make sure you click OK instead of Apply.

If it still doesn't work, you can do some heavy-duty mangling to get your program working properly. Making your program work correctly involves hands-on Linux work, so if you're uncomfortable with doing such things, take a deep breath and promise yourself ice cream afterward.

Open your file manager and locate the following directory:

```
opt/kde/share/apps/kdisplay/app-defaults
```

Phew! That's a mouseful. After you locate the directory, you need to either delete or rename the directory. Doing this keeps the X Window System from locating the default Kdisplay resource files (the ones that the X Window System uses to assert KDE styles over the non-KDE application's defaults).

In cases where you have the option to either delete or rename a file or directory, you're almost always making the better choice to rename the file or directory (and to make a note of both its original name and the one you used for renaming). In the event that you need to put the file back, you still have it. If the file's deleted, you may have to go all the way and reinstall from scratch. Renaming saves time.

After you rename or delete the directory, log out of your user account and then log back in. Logging out causes X to restart and allows the non-KDE program to use its own settings.

Okay . . . but It's Still Not Working

If you have different problems than the ones noted above, or if these tricks still aren't getting your problem solved, you may want to find an expert somewhere. Consult Chapter 16 and Appendix B to find places where KDE-savvy people hang out on the Internet. Chances are, if you're experiencing problems with a popular non-KDE application, you are not the first one to find the KDE feature that's holding you back.

You may also want to check out the non-KDE application's Web site to see if there are known conflicts with KDE. Sometimes all you have to do is download and install a bug patch.

Part IV
Under the Hood

In this part . . .

*H*ere's an easy riddle: How do you know someone is stranded on the freeway? Answer: The car's hood is up, saying (in effect), *There's an engine in here — how am I supposed to know what to do with it?* Well, not everybody has access to a shade-tree mechanic who can demonstrate which loose wire to connect, but as technology users go, the Linux crowd is made of hardier stuff. They're more like the European drivers who carry a toolkit in the trunk.

Even as you enjoy the creature comforts of KDE, it's wise to know what's going on under that well-appointed surface. So this section gives you some handy pointers on how Linux actually works — and how you can take command of its workings when you need to. Talk about empowerment.

Chapter 13

It May Look Different, but It's Still Linux

*I*t's easy to forget, sometimes, that KDE is simply the user interface to the powerful and flexible Linux operating system. After all, KDE succeeds at its goal of making the use of a Linux computer something that's simple and comprehensible for everyone, not just for people who write code for fun and memorize arcane commands like the rest of us try to remember the grocery list.

Part of the reason the masses haven't converted to Linux — even though there's a general feeling of interest and benevolence toward the operating system among the computer-savvy public — is that the administration of a Linux machine is perceived as strange. Complicated. Technical. Described in documentation that appears to have been written by yaks at midnight. Filled with stuff you have to do or otherwise send your machine into a fit of exploding flames.

Some of that is true, and some of it isn't. (We're not going to make a call on the yaks.) Linux administration can be quite complex. Some of the things you need to keep an eye on may slip your mind, but that's true of almost anything, whether involving computers or not. Much of the documentation doesn't do a very good job of explaining why you need to do something.

This is where KDE comes in. We won't tell you that KDE tools make it as simple to run a Linux system as it is to run an iMac, because that's not true. You have much more control over the operating system in a Linux environment than you do over the Macintosh operating system. More control means more effort, in computing as in life. This chapter provides you with two things: an understanding of the administrative tasks you have to perform because you're running Linux and a guide to the KDE tools that make those tasks a little easier.

The Multiuser Environment

The key concept to keep in mind as you work with your Linux machine is that you're in charge of a *multiuser environment*. Linux provides a way for several people — or one person pretending to be several people — to use a single computer. Users share the applications and system resources, but each individual account is private and has its own storage area. The system administrator can see what the users are doing or what they've stored on the hard drive, but users can't see anything related to other users' activities. Oh, the power! Oh, the possibilities!

When you installed Linux on your system, you created a special account called *root,* and you probably also created a personal account for yourself. As soon as you completed those account creations, you had a multiuser system. Yep, as easy as that! Yes, you're both root and trixiebelle, but your computer doesn't know that. Your computer sees the two as separate entities, and gives root complete access to everything on the machine, but requires trixiebelle to follow the rules.

As you go through this section, remember that the multiuser information applies to you even if you are the only human using your machine. Because you have access both to root and to your user account, you have multiuser concerns as much as if you also created accounts for your partner or roommate. If you do have other users on your machine, you have some interpersonal concerns as well. Those are mentioned later in the chapter, and there are some ideas about being a good system administrator as well as a good friend.

Let's talk for a moment about root. That root account you created for yourself is pretty darn special. Any time you need to make changes to your operating system, you likely need to do them as root. Root has access to all files on the system — even the personal ones in user accounts — and root can run any program: even the programs that will completely destroy your computer. Using your root account for day-to-day business is a bad idea. Use your user account for everything you'd usually use your computer to do. If you need to do something as root, you can log in specially to take care of the issue, and then log back out.

Creating user accounts

Because you created a user account for yourself when you installed Linux the first time around, you've probably done this already. However, depending on your distribution, you may have created a user account within the installation procedure and not as a regular root activity.

Adding users is an extremely simple procedure. In fact, you'll think longer about whether to give your nephew Larry an account on your machine than you will spend actually adding him.

1. **Log in as root.**

   If you're logged in to your user account, you can either log out and log in again as root, or you can use the KFM superuser mode described in the "Using KFM as the superuser" section later in this chapter.

2. **Open a terminal window.**

3. **Type** `adduser <username>` **at the command prompt.**

   Obviously, substitute your user's choice of login ID for `<username>`. Add Lulu with the command `adduser lulu`.

4. **Type** `passwd <username>` **at the command prompt.**

   You are prompted for a new password.

5. **Enter a password.**

   This initial password can be anything you like and can violate all rules of correct passwording.

   You are prompted to verify the password.

6. **Enter the same password again.**

   The user has been successfully added.

7. **Exit the terminal window.**

8. **Inform the new user of her username and password.**

   The new user should change her password immediately upon logging in for the first time. She can do this by typing `passwd` at a command prompt.

Using KFM as the superuser

Assume you know that root is a powerful thing (as described in the section earlier in "The Multiuser Environment" earlier in this chapter) and that you're happily logged in to your user account, doing whatever it is you like to do on your computer. You have this book open nearby, and as you scan through it, you realize there's something you need to check while wearing your root hat.

How do you get to root if you're logged in as a user? Sure, you can log out of your user account and come back in as root, but that means shutting down all your active programs. That can be a little tricky if you're chatting with Ksirc or listening to a CD.

The trick lies in KFM. Use the file manager's *superuser mode* to access root capabilities, get your task done, and then get back to whatever it was you were doing before:

1. **Open the KDE menu and choose System⇨File Manager (Super User Mode).**

   A terminal window appears; it is not the regular KFM window. The terminal window contains a prompt for the root password, as shown in Figure 13-1.

Figure 13-1:
Use KFM to get rapid access to root's capabilities.

2. **Enter the root password and press Enter.**

   KFM appears. Notice that it's showing the /root directory, which it doesn't do when in regular mode.

3. **Access the file or run the program for which you need root access.**

4. **Choose File⇨Close to exit KFM.**

This is a useful way to check something quickly — a configuration file, for instance.

The perils of multiple users

Let's face it. People can be weird. Sometimes they can even be offensive. More often, they can get themselves into trouble without even knowing it.

That's really quite easy in a Linux environment, especially if your users are new to Linux in general.

What's the systems administrator to do? Educate and inform. With proper explanations, your users are likely to feel more comfortable working on your system. You should also decide on some system policies and let your users know what they are. Better safe than sorry, right? Here are some ideas:

✔ Control password choice and change frequency. (See "Keeping Your Privacy Intact" at the end of this chapter for more ideas about passwords.) Make sure your users know that you will not tolerate sharing passwords.

✔ If you set a size limit on user accounts, let users know.

✔ Encourage your users to learn more about Linux, perhaps by working through *Linux For Dummies,* 2nd Edition (IDG Books Worldwide, Inc.) or a book specific to your Linux distribution (*Red Hat Linux For Dummies, Caldera OpenLinux For Dummies,* and the like). If you have a budding programmer on your machine, be clear about what kinds of programs you will and will not permit to be run.

✔ Offer help with file permissions and check over user accounts regularly to make sure permissions are set properly. (You don't have to read the files, just check the permissions.)

✔ Explain to users how to check what programs are running in the user account (***hint:*** type ps x at a command prompt — see Figure 13-2 for an example of the output) and how to get rid of processes that aren't being used (kill -9 processnumber). This is especially useful if your machine has a tendency to crash.

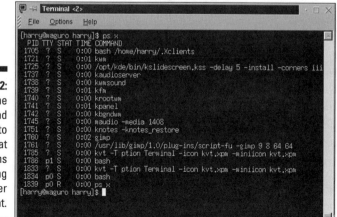

Figure 13-2:
Use the command ps x to learn what programs are running in your user account.

Consider using the Message of the Day feature to inform your users of certain things. The message appears when using a text-based login; the user logs in and the message scrolls up the screen. You could provide a Tip of the Day, notice of impending downtime, or a reminder of system policy. If you use a graphical login, users can access the Message of the Day by opening a terminal window and typing **motd** at the prompt. Here's how to set up a Message of the Day, or MOTD:

1. **Log in as root.**

   If you're logged in to your user account, you can either log out and log in again as root, or you can use the KFM superuser mode described in the "Using KFM as the superuser" section earlier in this chapter.

2. **Create the file** /etc/motd.

   You can do this in a terminal window or with KFM.

3. **In the file** /etc/motd, **enter whatever text you'd like to display to your viewers.**

   This file may contain a joke, a system downtime warning, or a reminder like "Change your password today."

4. **Save and exit the file.**

Now that you've created the /etc/motd file, it is displayed whenever a user (including you) logs in using a text-based login. If you want to change the message, just edit the file. Encourage your users to pay attention to the MOTD. A sample MOTD is shown in Figure 13-3.

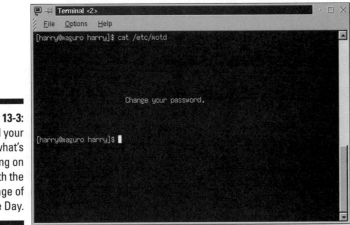

Figure 13-3:
Tell your users what's going on with the Message of the Day.

Package Management

In the Linux world, packages aren't something that Federal Express or United Parcel Service employees bring to your door. Rather, *packages* are a handy way to bundle various programs that you need in order to install software on your computer. With the advent of multiple distributions of the Linux software, several specialized package formats have appeared, including the Red Hat RPM format and the Debian deb package format.

Way back when the earth was still cooling, when geeks were geeks and wrote assembly code for coffee-break fun, all Linux software had to be installed by compiling it directly from raw source code. Although it's still a good idea to have a clue about installing software in this way, it's certainly a bit more complicated than many people liked. It also takes some time to install from source code.

Interested in learning about source code installation? Check out Appendix A. Although the appendix describes installing KDE source code itself, you can get a pretty good idea of the process by reading through it. You use much the same method to install any software that needs to be installed directly from source code.

A couple of the better-known Linux distributors (the aforementioned Red Hat and Debian) had a bright idea. "Wouldn't it be easier for our users," they thought, "if we had a specialized format that did most of that tedious work automatically?" Thus, the *package* was born.

Packages contain precompiled binary software, software libraries, and other things required to provide a complete and functioning installation of the given program. If you installed Red Hat or Debian Linux, you also have a program that lets you deal with their specialized package formats. Probably the best known of these management programs is the Red Hat Package Manager, or RPM. RPM allows you to install, uninstall, upgrade, and obtain information about a package. Package managers for other distributions that use them have similar features, so the Red Hat manager is focused on here.

If you're not running Red Hat, it's a good idea to check out the specs for your particular package manager at the distribution Web site. If you run a distribution that doesn't use package managers, just skip this section and move smoothly to the next.

For your package-management needs, KDE provides a neat little tool called Kpackage. Kpackage gives you an easy-to-use graphical interface to RPM, dselect (the Debian package manager), and other, less well-known managers.

1. Open the KDE menu and choose Utilities⇨KPackage.

The Kpackage screen appears, as shown in Figure 13-4, with a directory tree in the left window. The directory tree shows packages that are currently installed.

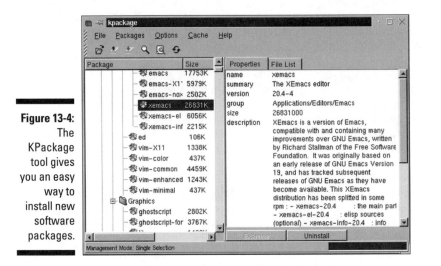

Figure 13-4:
The KPackage tool gives you an easy way to install new software packages.

2. Click one of the installed packages.

Information about the package appears in the right window.

3. Click the File List tab, which is above the right window.

A list of files appears in the right window, as seen in Figure 13-5. This lists all the files contained in that package.

4. If you want to uninstall the package, click the Uninstall button (at the bottom of the right window).

5. Choose File⇨Exit to exit.

You can also use KPackage to get an easier installation of packages that you've downloaded, whether from CD-ROMs or from the Internet:

1. Open the KDE menu and choose Utilities⇨KPackage.

The main KPackage screen appears.

2. Select File⇨Open.

A navigation window appears. Use it to find the uninstalled package that you want to install. The navigation method is the same as the one you use to move throughout KFM.

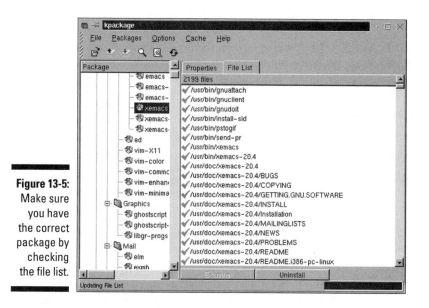

Figure 13-5:
Make sure
you have
the correct
package by
checking
the file list.

3. **Click the uninstalled package to select it.**

4. **Select from the left window the installation options you want to use, as shown in Figure 13-6.**

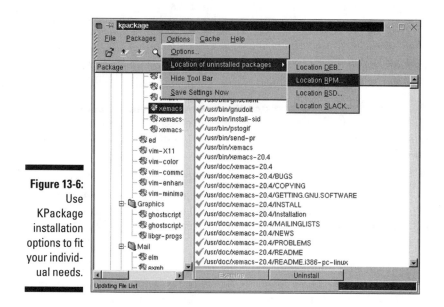

Figure 13-6:
Use
KPackage
installation
options to fit
your individ-
ual needs.

5. **Click Test (Do Not Install).**

   This option lets the machine perform a dry run through the installation procedure. It informs you if there is a problem with the package. It's a good idea to use the test option so that you don't accidentally cause system problems during a corrupted installation.

6. **If the test was successful, click Install.**

   Kpackage automatically performs the installation.

7. **Repeat this process for each package you want to install.**

8. **Choose File⇨Exit after you have finished working with KPackage.**

It's a Server, It's a Workstation. . .

Like any operating system, Linux runs a lot of programs in the background, meaning that you don't see windows or meters showing them in progress. These programs include the mouse driver, the program that handles e-mail, network utilities, and so on: all the little programs that keep your computer running properly.

Because Linux is Linux, you have the ability to work with these programs and decide how (or if) they run. That's all part of the UNIX philosophy! Not only that, but you can select one of several ways for these programs to run and shift between these ways as you need. It's highly flexible and configurable, and that's one of the best reasons for choosing Linux in the first place.

How does this all work? Through the magic of run levels. A *run level* is, in very simple terms, a shortcut. That is, each run level can be defined to contain a certain set of actions. When you invoke that run level, the actions contained within it either start or stop. For the purposes here, that's a complete enough definition. If you become entranced with run levels, you've moved beyond the scope of this book and need to check out an intermediate Linux book.

In keeping with traditional UNIX conventions, there are seven run levels. Run Levels 0, 1, and 6 have specialized functions, while Run Levels 2, 3, 4, and 5 are levels that you can define. See the "Run, run level, run!" sidebar for specific information about each run level. The most important Run Levels here are 3 and 5; they are the modes in which most Linux computers run most of the time.

Run Level 3 is a standard multiuser mode that starts out in text mode. When you boot up and log in, you start out at a command prompt. In order for graphical elements like KDE to begin working, you need to start the X

Window System by hand. Run Level 5, however, invokes the X Window System when it boots up. If your first sight after booting up is a graphical login screen or KDE itself, you're running in Run Level 5. (You need to know the difference between these two levels when reading Chapter 14 and the discussion of the graphical login screen.)

Run, run level, run!

Although you could manually start and stop each individual function that Linux uses in operating your computer, it makes sense to automate the process as much as possible. Not only is it more convenient (and requires less typing), but using run levels guarantees that you won't forget to start a critical process as you work through your list. Traditionally, each run level has a different function; in ordinary use, you don't need to shift between them very often.

Note: The run level functions described here are the standard functions for Red Hat Linux. They're similar in all Linux systems. If you want to see how your distribution defines run levels, take a look at the file /etc/inittab. Do not edit inittab! Just look at it.

Run Level 0 is a specialized level that puts the computer into shutdown mode. When this mode is invoked, all processes currently running close themselves. When the processes are completely stopped, Linux shuts itself down.

Run Level 1 is another specialized level, this one defined as single-user mode. This level is usually used as a diagnostic mode when something is drastically wrong with the system. Run Level 1 starts the minimum number of functions, those necessary for the core operation of Linux, and lets you handle every other function manually. If you're lucky, you'll never need Run Level 1.

Run Level 2 starts the computer in multiuser text mode, like Run Level 3, but does not start NFS

(network file service). If you're using a standalone machine, you won't notice a difference because you don't have a need for NFS. If you're part of a network, Run Level 2 causes your machine to behave like a standalone without any network services available.

Run Level 3 is one of the two standard run levels that you're likely to use. Run Level 3 starts the computer in multiuser mode, but doesn't start the X Window System. That is, you can operate everything on the machine that's in text mode without doing anything else. If you need anything graphical, you need to start the X Window System by hand (or switch to Run Level 5).

Run Level 4 is not currently designated for a particular purpose.

Run Level 5 is the other standard run level that you're likely to see. Like Run Level 3, Run Level 5 boots in multiuser mode. However, in 5, the X Window System starts automatically and you need to use KDE terminal windows to get to text mode. This is the mode to use if you want KDE to start automatically when you boot up.

Run Level 6 is the final level, and it's another specialized one; this is the reboot level. Like Run Level 0, invoking this level causes all the running programs to close down; unlike Run Level 0, when the programs have stopped, Linux reboots itself and powers back up.

What if you want to add a certain function to a given run level? Perhaps you have Linux installed on a machine that uses PCMCIA cards to provide certain devices. (PCMCIA cards are those small, heavy cards that many laptops use for modems; they also can be used for networking and for extra hard drive space.) Because you use a PCMCIA card to handle your network needs, you want to make sure that the `pcmcia` configuration script runs automatically at bootup. You boot in Run Level 3, so you want to add the `pcmcia` script to that level.

1. **Log in as root.**

   You can either log out of your user account entirely or use the KFM superuser mode described in the "Using KFM as the superuser" section of this chapter.

2. **Open the KDE menu and select System⇨SysV Init Editor.**

   The run level editor screen appears, as shown in Figure 13-7. There are two windows for each run level just below the toolbar; the top window contains programs that are started when that run level is invoked and the bottom window contains programs that are stopped when the run level is invoked.

   To the left is a window labeled Available Services. This window contains all the background programs available for you to install.

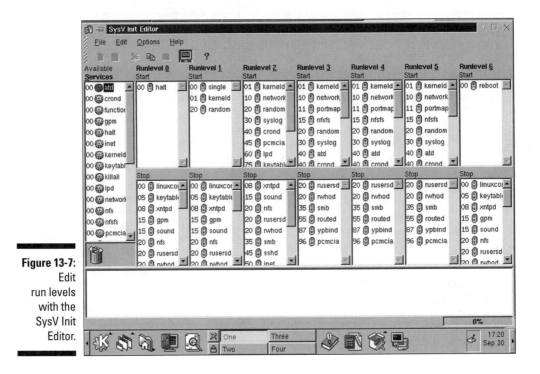

Figure 13-7:
Edit
run levels
with the
SysV Init
Editor.

The Available Services window lists the files that are contained in the directory `/etc/rc.d/init.d`. You won't need to memorize that, but it's useful to know in case you want to talk about run levels to someone used to working with them in text mode, rather than with a graphical run level editor.

Locate the program you want to add.

3. **Use your mouse to click and drag the program from the Available Services window to the appropriate run level window.**

   Remember to use the top window for programs you want to start and to use the bottom window for programs you want to stop.

   For this example, you would drag the `pcmcia` script from the Available Services window to the top window under Run Level 3.

4. **Click the Save icon (which looks like a floppy diskette).**

   The new configuration saves to disk. The next time you start your computer in this run level, the new program starts automatically.

5. **If you want to start the program immediately without rebooting, right-click the program in the Available Services window.**

6. **Select Start from the pop-up menu.**

   As you can see in Figure 13-8, the pop-up menu allows you to start and stop services from within the run level manager.

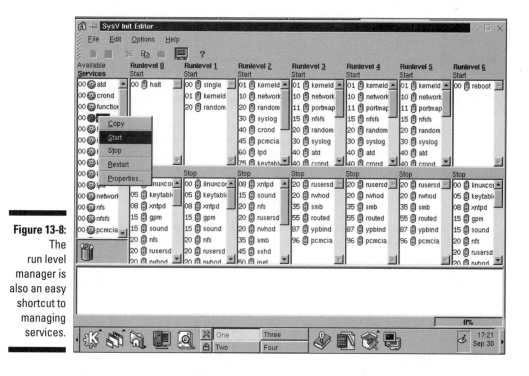

Figure 13-8:
The run level manager is also an easy shortcut to managing services.

If you want to add or remove a service from a given run level, you need to know exactly what the service is, what it does, and why you want to add or remove it. If you play around with this tool and add or remove services without understanding what they do, you can inadvertently cripple your machine by removing a critical program — and it is very hard to fix run level errors if they involve basic services.

Mounting File Systems

If you're new to Linux but have used Windows or Macintosh computers before, you may find the Linux method of file-system management quite odd. In fact, Windows and Mac users often don't even think of what they're doing as file-system management because of the way their operating systems handle floppy and CD drives.

Linux works under a *conservation of resources principle*. You don't need to have access to all your storage devices, or *drives,* all the time; you just need them when you need them. With Linux, you need to *mount* or *unmount* file systems as the occasion requires.

What does it mean to mount a file system? Well, it doesn't mean that you climb atop a pile of CD-ROM jewel boxes and begin to declaim the poetry of Henry Wadsworth Longfellow. To understand the phrase, first read the term definitions:

 ✔ **File system:** A file system can be anything from a hard disk to a floppy disk, a tape drive, a CD-ROM, or a single directory. In general, Linux folks use the term *file system* to refer to any given directory and all of its sub-directories. For example, a CD-ROM copy of the *Encyclopaedia Britannica, A-F* will have a top-level directory and a number of subdirectories that contain the actual entries.

 ✔ **Mount:** After you have your file system, you need to mount it. *Mounting,* in Linux terms, means to make the file system available to the local system. Here, *local* means your particular computer.

Some file systems mounting happens automatically. When you installed Linux for the first time, you created a number of partitions on the hard disk. Each of these partitions is a separate file system. When you boot up the computer, part of the start-up process is the automatic mounting of these file systems. You can also unmount and remount these hard disk partition file systems by hand, just as you can mount and unmount storage device file systems by hand.

This system of mounting and unmounting file systems has both disadvantages and advantages. The main disadvantage of the mounting method is that you have to mount the file system every single time you want to use the floppy drive or the CD-ROM drive. Compared to the ease of use with Windows or Macintosh, mounting drives can be a real pain.

The advantages outweigh the inconveniences, though. With the mounting method, you have greater control over the file systems. If there appears to be a problem with your floppy drive, such as signs of corruption, you can just unmount the file system and work on the problem without compromising your main system. You also have the ability to mount file systems from remote machines and work with them just like they were part of your own computer. This is done using the Network File System, or NFS.

If you're interested in the possibilities of remote file sharing across a network, but you're the only Linux fan in a roomful of Windows users, take a look at a nifty program called Samba. Samba allows you to share file systems across a mixed-OS network composed of Linux and Windows machines; much of this book was written across a Samba network. Windows 98 Networking shares some features with the Linux implementation of NFS; after you have the network set up, both the Windows machines and the Linux machines can use file systems on all the machines in the network.

True to form, KDE gives you a specialized tool that makes the mounting and unmounting of file systems a snap.

1. **Log in as root.**

   If you're logged in to your user account, you can either log out and log in again as root, or you can use the KFM superuser mode described in the "Using KFM as the superuser" section of this chapter.

2. **Open the KDE menu and choose System⇨KDiskFree.**

   The KDiskFree screen appears. If you've looked at Chapter 14, you'll remember KDiskFree as a helpful tool to assess the fullness of your drive, but it's also a useful mounting tool if you're logged in as root.

   The KDiskFree screen displays the various file systems available on your computer. If the file system is already mounted, it is black and clickable. If the file system is available but unmounted, it is greyed out.

3. **Click the icon of the file system you want to mount or unmount.**

   KDiskFree displays a message and then mounts or unmounts, as you selected.

4. **Choose File⇨Exit after you have finished.**

Keeping Your Privacy Intact

Linux is a multiuser system, even if you're the only user. One of the problems that arises from the capability to set up accounts is the issue of security and privacy. Think about it: When you log in to your Internet provider to check your mail, or you save a document to your hard drive, or you visit sites on the Web that give you cookies, that information is stored in your user account files.

In the ideal world, nobody would care about your private stuff. After all, you're not a celebrity, right? Who cares if you have a couple of e-mail accounts with pseudonyms? Who cares if you keep your painfully honest and private diary in a text file? Who cares if you visit the "Fluffy Bunny News Page" so often that the front page of the site mentions you by (pseudony-mous) name?

You do. We all do. Our stuff is ours, and we don't want people to see it with-out authorization to do so. Linux handles these issues with something called a *permission profile*. Each file has one. The permission profile determines who has permission to access the file and what kind of access they can have. Three types of permissions exist:

- ✔ **Read:** Read is the most basic type of permission. It means that the file can be viewed, but not altered in any way.

- ✔ **Write:** Write is the middle kind of permission. When you place write access on a file, it can be altered by whomever has write access to it.

- ✔ **Execute:** Some files are executable, which usually means that they're programs or scripts. Execute permission means that whomever has exe-cute access to the file may run the script or program — in the directory where it lives. This can be dangerous if it's a destructive program.

Just like the three types of permission, three levels of access exist:

- ✔ **User:** This is you, or whoever owns the user account. Generally, you have full access to all the files in your account (unless you mess up the permissions somehow).

- ✔ **Group:** After you create the user account, you may have created special groups. If not, the group is the entire user base of the machine. Group access means that anyone within your group can view your files under the type of permission you attached to the file (read, write, or execute).

- ✔ **Global:** Exactly what it says. This is a dangerous level, with one major exception. It may not seem like it's much to worry about, and if your machine is a standalone box with no cords trailing out the back, it may be that you're okay. But one of the major assumptions made throughout this book is that you have Internet access. After you've connected your Linux box to the Internet, anyone who knows you're there can access files set with global access privileges and use them according to the per-mission level. Do you really want to give some guy in Uzbekistan execute permission on your home directory? We didn't think so.

The World Wide Web is an exception to the "Global access is dangerous" rule. Assume for a moment that a Web server is running on your Linux machine. (It's unlikely that you'd need this book if you were doing so.) The Web server allows people on the Internet to view all the globally accessible pages on the machine. Users most often create their own Web pages by building a directory structure within a particular directory that is globally accessible. That is, you'd create a directory called WWW and make it globally readable. Everything and anything that goes into that directory is visible on the Web; it wouldn't be visible if it weren't globally accessible. Still, it's a conscious choice to move files into that directory.

Be aware of your permissions; if you're connected to the Internet, there's always a chance that some curious or malicious person will test your permissions.

All of this permission stuff can get confusing, because you can have three levels of access for each of the three types of permission. If you think well in spatial terms, imagine the permissions profile as a matrix, with types of permission along the X axis and levels of access along the Y axis: The most tightly controlled files, user-readable, are snugged tightly to the center, while the most available files, global-executable, are way out there in the ether. (If that image doesn't work for you, try thinking of something else. Or perhaps the basic definition of permissions works for you, in which case you get the gold Linux star!)

The traditional UNIX system for defining permissions is a little esoteric, so KDE added a highly useful permissions feature in KFM.

1. **Open KFM.**

2. **Navigate to the file on which you want to check permissions.**

3. **Right-click the filename.**

4. **Select Properties from the pop-up menu.**

   The properties screen appears, as shown in Figure 13-9.

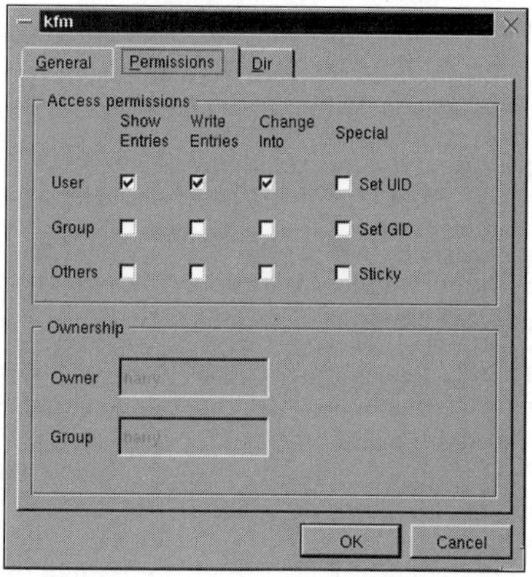

Figure 13-9:
Pop-up KFM menus are an easy way to handle file permissions.

5. Select the Permissions tab.

The permissions profile for the selected file is shown.

6. Select the checkboxes to set the permissions profile as you want it.

Remember to keep your own level of access to the file. You usually need at least write access to your own files so that you can alter them.

7. Click OK to exit the Properties screen.

The new permissions apply to your file after you click OK.

If you're logged in to your user account, you can only set permissions on your own files. If you're logged in as root, you can set permissions on any file on the machine, including those in other user accounts.

Be careful when messing with files in other people's accounts. Root has a lot of privileges that can screw up everyday relationships if you let the "power of root" go to your head. Use root powers to fix obvious security holes and help your users keep their data secure. Don't use it to get revenge by making your roommate's journal publicly readable.

A lot of the problems that people normally encounter when working with Linux are file permission problems. It's easy to get permissions set wrong without really noticing it. If you have some sort of access problem with a particular file or directory, check the permissions profile before you try anything else. You can often fix a frustrating situation with an easy click or two.

You should know about a couple more of security's finer points. These are especially important when you have other users on your machine.

- ✔ The biggest "D'oh!" we can think of is leaving passwords taped to your monitor or keyboard. Particularly the root password. Memorize it and don't leave it lying around in the open.

- ✔ We also strongly advise against doing routine work in your root account. Save root for special stuff. Use your user account for daily stuff.

- ✔ If you're not using a graphical login screen, make sure you log out of your shell account as well as log out of KDE at the end of a session.

- ✔ Get into the habit of picking a secure password: not your name, not your street name, not your phone number. A good tip is to mix numbers and letters, both upper- and lowercase.

- ✔ If you really want to enforce password security, install a program that forces your users to change passwords every 30 days and doesn't permit repeat use of the same password. Such programs can be found in various archives on the Internet. Be aware, though, that rapid password turnover can often lead to the direct opposite of the desired effect: Users who find it hard to remember passwords will just write the new one down and tape it to the monitor. (See the beginning of this list.)

Chapter 14

Taking Control — the KDE Control Center

*I*n the course of familiarizing yourself with KDE, you've probably used its many configuration tools to make your desktop uniquely yours. Perhaps you changed the theme, or you put certain icons onto the panel and removed others. One of the nice aspects about KDE is how configurable it is; that's one reason why KDE is so popular.

In much the same way that you configured the appearance of your desktop with KDE tools, you can configure your computer itself with other KDE tools. KDE gives you simple ways in which to work with the level that lies underneath your desktop: Linux itself. Most of the Linux configuration tools are located in the KDE Control Center, the focus of this chapter. You can access the Control Center via its icon in the panel: a half-monitor, half-circuit board icon.

You find two different kinds of tools in the Control Center. You can use options that affect individual user accounts no matter how you're logged into the machine. But if you want to use a tool that affects your entire system, you need to log in as root. You can access the root account with two different methods: Either log out of your user account and relogin as root or use the KFM superuser mode, as described in Chapter 13. Either way, be sure that you log out of the root account after you finish your task, because you don't want to leave the root account open without needing it to be available.

As we mention before, logging in as root can be dangerous. Making irrevocable changes without realizing it is quite easy. Make a habit of logging into your regular user account; if you really need to log in as root, you can do so intentionally.

Setting Up a Graphical Login Screen

Admit it — part of the reason you installed KDE in the first place was that you simply find the graphical interface more pleasing than plain old white text on black background. So maybe it bugs you that you have to exit KDE and go back out to the text prompt after you're done with your session, leaving your computer to look like any other UNIX-type machine with its simple little `login:` prompt sitting there quietly.

The solution is to create a graphical login screen. After you have it set up, you never need to stop running KDE if you don't want to. Go ahead and log out as you normally do. Instead of exiting KDE, though, your computer returns to a graphical login screen — but KDE is still going! No more typing `startx` after logging in, no more waiting for the desktop to appear.

We have to apologize to you, gentle reader. Normally, we stick in a couple of pictures to show you exactly what the graphical login screen looks like. In fact, we take screenshots, exactly as we describe the process in Chapter 11. Unfortunately, in order to take a screenshot, we have to be logged into the computer so that we can use KSnapshot. Do you begin to see the problem? We can't get the login screen on the monitor until we log out — but we can't take a screenshot until we're logged in. So, you have to trust us that this works; give it a try to see what your login screen looks like. If you don't like it, you can always turn the screen off! (We did include some illustration of screens you use in setting up the graphical screen.)

You must log in as root to create a graphical login. You do not need to log in as root to use the graphical login; everyone with user accounts on your machine sees the graphical login screen after you set it up.

Here's how you set up a graphical login screen:

1. **Log in as root.**

   If you have to log out of your user account and back in as root, do so now.

2. **Open the KDE menu and choose Settings⇨Applications⇨ Login Manager.**

   The Login Manager screen ("KDM Configuration") appears, as seen in Figure 14-1.

3. **Click the Appearance tab.**

   This should be the default; if it isn't, just click it now.

   The Appearance tab contains a whole slew of options for you to choose from. You can decide whether to use a greeting message, a logo, or one of several "GUI styles" that set the overall look of the screen. Make your selections on this tab.

4. **Click the Fonts tab.**

   On this tab, you can select the font that you want to appear on your login screen. You can pick a larger font size because the size of the login screen doesn't change, no matter how small the font you select may be.

5. **Click the Background tab.**

   If you want a particular background on your login screen, you can select it on this tab. Select the Browse option to locate a particular background image file on your machine.

6. **Click the Users tab.**

   This tab enables you to enter certain users into a drop-down box on the login screen, saving those users the keystrokes of typing in their user IDs. (Users still have to type passwords by hand, though!)

7. **Click the Sessions tab.**

   On this tab, shown in Figure 14-2, you can identify the users who are allowed to issue shutdown and reboot commands directly from the login screen. Be very careful with this option; putting your own user ID here is usually okay, but don't give everyone on your system shutdown powers. You never know what your housemates may get up to.

8. **Click OK after you finish with all the tabs.**

   The Login Manager screen closes.

9. **To start graphical login mode, issue the command** init 5 **while you're logged in as root.**

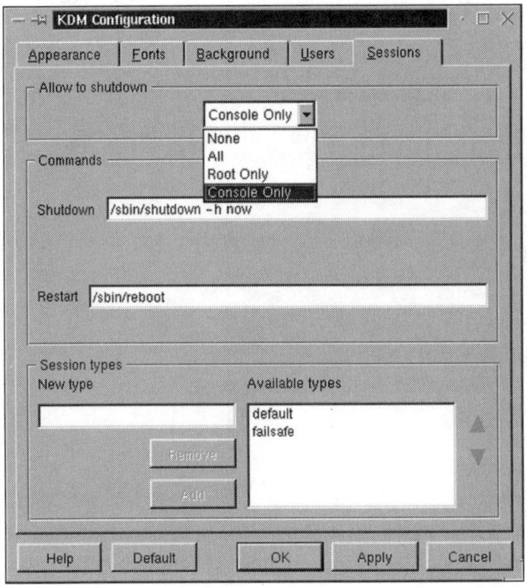

Figure 14-2:
Determine
who has
"The
Power" and
who doesn't
on the
Sessions
tab.

Do this in the same way you'd issue any command-line messages; open a terminal window and type init 5 at the prompt.

The next time you log out, the computer resets itself to graphical login mode and the login screen appears.

Using the graphical login screen means that you save a little bit of time during the login process. Because KDE continues to run in the background when you are in graphical login mode, you don't lose the time taken up by loading the desktop GUI each time someone logs in.

You may find that you simply don't like the graphical screen, or you may want to use your computer in text mode enough that the graphical screen is inconvenient. Luckily, turning off graphical login mode is as simple as turning it on. To return to text login mode, use these steps:

1. **Log in as root.**

2. **If you're in graphical mode, open a terminal window or exit to text mode.**

3. **Type** init 3 **at the command prompt.**

   You just changed run levels (see Chapter 13) from Run Level 5, which automatically starts the X Window System, to Run Level 3, which automatically starts in text mode.

4. **Log out of the root account.**

Should you ever want to return to the graphical login screen, just log in as root and type init 5 at the command prompt. This changes the run level back to Run Level 5 and enables the graphical login again. You can reconfigure its appearance in the Login Manager, as you did above.

Getting the Lowdown on Your System

As soon as you make the commitment to running Linux, you enter the world of information. You can find out anything you want to about your system, and getting to that information isn't usually a matter of navigating through many submenus to choose an oddly named tool. People who run Linux tend to be the sort of people who want all the information they can get about their systems anyway. As with many other things, KDE makes this easier for you by putting a lot of the tools you need right at your fingertips in the Control Center.

You don't have to be obsessive about monitoring your system. You have no reason to check each of these tools two or three times during the day. Do make a habit, though, of checking them regularly — maybe once every week or two, or more often if you know you've put a bit of stress on your system by downloading large files from the Internet or adding a lot of new software.

How much disk space do I have left?

Ah, probably the most frequently asked question in the computer world. How much disk space have I got left? Do I need to clean out some directories, stop automatically downloading Backstreet Boys fan fiction, change the cache size in Netscape, transfer my 3,000-page novel in progress to a Zip disk? Or, do I just need some sort of justification so that I can go to the computer store and pick up a new multi-gig hard drive? (Hey, take your excuses for new hardware where you can find them.)

To find out how much disk space you do have left for those high-resolution Ricky Martin pictures, use this process:

1. **Click the Control Center icon in the panel.**

2. **Choose Information⇨Block Devices.**

   The Block Devices window opens.

3. **Click the KDiskFree tab.**

   The KDiskFree window appears, as seen in Figure 14-3, showing each partition on your hard drive, its size, the amount of free space left, and how full it is (expressed as a percentage).

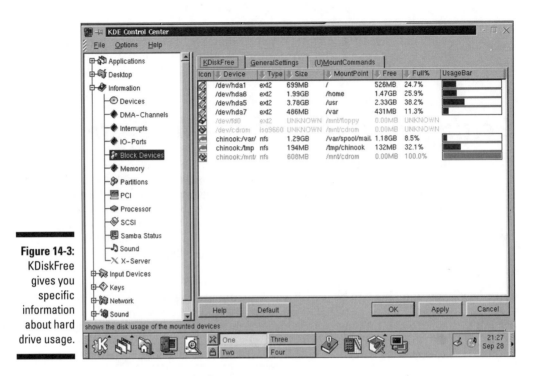

Figure 14-3:
KDiskFree
gives you
specific
information
about hard
drive usage.

4. **To change the information shown, click the General Settings tab.**

Here, you can control what information appears after you open KDiskFree and how often that information is updated.

KDiskFree opens by default whenever a partition becomes critically full. You can turn that behavior off on the General Settings tab, but please don't. The default is quite useful, especially if you don't realize you're putting such strain on your diskspace.

5. **Click OK after you finish looking at KDiskFree.**

The Block Devices screen is a useful feature to have around for information other than that in KDiskFree. You can use Block Devices to see what file systems are currently mounted, such as a CD-ROM drive, a floppy disk, or a network file system if you're networked.

You can use the Block Devices screen as a regular user in order to determine what's mounted. But, if you're logged in as root, you can also use Block Devices to mount and unmount disks and network partitions. See Figure 14-4 for a Block Devices screen accessed by the root account on a networked computer.

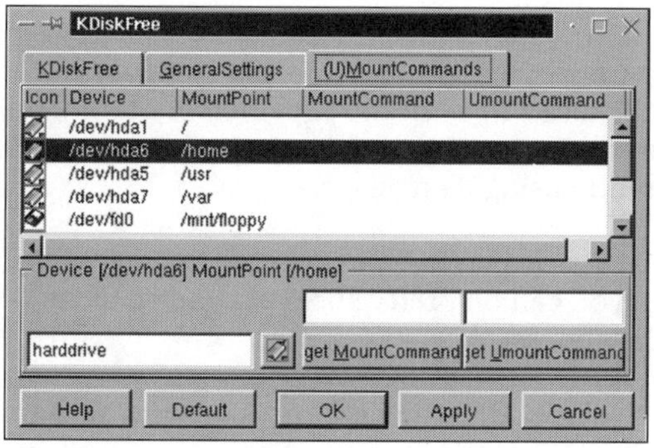

Figure 14-4:
Block
Devices is
even more
useful if
you're
logged in as
root.

You have no universal standard to judge how full your disk partitions should be. You may have perfectly good reasons for packing partitions as full as you can, or you may be the sort of person who gets antsy if you have less than 60 percent or 75 percent of disk space available. A good rule to follow is if you have to check to see if you have space available every single time you want to download something or add a new program, you probably need to clean out your hard drive.

With the price of drives dropping by the day, and the amount of space needed to hold most programs being released, hard drives that hold a gigabyte or more of information have become the new standard. You can blur the edges a bit if you use removable media such as Zip or Jaz drives, or even 1.44MB floppy disks, and Linux itself is simply smaller than Windows 95 or 98. Still, if you worry about disk space, invest a hundred bucks or so and pick up a larger hard drive. It's a hardware investment that's difficult to regret.

How much memory am I using?

Just like hard drive space, everyone wants to know about their computer's memory usage. Rightly so! Memory is the difference between a three-cylinder Geo Metro engine and the raw horsepower of a Lamborghini, all in the same machine case. If you ever wonder about your own memory use, let the KDE memory tools give you the answers.

Of course, you have the most basic memory tool at your disposal already. If the computer just seems sluggish, or if routine tasks are taking longer than usual, memory is probably the issue. If you ask your computer to perform more tasks than it has available memory to complete, it needs to swap out that precious memory space — and that takes time. The more you work with your computer, the easier it will be to sense a memory problem.

Just the facts

If you just want to know how your computer is using memory, use Control Center⇨Information⇨Memory to open the KDE Memory tool. The Memory screen, shown in Figure 14-5, gives you a variety of information about how your computer is currently using its memory.

If you see that you have little or no free memory, or that a lot of swap memory is being used, you can be pretty sure that you've located the source of your machine's sluggishness.

Swap memory isn't actually RAM. Rather, swap memory is an amount of space on your hard drive that you allocated when you set up Linux for the first time. If you ask your computer to perform an action that takes more memory than it has available, your computer will move some items from RAM onto the swap space on the hard drive, and exchange items between RAM and swap until the requested actions are completed. If your computer swaps a lot, you need to add RAM to reduce the system load.

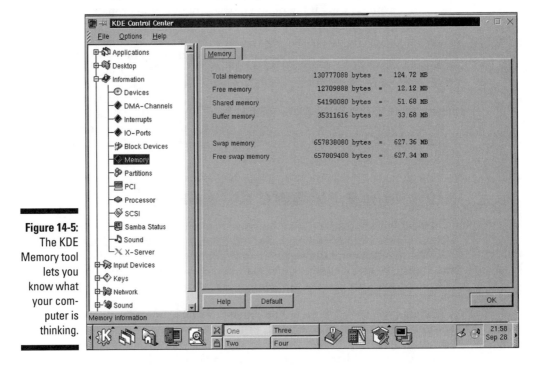

Figure 14-5:
The KDE Memory tool lets you know what your computer is thinking.

More information, please

So, you determine that your memory is indeed working overtime. What's causing the problem? It can be anything from too many programs open at one time, to a background process you didn't realize was running, to an otherwise innocuous program with a slow memory leak. To find the culprit, let the KDE Process Management tool tell you what's going on.

Open the KDE menu and select Utilities⇨Process Management to open the Process Management screen. In this window, like the window shown in Figure 14-6, you see a list of all the programs currently running on your machine — both system programs and programs you opened.

Next to each program listed, you see the percentage of system memory that program is currently using. If you have a program using an unusually large amount of memory, you may want to exit it. You can also close down other programs to give the memory hog more room in which to work, if you need the larger program open for a particular reason.

When you look at the process table, you notice that KDE itself uses a large chunk of memory for its various functions. This memory use is something you just have to accept; KDE uses quite a bit of memory to keep the graphical interface working seamlessly. This large memory use is probably the biggest drawback to graphic interfaces for Linux, because you have no way around the fact that graphics need memory.

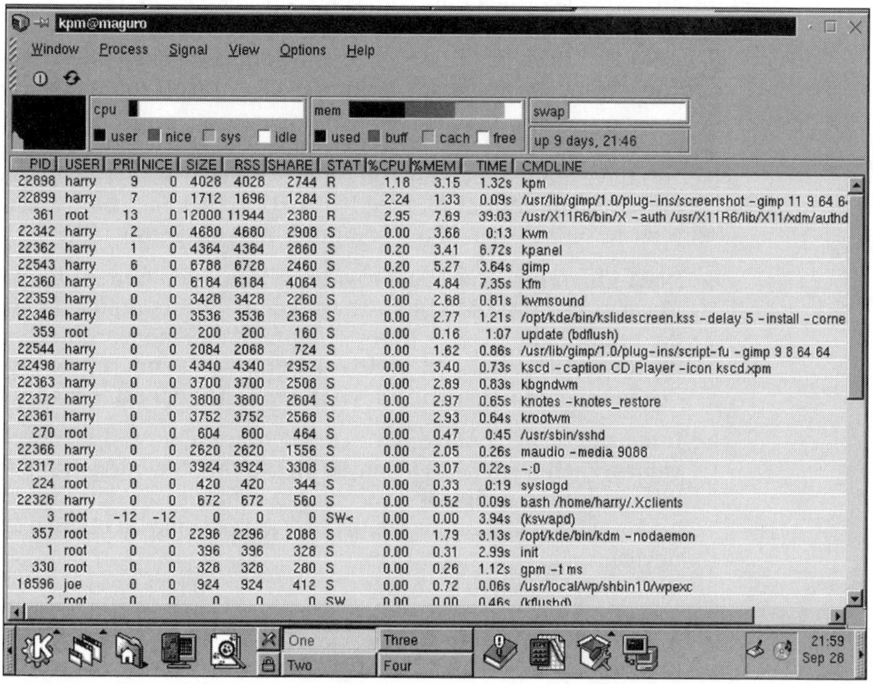

Figure 14-6:
Use Process Management to get useful details about memory usage.

So what do you do if you don't have enough memory to go around? First, find out what kind of memory your computer uses. You can find this out with a quick browse through the manufacturer documentation or Web site or with a not-so-quick call to customer service. Most memory is pretty cheap these days, if your machine takes a popular module such as SDRAM. For those of you with machines that are more finicky and require something slightly more obscure, such as 72-pin DRAM DIMMs, expect to pay a bit more — two or three dollars per megabyte, rather than a dollar.

Regardless of the price, a memory upgrade is one of the cheapest ways to spiff up your computer. You will definitely notice the difference in the performance of KDE and probably in your favorite applications as well. Working comfortably in simultaneous windows, while running KDE, is hard to imagine without at least 32 megabytes of RAM. Many folks insist that you can't run KDE and other programs with less than 96 or 128 megabytes of RAM. The exact number is quibble-worthy, but the point is clear: You work faster and your machine strains less if you add RAM.

What else can you tell me?

Several other information tools are in the Control Center, described in the following list. Taking a look at all of them is worthwhile. You can find out all sorts of details about your computer: where the interface to your hard drive is stored in the memory, what PCI devices you have installed already, and so on. Sure, you may think that you will never need this kind of information and that having specific tools dedicated to this information is a waste of resources, but trust us. There will come a time when you need to know, and you'll be glad of a specialized tool that will save you some time.

- **Devices:** The Devices tool tells you, perhaps obviously, what devices you have loaded on your computer. A device is anything that provides input or handles output (see I/O ports in this list), but is often used to refer to those parts of the computer that are removable and upgradable.

- **DMA-Channels:** This tool provides information about Direct Memory Access, or DMA. DMA helps to speed up your computer by permitting data to be sent directly to the computer's memory from an attached device (such as a CD-ROM drive). Because the microprocessor chip doesn't have to be involved, your computer operates more quickly.

- **Interrupts:** This tool helps you mind your IRQs, or Interrupt Request values. Each device has a unique IRQ so that the computer knows how to interpret various signals it receives as it processes data. You can cause huge snafus if you inadvertently assign the same IRQ to two different devices.

✔ **IO Ports:** IO ports, or Input/Output Ports, can cause quite a bit of hassle if you don't know which device uses which port. An I/O device is anything attached to your computer that either provides data to the computer, or handles data created by the computer: keyboards, monitors, scanners, and so on.

✔ **Partitions:** Don't know how your hard drive is partitioned? Check it here. (Partitions allow you to manage the space on your hard drive more efficiently.)

✔ **PCI:** What's occupying your PCI slots? (Knowing this information can be very handy if you're faced with a great deal on an eBay auction, but you're not quite sure if you have any available PCI slots for the new toy.)

✔ **Processor:** This tool gives you some extremely useful information about the processor on your motherboard. You can learn the type of processor, manufacturer, speed, and all the other information you need to get into a bragging war.

✔ **SCSI:** Got SCSI devices installed on your machine? Check 'em here.

✔ **Samba Stats:** If you're running Samba for your local network, you can check it out here. (Samba is a program that allows you to share files over a network with both Linux and Windows 95 or 98 computers.)

✔ **Sound:** This tool is currently not supported. In future releases of KDE, it will contain information about your sound card.

✔ **X Server:** For information about your X Window System server and useful if things go kablooey and you have to explain your set-up to someone who understands X. (And if you find that person, treat her nicely! Such people are worth a great deal).

Tweaking Your Keyboard and Mouse

True, most of us just plug in our input devices and go our merry ways. You can make your keyboard and mouse more responsive to your individual habits, though, with a few nifty KDE tools.

In the KDE Control Center, you find several keyboard tools that allow you to minimize the number of keystrokes it takes to perform a given action, to get your keyboard responding properly to the way you type, and to permit the use of non-English keyboards. Mouse tools let you set speed and responsiveness of the cursor. We also include a non-computer procedure in this section, so that you can keep your mouse clean and happy, thus avoiding one of the major reasons for mouse trouble.

The mysterious configuration file

Keep in mind that KDE, despite its many graphical features, is still just an overlay on top of Linux itself. After you click an icon on the KDE desktop, the computer interprets that click as an issued command — the same as if you typed the command at a text prompt. KDE gives you the option to use graphical tools instead of learning the text commands.

In the same way, if you use the Control Center to change your mouse's behavior or to set up a graphical login screen, you're really editing your configuration files. A *configuration file* is a text file, and you have several scattered throughout your directories that control different facets. (You sound "in the know" if you refer to them as config files.)

To see a sample configuration file, fire up KFM and open your home directory. Choose View⇨Show Hidden Files. Now, in the file listing, look for a file called .kderc. This file is the main config file for your personal KDE configuration for features such as icons, themes, global keys, and so on. Here's an excerpt from the .kderc file on one of the computers we used to write this book:

```
# KDE Config File
[KDE]
widgetStyle=Motif
macStyle=off
[Global Keys]
Kill window
    mode=CTRL+ALT+Escape
Pop-up system menu=ALT+F1
Window toggle sticky=
Window move=
Task manager=CTRL+Escape
```

The sample shows how we configure the basic appearance of KDE and a few global keystroke combinations.

You can find other personal configuration files in your .kde directory (be sure to include that leading dot). Config files for the whole system are located in various subdirectories under /opt/kde. (You may need to log in as root to view these.)

As a general rule, don't muck around in these files for fun, or you may find yourself unable to use your computer. Knowing that the files are there, however, is still good. Should it come to pass that something is so broken that a KDE Control Center tool can't fix it, or that your Control Center is somehow corrupted, you know where the config files are so that you can edit them by hand.

Typing up a storm

If a hundred chimpanzees with Smith-Corona manual typewriters may eventually compose *Hamlet,* just imagine what you can do with a streamlined and personalized keyboard! You can configure several things in the KDE Control Center, including custom keystroke combinations, keyboard layout, and basic settings to match your typing style.

The perfect (keystroke) combination

One of the more useful features you can do with your keyboard is to set up keystrokes, or combinations of keystrokes, that perform given functions. That is, you can assign a common action to a keystroke combination, rather than using a multi-click process to get the action completed.

You can see the standard keystroke combinations, already assigned by KDE, by choosing Control Center⇨Keys⇨Standard Keys. Don't duplicate these when you create your own!

To assign keystroke functions, choose Control Center⇨Keys⇨Global Keys. To give you an idea of how the process works, here's how to set up your keyboard to manage your virtual desktops (see Chapters 1 and 3 for more information on virtual desktops). In this example, you set the keystroke combination Ctrl+→ (Control plus right arrow) to move to the virtual desktop immediately to the right of the one you're now working on.

1. **Choose Control Center⇨Keys⇨Global Keys.**

   The Global Keys window appears, as seen in Figure 14-7.

2. **Select the Switch One Desktop to the Right option in the Action box.**

   The Action box is the area where you choose the action that you want to link to the keystroke sequence.

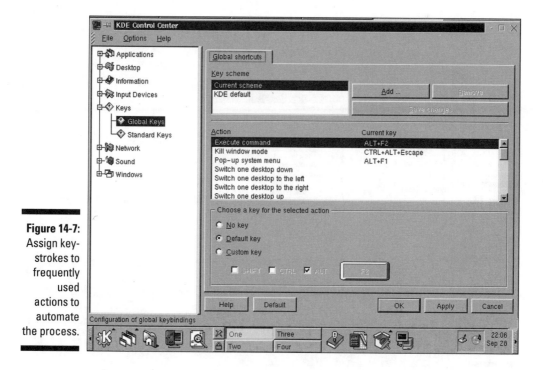

Figure 14-7: Assign keystrokes to frequently used actions to automate the process.

3. Click the Custom Key radio button.

With this button, you begin the process of defining which keys are to be associated with the action you choose.

4. Click the CTRL checkbox.

Here, you set the keystroke sequence to include the Control (or Ctrl) key. Using the Ctrl key is a good idea because it requires you to perform the keystroke sequence intentionally. If you assign actions to single keystrokes, you run the risk of setting off actions while you're typing normally when you really want to use the keys for their original purpose.

5. Click the rectangular box that looks like a key.

The key box is highlighted. The next key you press on the keyboard assigns the keystroke combination.

6. Press the right-arrow key on your keyboard.

The word Right appears in the key box, and Ctrl+Right appears in the key table above the key box. Your window looks like the one in Figure 14-8 after you complete the task sequence.

7. Click OK.

The Global Keys window closes, and your keystroke combination is complete. Now, each time you press the Control key and the right arrow key at the same time, your monitor shows the virtual desktop to the right.

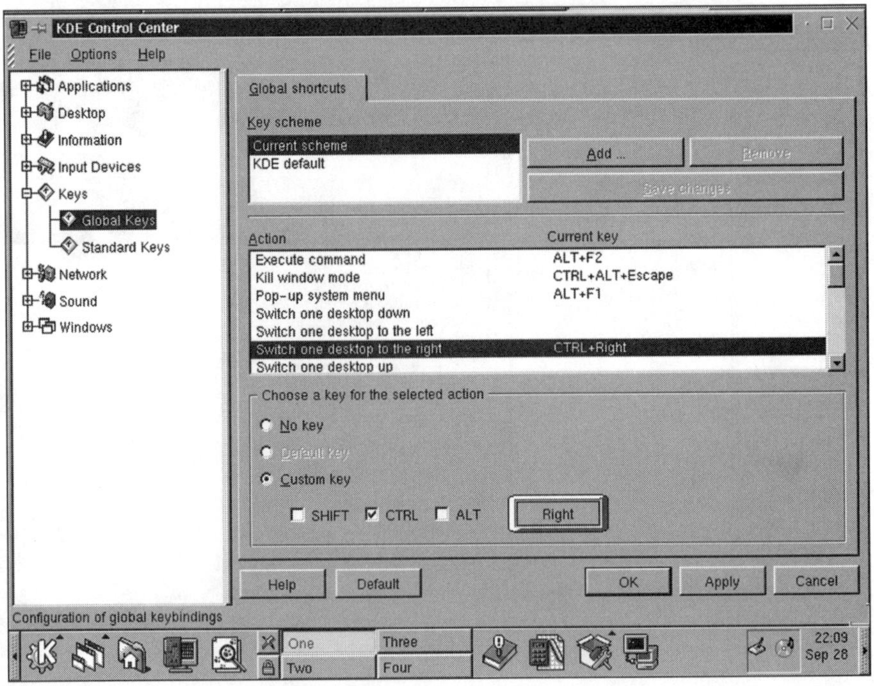

Figure 14-8: The Global Keys window looks like this after you finish assigning the keystroke combination.

Keystroke combinations are wonderful timesavers for frequently performed actions. You can easily go a little nuts with them and try to assign combinations to every action you may ever want to perform, but remembering just a couple of combinations is easier. Figure out what you do frequently that requires a lot of clicking or sequential menus, and assign those extra clicks to a keystroke combination.

You can always clear keystroke combinations by going back into Control Center⇨Keys⇨Global Keys and deleting that particular key association to the action. You may have chosen a key combo that isn't quite intuitive enough if you can never remember whether it's Ctrl+F3 or Ctrl+3.

Give your brain a hand if you construct keystroke combinations. Use combinations that make sense, rather than combinations that are built almost wholly at random. To use a familiar example, doesn't Ctrl+S for Save make more sense than Ctrl+9? Try to stick with combinations that use spatial or alphabetical triggers — psychologists say that such mnemonic devices make it easier for us to remember abstract information such as key combinations.

Your keyboard's a polyglot

Take a minute to think about this — not every language uses the same alphabet as English, right? How do you suppose people who write in other languages handle their keyboards? The trick is in keyboard layout configuration. You can find a keyboard suited to almost every language where computers are used; then, you just need to load the proper keyboard drivers into the system, and away you go.

If you want to use a keyboard different from the standard English keyboard used by Americans, Anglophone Canadians, and the rest of the English-speaking world, take a look at the list below. Given the international appeal of KDE, you'll likely find a keyboard layout right for you.

- ✔ Bulgarian
- ✔ Canadian French
- ✔ Croatian
- ✔ Czech — KDE provides drivers for three different Czech keyboard layouts.
- ✔ English (Dvorak layout) — The Dvorak layout is different from the standard QWERTY keyboard. Aficionados of Dvorak claim this layout increases typing speed and reduces error.
- ✔ European (Western)
- ✔ Finnish
- ✔ French (Switzerland)
- ✔ French
- ✔ German (Switzerland)

- German

- Greek — you can find two Greek keyboard layouts, one using the Hellenic alphabet and one using the Latin alphabet

- Hebrew

- Hungarian

- Icelandic

- Italian

- Lithuanian

- Norwegian

- Polish — you can find two Polish keyboard layouts available

- Romanian

- Russian — winning the multiple-layout prize with six, you can use a wide variety of Cyrillic or Latin alphabet keyboards

- Slovak

- Spanish (Latin America)

- Spanish (Spain)

- Swedish — two Swedish keyboard layouts available

- Thai

- Ukrainian — like Russian, multiple keyboard layouts for Ukrainian KDE users are available

To install a new keyboard layout, choose Control Center⇨Input Devices⇨ International Keyboard. Select the appropriate layout from the scrollbox, shown in Figure 14-9, and click OK. You need to shut down the computer, install the new keyboard, and reboot in order for the change to take effect.

It's in the way that you type it

Don't forget to make a couple of quick setting changes to match the way you like to type. These settings are personal choices; you may hate what we love, and vice versa.

1. **Choose Control Center⇨Input Devices⇨Keyboard.**

   The Keyboard Configuration screen appears, as seen in Figure 14-10.

2. **Click AutoRepeat on or off, according to preference.**

   AutoRepeat (Keyboard Repeat) determines what happens if you hold down one key for some time. If AutoRepeat is on and you hold down the N key, you see nnnnnnnnnnnn on the screen. If AutoRepeat is off, you can hold the N key down all day and you still only see n.

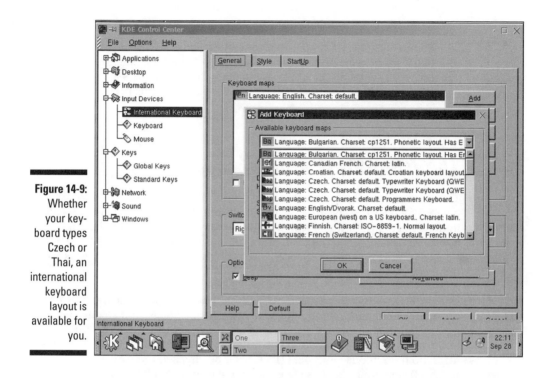

Figure 14-9:
Whether
your key-
board types
Czech or
Thai, an
international
keyboard
layout is
available for
you.

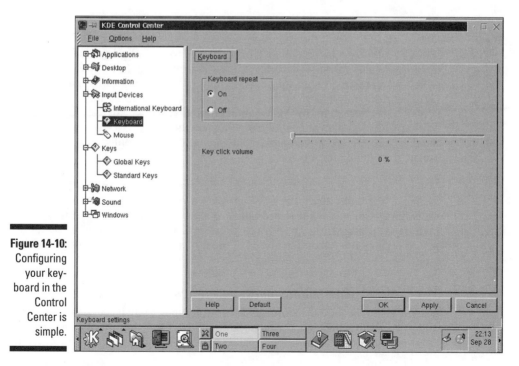

Figure 14-10:
Configuring
your key-
board in the
Control
Center is
simple.

3. **Set Key Click Volume to your preference.**

   Some folks really like to hear themselves clickety-clicking along. If you like that, turn on the key click to set the volume by gliding the slider button; you get a little chirp sound every time you press a key. If you think the physical sound of typing is enough, turn this preference off.

4. **Choose File⇨Exit to leave Control Center.**

The friendliest kind of mouse

The mouse — it seems indispensable, doesn't it? It's hard to imagine personal computing over the last 10 or 12 years without the mouse. The mouse is an integral part of both the Macintosh and Windows systems. Still, the mouse is a relative newcomer to the UNIX and UNIX-based world. In fact, running complicated and large Linux networks with nothing more than a keyboard is still quite common for many folks.

The problem with living mouselessly is that you have to remember all sorts of arcane commands, command syntax, specialized flags, and so on, which gets rather complicated. If you're the sort of person who chose KDE because it is graphical, then you'd not be very happy if we told you that from this day forth, no more mouse for you. (Heck, we'd be cheesed too! We like our mouses!) The mouse makes life easier, no matter what platform you're using.

You may not have a mouse. No, we're not thinking that you're some techie wizard who knows all the secret command-line words. Rather, we're thinking that you may be a gadgeteer. (It's okay. We are too.) A two-button mouse is so boring! Even a three-button mouse is still pretty standard these days, so what's a self-respecting gadget junkie to do? Well, you can investigate the fabulous world of input devices: trackballs, pen/tablet combinations, touchscreen pads, and so on. We're assuming that, if you have such a device, you have appropriate Linux drivers and you know how to use it. We can't guarantee that your device will be affected by any of the KDE configuration tools meant specifically for mouses.

KDE understands that most people are comfortable using the mouse to manage their computers. Back in Chapter 1, we described some basic mouse skills that we assume you already have, so we won't cover the basics here. Instead, we show you some ways to get your mouse up to top speed. Dealing with the mechanical complications of the mouse is frustrating enough without having to fight with its action on-screen as well!

Mechanical mouse maintenance, my my my

It's surprising how often people just throw mouses away if they start working oddly. Maybe it's because the devices are cheap enough to treat as a disposable, or because the users don't realize how easy it is to clean a mouse. While it may not seem directly relevant to KDE, mouse maintenance makes your life easier, and it's something that many people don't know how to do (you'll look like a genius at work). Here's how to give your mouse a bath:

1. **Turn the mouse facedown in your left hand.**

   If you're a leftie, reverse the directions.

2. **Turn the plastic ring around the trackball.**

   The ring usually turns about an eighth of the way and stops. Remove the ring after it is loose and place it on your desk.

3. **Tip the trackball carefully out into your right hand and place the trackball on the desk.**

   This keeps the trackball safe and clean. Inside the trackball cavity, you see several small plastic rollers, probably covered with dust mats.

4. **Dampen a cotton swab with some rubbing alcohol and clean the rollers carefully.**

   Get those dust mats out, as well as any other stray dust in the cavity. The dust is the cause of most malfunctioning mouses.

5. **Replace the trackball and the ring, locking the ring into place.**

   Your mouse should now be working correctly, saving you the cost of buying a new one. (Unless, of course, you want a new one. In that case, ignore this entire procedure.)

Mouse behavior: A controlled study

Now that your mouse is spiffy clean and rolling free, take a look at the software side of mouse maintenance and behavior. If you think you are stuck with the speed and configuration that shows up after you plug in your mouse, think again! KDE lets you set all those parameters to your individual taste, whether it's screamingly fast or deliberately paced.

To use the KDE mouse configuration tools, follow this procedure:

1. **Choose Control Center⇨Input Devices⇨Mouse.**

   The Mouse screen appears, as shown in Figure 14-11.

2. **Set the mouse acceleration speed with the Acceleration slider.**

   Acceleration is how fast the cursor on the screen moves, compared to how far you move the mouse physically. Some people prefer to make large gestures with the mouse, while others want hair-trigger response.

3. **Set the mouse threshold with the Threshold slider.**

   Threshold is how far you have to move the mouse before the acceleration kicks in. Over small areas of the screen (such as a slider bar), acceleration is at a minimum in order to allow you to use the mouse for precise work.

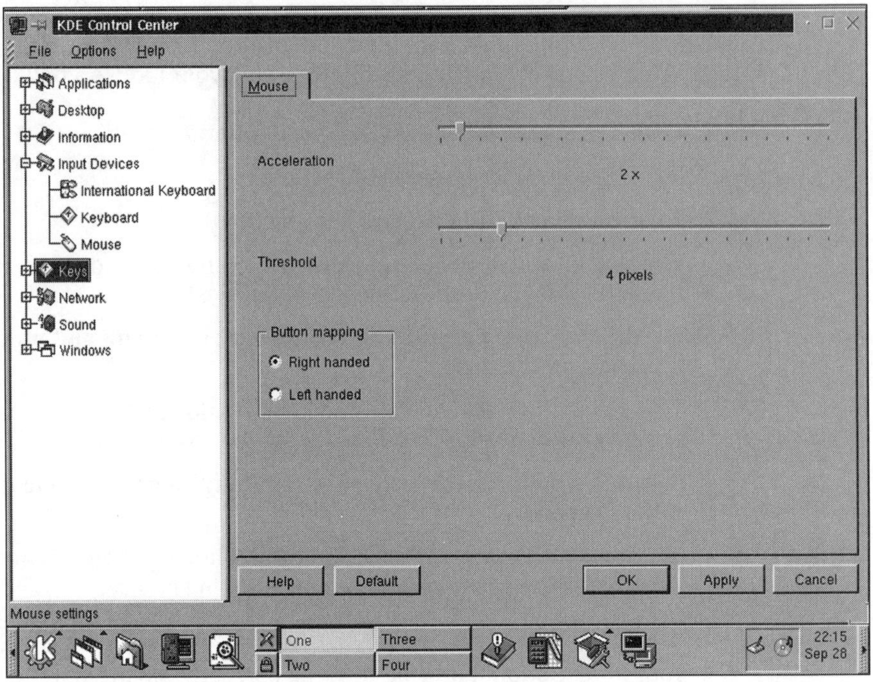

Figure 14-11:
Configure
your mouse
with the
KDE Mouse
tool.

4. **Select a mouse button configuration.**

Left handed? You can reverse the button configuration so that you can use the mouse easily with your left hand, and not have to think about which button to push in order to mimic righty clicks. If you select left-handed configuration, a left-handed left click functions as a right-handed right click, and vice versa.

5. **Click OK after you finish.**

You probably need to tinker a bit with the acceleration and threshold settings until you're happy with cursor speed. Just reopen the Mouse screen within the Control Center and change the setting.

Part V
The Part of Tens

The 5th Wave   By Rich Tennant

"Okay, Darryl, I think it's time to admit we didn't load the onboard mapping software correctly."

In this part . . .

Think of this part as the basic kit a cyber-pioneer takes along into the new worlds of Linux — a collection of highlights to consult for guidance as you begin your adventure. Here, gathered for your enlightenment and delight, are the ten things every new KDE user should know, ten friendly help providers, ten ways to have perfectly legal fun with KDE, and the ten great themes every KDE user should know about. (Gee. It's feeling more civilized around here already.)

Chapter 15

Ten Things I Wish Someone Had Told Us

As a KDE user, you'll want to look like a pro. So do this stuff.

Resolve to Increase Resolution

KDE is compatible with any video resolution supported by the combination of your graphics card, monitor, and X Window System drivers. However, although you can use KDE at 640 x 480 resolution, KDE really works best on a higher-resolution display.

To get the most from KDE, you need enough on-screen space available for the KDE panel and taskbar, plus room to spread out multiple windows. As a result, you'll probably be happier running KDE at 1024 x 768 or higher resolution, as shown in Figure 15-1. Of course, running KDE at this resolution requires a good-sized monitor (at least a 17-inch, preferably a 19-inch or larger) in order to produce text and icons of a legible size. If your video card and monitor won't support a high-resolution display, it may be time to consider an upgrade.

Figure 15-1:
KDE running
at 1024 x 768
resolution.

Many KDE dialog boxes and default windows are sized to fit comfortably on
the desktop when KDE is operating on a high-resolution monitor. Running KDE
at 640 x 480 or 800 x 600 resolution means that those dialog boxes and windows are too big to fit on the desktop (see Figure 15-2). As a result, some of
the options and buttons may be inaccessible unless you move the dialog box.

Of course, video resolution isn't something you can set or control from
within KDE. You need to configure X to run at the desired resolution before
starting KDE. You may need to use a utility such as Xconfigurator to change
your X settings. (Refer to a good book on Linux or X Window System for
instructions on configuring X.)

Most of the figures in this book were captured from a system running KDE at
800 x 600 resolution. We chose this resolution for its capability to produce
readable figures. Using this resolution isn't preferable if we are actually working with KDE.

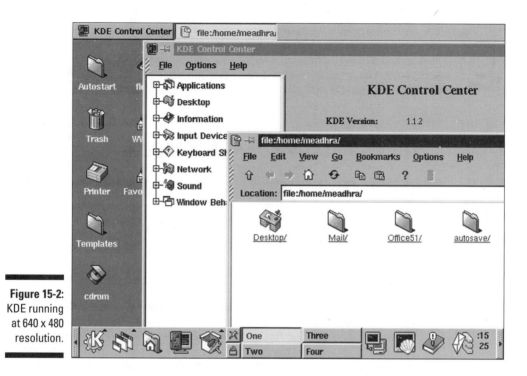

Figure 15-2:
KDE running
at 640 x 480
resolution.

Alt+drag to Move a Window

Normally, to move a window on the KDE desktop, you simply click and drag the window's titlebar with the mouse pointer. KDE deposits the window in its new location after you release the mouse button. But what if the window's titlebar is inaccessible — hidden behind the taskbar or panel, or the window extends off the desktop — how do you move the window if you can't drag the titlebar?

If a window's titlebar is inaccessible, you can press and hold the Alt key as you click and drag the mouse pointer anywhere on the window or dialog box you want to move. KDE moves the window, just as when you drag the titlebar. Release the mouse button to drop the window in a new location.

This technique comes in especially handy if you need to use KDE on a lower-resolution display such as a laptop computer. Some of the standard KDE windows and dialog boxes are too large to fit on the screen at lower resolutions and you must move the window or dialog box around to bring options and buttons in different areas into view.

You can use a similar technique to resize a window if the corner sizing handles are inaccessible. Press and hold the Alt key as you click the right mouse button and drag. The nearest window corner jumps to the pointer position and you can drag to move it to a new location. Release the mouse button to fix the window at its new size.

Quick Access to Web Addresses

If you want a quick way to open your browser and load a Web page for viewing, try this:

1. **Right-click the desktop and choose Execute Command from the pop-up menu that appears.**

   KDE opens the Command box.

2. **Type the Web page URL and press Enter.**

   KDE closes the Command box, opens your browser (usually KFM), and then loads and displays the Web page you requested. Of course, if the Web address is located beyond your local file system or network, you must have an Internet connection active or else have your system configured to automatically initiate a dial-up connection.

If the server name portion of your Web address starts with www, you can omit the http:// part of the URL.

Getting to the Root of the Matter

If you find yourself often needing to switch user modes between a regular user and the superuser after you perform command-line operations, you can appreciate the Konsole utility's Root Console feature. It's very useful for mounting CDs and floppy disks and other such tasks. To use the Root Console, follow these steps:

1. **Open Konsole. (Choose KDE Menu⇨Utilities⇨Konsole or click the Konsole button on the panel.)**

   KDE opens a Konsole terminal emulation window and the command line prompt appears. At this point you log on under your normal user name.

2. **Choose File⇨Root Console.**

   Konsole starts a second terminal session as the superuser, root, and prompts for your root password. The new session is running in the same Konsole window.

3. **Type the password for root and press Enter.**

   The shell prompt appears for root. You are logged on with full superuser privileges.

4. **Enter commands in the root console session.**

   You can mount file systems and perform other administrative tasks that require superuser access.

5. **If you need to switch back to normal user mode, choose Sessions⇨Konsole.**

   Konsole returns the normal user's terminal session to the Konsole window. You can interact with the system as a regular user. You can use the Sessions menu to switch back and forth between Konsole and Root Console as needed.

6. **After you finish working at the command line, click the Close button in the Konsole titlebar.**

   KDE closes the Konsole window and both terminal sessions.

Die, Window, Die!

Unlike some other very popular operating systems, where program crashes are a common occurrence, KDE programs don't crash or freeze very often. Still, a crash does happen occasionally. And when it does, it's good to have a way to clear the frozen window from your desktop without needing to shut down your system. You can use the following procedure to kill a window any time a program doesn't respond to the normal efforts to close its window.

1. **Press Ctrl+Alt+Esc.**

   The pointer changes to a skull and crossbones symbol — like the old-fashioned symbol for poison. That's appropriate because the pointer is now loaded with a poison that is lethal to program windows.

2. **Click the kill pointer on the offending window.**

   KDE closes the window and "kills" the associated program (or forces it to shut down).

This technique is deadly!!! Use it with care. This click of death is a way to deal with a broken program that has become unresponsive — Ctrl+Alt+Esc isn't a replacement for the Close button in the window's titlebar or other conventional techniques for properly exiting a program.

Pulling the Plug on X

On rare occasions, you may encounter a problem that causes KDE and your X Window System to stop responding. If you were using a different operating system, you'd probably have to power down and reboot your computer to recover from this kind of problem. But KDE users have a less drastic solution available:

1. **Press Ctrl+Alt+Backspace.**

   The system immediately halts your X Window System server. After X shuts down, you find yourself back at the login screen or command prompt.

2. **Log in normally at the graphical login screen or type** startx **at the command prompt to return to normal operations in KDE.**

This technique enables you to reboot your graphical user interface (X and KDE) without rebooting the underlying operating system (Linux/UNIX) or shutting down the computer hardware. As a result, you get back to work faster and you don't have to reset network connections, remount file systems, or disrupt other users who may be connected to your computer.

Taking the Shortcut Home

Although graphical user interfaces, such as KDE, are designed to enable you to make selections and issue commands by pointing and clicking with your mouse, keyboard shortcuts often come in handy. Here's one of the handiest — a keyboard shortcut for gaining access to your home directory with KFM:

1. **Press Alt+F2.**

   KDE opens the Command window.

2. **Type ~ (the tilde character) and press Enter.**

   KDE opens a KFM file manager window and displays the contents of your home directory.

Instant Access to the KDE Menu

Sometimes doing things with the keyboard is just easier than using a mouse. This is especially true if you're using a laptop computer and your mouse is really a touchy touch pad or one of those eraser-head-in-the-keyboard things. So, for those times that you're stuck using a laptop with an awkward pointing device, here are some tips for using the KDE menu to launch programs — and doing it *sans* mouse:

✔ Press Alt+F1 to open the KDE menu.

✔ Press the up and down arrow keys to move the highlight to the menu item you want.

✔ Press the right arrow key to open a submenu if the highlighted menu item has one.

✔ The up and down arrow keys work in the submenus, too.

✔ Press Enter to select the highlighted menu item, which is the equivalent of clicking the menu item to choose it. KDE launches the selected program.

What Desktop Am I Using?

Virtual desktops are a great innovation, but they can be confusing, too. Sometimes it's hard to tell which of the virtual desktops you're currently using.

Getting disoriented is particularly easy if you engage the magic borders feature, which enables you to switch desktops by simply moving the mouse pointer to the edge of the screen. Magic borders make switching desktops fast and easy — sometimes too easy. A slip of the mouse can switch desktops by accident. The switch happens in the blink of an eye. If KDE unexpectedly switches to an empty desktop, you may think the program windows you were using on the other desktop suddenly disappeared.

Of course, you can always tell which virtual desktop is active by checking the desktop pager buttons in the KDE panel. The button that looks depressed indicates the active desktop. To select a different desktop, simply click the corresponding pager button.

Another good way to help keep track of your virtual desktops is to color-code each desktop with a different background color or wallpaper. To configure your virtual desktops with distinctive colors, follow these steps:

1. **Right-click the desktop and choose Display Properties from the pop-up menu that appears.**

   KDE opens the Display Settings dialog box and displays the settings on the Background tab, as shown in Figure 15-3.

2. **Deselect the Common Background checkbox in the Desktop area.**

   This allows you to set separate background treatments for each of the virtual desktops. If the Common Background option is selected, all your virtual desktops will look the same.

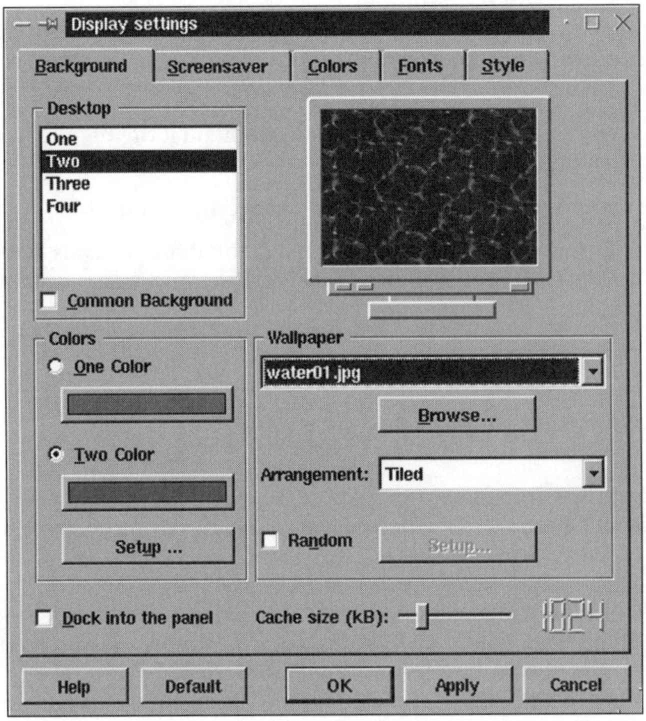

Figure 15-3:
You can
configure
each virtual
desktop
separately.

3. **Select a desktop name in the Desktop list box.**

   The remainder of the settings on the Background tab apply to the
   selected desktop.

4. **Adjust the settings in the Colors and Wallpaper areas as needed.**

   See Chapter 6 for more details on setting desktop colors and wallpaper.

5. **Repeat Steps 3 and 4 for each of the other virtual desktops.**

   The goal is to make it easy to identify which of your virtual desktops is
   active just by glancing at the desktop background, so pick colors or wallpapers that are distinctively different. No two virtual desktops should
   look the same.

6. **Click OK.**

   KDE closes the Desktop Settings dialog box and applies the settings to
   your desktops. Try paging through each of the virtual desktops to see
   the different backgrounds.

Capitalization Makes a BIG Difference

News flash: Linux and KDE filenames and path names are *case sensitive*!!!

This is no surprise to longtime Linux/UNIX users, but it may come as a shock to former Windows users.

Windows path names are *not* case sensitive. `Filename`, `FILENAME`, `FiLeNaMe`, and `filename` are all equivalent in Windows. To make matters worse, various Windows programs and utilities routinely change the capitalization of the file and directory names they display. As a result, most Windows users have developed a habit of ignoring capitalization in file and path names. That's a very bad habit for anyone using a UNIX-based computer!

You must pay attention to proper capitalization of file and path names. Unlike in Windows, `Filename`, `filename`, and `FILENAME` are three separate and distinct filenames in Linux. The names aren't equivalent at all. Therefore, if you need to find the file `Office51`, and you enter `office51` in the Named box of the Find Files utility, the program will not find the correct file.

Chapter 16

Ten Sources of Help

*U*nless you are some sort of KDE superhuman, you're probably going to have questions that aren't covered in this book. (Alas! It's true!) As mentioned frequently, KDE is an international volunteer project. That means that your best help is going to come from the same place that fostered the project in the first place: the Internet.

KDE help on the Internet comes in several flavors. You'll find a lot of good information collected on various Web pages, whether it's a formal help document or a collection of previous questions and answers on a given topic. You'll find talkative mailing lists, where users and developers chat via e-mail about their problems and neat ideas. You'll find newsgroups that talk about KDE, and you'll even find real-time chat on IRC. If you've found yourself interested in contributing to the project, there's help for you, too.

Jumping In with the Quick Start Guide

The Quick Start Guide is a Web resource that does exactly what its name implies. It's a very basic KDE introduction, which covers installation, window management, launching and using applications, configuring your desktop, and logging out. Fire up a Web browser or KFM and head over to

`www.kde.org/documentation/quickstart/index.html`

You should be aware that the Quick Start Guide uses the term *Application Starter* to refer to the button we call the *KDE menu* throughout this book. That's the term that KDE developers used a while back, which is when the Quick Start Guide was written. If the guide is revised when new versions are released, that term will likely change to something people actually use.

Although this book is more comprehensive than the Quick Start Guide, you may not always be able to lug a book around. Print out the Quick Start Guide and put it next to your terminal, or give it to a friend who may not be quite as convinced about the utter coolness of KDE as you are.

Using the User's Guide to KDE

If the Quick Start Guide is too basic for you, give the User's Guide to KDE a try. The User's Guide is written from, obviously, a user's perspective. The guide covers installation requirements, window and desktop management, some cool games and graphics viewers, and a few hints for better use of KDE. You can find it at the following address:

www.kde.org/documentation/userguide/index.html

Again, you'll find more detailed information in this book than you do in the User's Guide, but it's a helpful URL to keep bookmarked in case you have a quick question and don't want to flip through the book lest you be side-tracked by a funny cartoon.

Getting the Facts with the KDE FAQ

If you've spent much time on the Internet, you're probably familiar with the term *FAQ*. It stands for Frequently Asked Questions and is a compilation of the answers to questions that are asked, well, frequently. Finding and using the FAQ is a good first step for almost any problem you may need an answer to, and the KDE FAQ is no exception. Find the KDE FAQ here:

www.kde.org/documentation/faq/index.html

If you want to sound in the know when you're talking about FAQs, pronounce it *fack* instead of spelling it out as *eff-ay-cue*.

The KDE FAQ is the document that is updated most often of the three listed so far. The authors expect you to have a reasonably good understanding of your UNIX-based operating system, and the answers often send you off to work in a terminal window. Even if you're a die-hard non-techie, you'll find much of interest and help in the KDE FAQ, and the technical information will become easier to understand as you work more with your operating system.

Signing Up for the kde Mailing List

If you like to get a lot of e-mail about subjects that interest you, consider joining one of the many KDE mailing lists. The granddaddy of all is the kde mailing list. It's a general discussion list, which means that just about any KDE-related topic is fair game. Because there are specific lists for other KDE topics, you may be asked to post your questions to a more appropriate list. Still, the kde list is quite active; if you subscribe, expect to receive anywhere from 600 to 1,000 posts a month (an average of 20 or 30 a day).

Not familiar with lists? A *mailing list* is a way for all the people subscribed to that list to send e-mail to one central address. The computer at that address redistributes the messages to all the subscribers. It's good netiquette to stay quiet and just read the messages for a few days until you get a feel for the group.

Subscribe to the kde list by sending e-mail to the automated request handler software at the list's email server:

✔ Address your message to

kde-request@kde.org

✔ Leave the Subject line blank.

✔ Type the following line in the body of your message:

subscribe kde your-email-address

✔ Replace the term your-email-address with your actual e-mail address. Don't put anything else in the message; a computer is going to read it, not a person.

Finding Your Peers at kde-user

A mailing list populated mostly by users like you, the kde-user list is a good place to seek help from other folks using KDE. You may be able to get a simpler explanation of a troubling issue on kde-user than you would on the kde list or in the KDE FAQ. The main drawback of the kde-user mailing list is the volume of e-mail that it generates. In 1999, the list has averaged over 1,400 posts a month, or more than 40 a day. In some months, the list receives nearly 2,000 posts.

Subscribe to the kde-user list by sending e-mail to the automated request handler software at the list's e-mail server:

✔ Address your message to

kde-user-request@kde.org

✔ Leave the Subject line blank.

✔ Type the following line in the body of your message:

subscribe kde-user your-email-address

✔ Replace the term your-email-address with your actual e-mail address. Don't put anything else in the message; a computer is going to read it, not a person.

Getting the Headlines at kde-announce

You can subscribe to a mailing list that sends much, much less e-mail than either the kde list or kde-user. The kde-announce list is moderated, which means that only approved posts are sent to subscribers. The only messages that you receive from kde-announce are formal announcements from the KDE team. It's rare for a month to go by in which the list has received more than 60 messages.

Subscribe to the kde-announce list by sending e-mail to the automated request handler software at the list's email server:

✔ Address your message to

kde-announce-request@kde.org

✔ Leave the Subject line blank.

✔ Type the following line in the body of your message:

subscribe kde-announce your-email-address

✔ Replace the term your-email-address with your actual e-mail address. Don't put anything else in the message; a computer is going to read it, not a person.

Fighting Overload with the List Archives

Although mailing lists are fabulous ways to get information to a large number of people in a straightforward fashion, they can be problematic — especially for people who don't like to get a lot of e-mail or whose mailbox space is limited. There is a solution! All the KDE-related mailing lists are *archived*. This means that all the posts to those lists have been saved and are available to anyone who wants to read them. Find the KDE mailing list archives at this address:

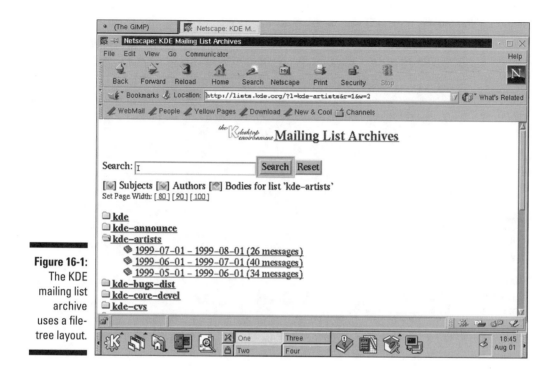

Figure 16-1:
The KDE
mailing list
archive
uses a file-
tree layout.

```
http://lists.kde.org
```

Select the file folder next to the list that you're interested in; the file tree expands and shows you a list of the posts archived by month. Pick a month and start reading. If you want to search, select a list and then enter the term you want to search for into the text box at the top of the page and click the Search button. Take a look at the archive layout as shown in Figure 16-1.

Protecting Yourself with Bug Reports

Sure, we can pretend that KDE is a perfect program — but who's ever heard of truly perfect software? Even the best programs have problems. For software that's in the early stages of its career, like KDE, those problems usually surface as *bugs,* or glitches that result from inadvertent programming mistakes.

KDE bug reports are archived at `http://bugs.kde.org`. A sample bug report is shown in Figure 16-2. Bugs are sorted into critical, grave, and normal categories. *Critical bugs* either prevent KDE from running or cause serious damage to your machine; *grave bugs* are serious but not as harmful; *normal bugs* are merely annoying. The bug report page also houses the *wishlist* items: things that users and developers would like to see in future releases.

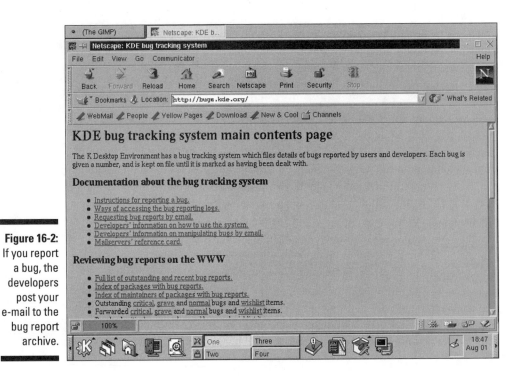

Figure 16-2:
If you report
a bug, the
developers
post your
e-mail to the
bug report
archive.

Checking Out comp.windows.x.kde

If you prefer newsgroups to e-mail or you want more interaction than a Web page can provide, there's the USENET newsgroup comp.windows.x.kde. Although most people using this newsgroup are KDE users, not developers, they can offer quick solutions to pressing problems. At the least, they can point you to other resources. It's a good place to start — especially if you're at a pretty basic level. Take a look at the message subjects for a random day in comp.windows.x.kde, as shown in Figure 16-3.

Most of the posts to comp.windows.x.kde (and, in fact, most posts to USENET groups regardless of hierarchy) are archived at www.deja.com. If you have a specific question and you'd like to see if it's been addressed somewhere on USENET, you can search the archives at Deja to find out.

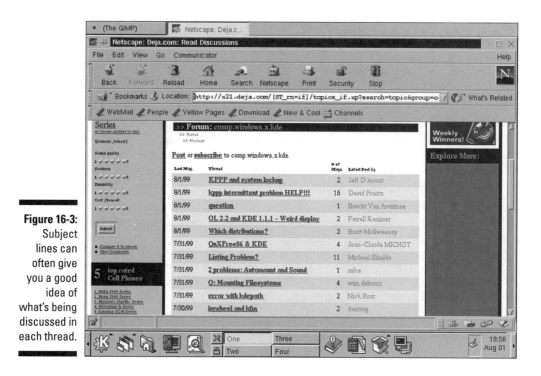

Figure 16-3:
Subject
lines can
often give
you a good
idea of
what's being
discussed in
each thread.

Hanging Out on #kde

Finally, if you like an equal part of chat with your technical discussion, join
the conversation at #kde, an IRC channel found regularly on various IRC networks. If you're looking for a server, try the following network home pages for
a list of available machines:

✔ EFnet is the oldest of the IRC networks. Find a list of EFnet servers here:

www.efnet.org

✔ IRCnet is mostly European. A list of servers is here:

www.ludd.luth.se/irc/servers.html

✔ Undernet is another of the major IRC nets. Its servers can be found here:

http://servers.undernet.org

Lending a Hand

Now that you have ten sources of help, here are two bonus resources that flow in the other direction. If you are interested in contributing to the KDE project, there are several other ways you can help.

- ✔ The KDE team welcomes contributions from programmers, artists, multi-lingual translators, and people with a variety of other skills. Start out by looking through the project list at www.kde.org/jobs.html. You can also browse the archives of some mailing lists that focus on particular aspects of the project: kde-artists, kde-look, or k-devel are good places to start.

- ✔ If you don't program or can't find something to do, but you still want to help, consider making a donation to defray some of the costs involved in keeping the KDE project going. The software will likely always be free and its code open source, but the Web site and hardware that support the development of KDE aren't free. You can find out more about this kind of assistance at www.kde.org/support.html.

Chapter 17

Ten Cool Toys

*N*ow that you've spent a lot of time setting up KDE, tweaking configurations, and doing a good chunk of work, it's time to play. (Yes, play! What good is a computer if it doesn't make you smile once in a while?) If you're not up for sharing your crayons, at least organize your work habits so that you have that time to goof off later.

One of the great things about using open source software is that many people concentrate their contributions on small programs. These programs can be games, information gatherers, helpers for your work habits, or themes for your desktop. Themes get their very own section of this book in Chapter 18, which focuses on the other small programs that make using KDE easy and fun.

The ten programs described in this chapter are included on the CD at the back of this book.

Because KDE itself is so new, third-party programs written for KDE are also new. Most of the programs described here, and those available in KDE file archives on the Internet, are *beta software*. This means that they may not work on your machine or that they may crash. As KDE grows more robust, so will the programs written for it.

KDE Keeps You Working

Use a few of the business-related KDE programs to automate things you do every day. You can save some time if you let your computer find certain information, and you can simplify a complicated process by installing a program that does only one thing — but does it well.

Here are five small work-related KDE programs to get you started. If you want to find more, look at some of the sites listed in Appendix B for programs released after the printing of this book.

WebMaker

Do you want to create good-looking and professional Web pages without having to code each and every HTML tag by hand? If so, you might benefit from a full-featured HTML editor like WebMaker. WebMaker has an attractive GUI interface and helps you keep track of your HTML tags with color coding and a nested layout. It previews all your image tags to make sure you're calling the right image file. Best of all, it's fully HTML 4.0-compliant, which means it meets the rigorous guidelines of the latest HTML standard.

Interested in WebMaker? There's more information at the program's Web page — created in WebMaker, of course:

```
www.services.ru:8101/linux/webmaker/
```

KStocks

A lot of investors like to keep right on top of their portfolio, checking stock prices and news throughout the day. KStocks brings some organization to that habit, letting you select up to 30 stocks to check at the same time. KStocks compares the stocks you enter against a Web stock ticker like the one offered by Yahoo!, imports the data, and displays it to you as a chart.

Learn more about KStocks and keep up with new versions at its home page:

```
http://mitglied.tripod.de/AndreasWuest/kstocks/indexstocks.
html
```

KPilot

If you're a techno-gadget kind of person, you probably carry a PalmPilot everywhere. However, you've probably noticed that Palm Desktop and HotSync software is primarily a Macintosh and Windows thing. No longer: Now there's KPilot. KPilot HotSyncs maintains your Palm Desktop calendar and contacts and runs under KDE. It even looks like Palm Desktop.

Be sure to check out the nifty animation on the first page of the KPilot Web site:

```
www.slac.com/pilone/kpilot_home/
```

Like all programs in active development, there are some things that KPilot doesn't quite have right yet. You may feel more comfortable using a development version with a personal Pilot, rather than a corporate palmtop. The developer lists all known bugs on the Web site; you can also download patches and updated versions there.

Kuickshow

Nothing is more frustrating than having a bunch of graphics files on your computer but not remembering what each file depicts. (Especially if you didn't give them clear names when they were saved!) Kuickshow is a handy utility that displays your graphics files. It has some basic graphic editing capabilities, its own file manager, and intelligent resizing for display. You can choose to show the files in a desktop window, or you can view them against a black background in full-screen mode.

Check out the Kuickshow Web page:

```
http://www.milleniumx.de/kuickshow.html
```

Empath

If you work with Microsoft products at your office or home (as well as at your Linux machine, of course), you may rely on Outlook to handle your e-mail. Empath is a fully configurable KDE program that handles your e-mail in a format just like the Outlook interface. You can change almost everything about Empath's appearance; you can have it run just the way you like.

The Empath home page is here:

```
http://without.netpedia.net/empath.html
```

Are We Having Fun Yet?

Whether it's because they're easier to write or because the world just needs to have more fun, entertainment programs are extremely popular among the KDE developer community. Here are five toys that will occupy your time in a most pleasant manner.

KVoicecontrol

If you're interested in speech-recognition software, whether for fun or for physical accessibility, KVoicecontrol allows you to try this powerful new interface on your KDE box. Attach a microphone to your machine, configure KVoicecontrol, and start talking. The current version supports only standard UNIX commands; with time, it may become robust enough to handle full speech input. For now, it's an interesting and different way to run your system.

To learn more about KVoicecontrol, visit its home page:

www.kiecza.de/daniel/kde/

KFortune

One of the traditional UNIX entertainment programs is a fortune-telling program. KFortune is the KDE version of fortune. Every time you run KFortune, it displays a random quote from its messages file. You can edit the messages file to include your favorite quotes, whether inspirational or just downright funny.

Visit the KFortune Web page:

www.fys.ruu.nl/~eendebak/kde/kfortune.html

Katchit

Do you like to play small games that don't take over your entire desktop? Do you enjoy chasing penguins? If you answer yes to either of those questions (if you answered yes to the second one, don't worry — we'll never tell), give Katchit a whirl. Katchit is a cute little game in which you have to reach Tux, the Linux penguin, before you're caught by whirling enemy beings. It requires the QwSpriteLibrary, which is also included on this book's CD.

Learn more about Katchit at its Web page:

http://perso.club-internet.fr/p_george/katchit.html

Kwintv

Is the multimedia content of the Internet just not enough sensory input for you? Do you long to watch television at the same time you're surfing the Web or playing video games? If so, Kwintv is your application, you multitasking genius.

If you have a TV card in your computer that's supported by a *video4linux* driver, you can run Kwintv, which places a small television window on your desktop and pipes TV straight into your computer. It also gives you an easy way to create screen and audio capture files. It even supports an infrared remote control if you install the right packages.

Learn more about Kwintv at its home page:

`www.mathematik.uni-kl.de/~wenk/kwintv/what.html`

KWebwatch

KWebwatch is a neat little utility that scans the Web for pages you've selected. When it finds that a page has updated, it moves that page to the top of its list and highlights it. Using KWebwatch means that you don't have to waste a lot of time reloading pages to see if anything has been changed since the last time you looked.

The KWebwatch Web page is found here:

`http://personal.atl.bellsouth.net/atl/s/h/shutton/`
`kwebwatch.html`

Tell the World that You Love a Dragon

The last item in this chapter isn't a program. In fact, it's not even something that you can load onto your computer. Instead, it's a way to show the world that you're a KDE fan. (It's also the only KDE-related thing in this book that you have to pay for, but it's so cool that we couldn't resist.)

What could this strange thing be? KDE clothing, of course. MieTerra has available two official KDE T-shirts at its online store (`www.mieterra.com/cgi-bin/store/web_store.cgi`). At the time this book was printed, each preshrunk 100% cotton shirt cost $14.99 U.S. plus shipping and handling.

The best part about buying a KDE shirt from MieTerra is that the company donates half the purchase price to the KDE project. Such a good deal: Get a great-looking shirt and support your favorite desktop at the same time!

Chapter 18

Ten Great Themes

*I*f you get in the mood to do a little redecorating in your home or office, you may start your project by perusing some magazines for ideas before heading out to the paint and wallpaper store for supplies. Without that advance preparation, the vast array of colors and decorating treatments that are available can easily overwhelm you. Similarly, this chapter provides a sampling of the many great KDE themes that you can find online (and on the CD included with this book), so that you can get an idea of the range of effects you can achieve by applying themes to your KDE desktop environment. Use the illustrations presented here to help you select a theme that you may want to use, or to get ideas for creating your own theme by combining elements from several themes.

All the themes shown in this chapter are available on the CD included with this book. You can also find all these themes, and many more besides, at the Themes.org Web site (`http://kde.themes.org`).

Are You Ready for the Arctic?

The Arctic theme (shown in Figure 18-1) features a cool, light blue color scheme and a full-sized photo of arctic scenery for your desktop wallpaper. The titlebar buttons exhibit clean, simple graphic designs, which contrast with the heavy snowcap effect of the top window orders. The overall effect is crisp, easy to read, and kind of soothing.

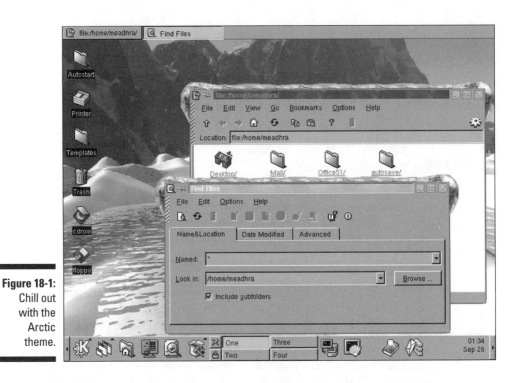

Figure 18-1:
Chill out
with the
Arctic
theme.

Paint Your Screen in Shades of Bluez

The Blue theme (shown in Figure 18-2) is named for its soothing, medium blue color scheme. The full-sized desktop wallpaper image seems to capture the trails of a swirling blue light. The window borders have a nice three-dimensional effect that is interesting without being too busy. The titlebar buttons look like LED lights over simple, easy-to-see symbols.

Figure 18-2:
Fight the
blues with
the Bluez
theme.

Grateful for the Dead (Theme)

The Dead theme (shown in Figure 18-3) tends toward the macabre with its heavy, dark gray color scheme, and red, dripping blood on the top edge of the panel and the active titlebar. The window borders and toolbar buttons are composed of bones. The wallpaper image depicts skeletons, barely visible in the darkness of a dungeon. This theme is designed to give you the creeps.

Figure 18-3:
Bones and
blood
dominate
the Dead
theme.

Getting Industrious

The Industrial theme's panel exhibits the distinctive black and yellow diagonal stripes that are so common in a factory setting. The theme (shown in Figure 18-4) features an interesting window border treatment and titlebar buttons that look as if they are stamped out of steel. You may expect a dark gray color scheme in this Industrial theme, but instead, the dominant color of the windows and the mottled background is a warm, reddish brown.

Mechanizing with the Mechanical Theme

The hallmarks of the Mechanical theme (shown in Figure 18-5) are its nicely executed charcoal gray color scheme and the wallpaper image by artist Neil Blevins depicting a futuristic factory scene. The text and active titlebar color are a light gray-green. The titlebar buttons have a stamped metal look and the window borders are thin, but functional.

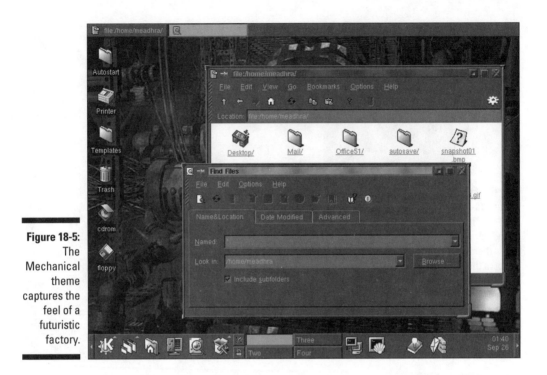

Figure 18-5:
The
Mechanical
theme
captures the
feel of a
futuristic
factory.

Giving Your Windows a Metal Edge

The Metal Edge theme (shown in Figure 18-6) gets its name from its window border treatment that simulates metal pipe or rounded metal edging. The dominant color in this theme is a teal blue that appears in the panel, windows, and in the mottled blue and green wallpaper. The stark white of the window background contrasts with the teal blue of the window surround, which gives this theme a crisp appearance.

Figure 18-6:
This edgy
theme is
named
Metal Edge.

Getting into Nature — Natural-E

Nature lovers are sure to appreciate the photo of a mountain stream that
serves as wallpaper in the Natural-E theme (shown in Figure 18-7).
Photographic images of rocks also show up in the window borders and
titlebars and as the background for the KDE panel. The theme's color
scheme is executed in shades of gray to blend with the rock images.

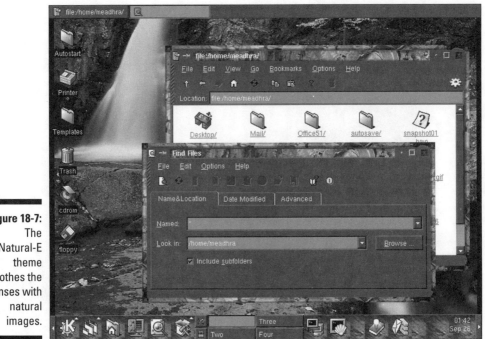

Figure 18-7:
The
Natural-E
theme
soothes the
senses with
natural
images.

Operating with the Operational Theme

The Operational theme (shown in Figure 18-8) is a study in simplicity. The light gray color scheme is almost the same as the KDE default color scheme, but a number of small touches set this theme apart from the default. The title-bars on inactive windows are the same light gray as the window surrounds, which makes the subtle monochromatic dot pattern in the active titlebar more than enough of a difference to mark the active window. The titlebar buttons feature simple, clean graphic symbols. The gradation in the panel background is a nice touch. The dark purples and grays of the abstract wallpaper pattern provide a contrasting background for the light gray foreground windows.

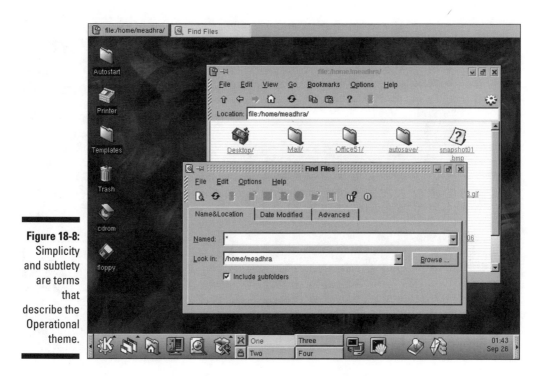

The Purple Tech Look of P-Tech

The P-Tech theme sports an unusual purple color scheme and window borders that are composed mostly of thin lines that are set off from the window just enough to allow a bit of background to show through. And what a background it is — mostly black with a large rendering of an evil-looking chrome, cyborg-like skull.

Figure 18-9:
The P in
P-Tech
stands for
purple.

Rippin with Rivenesque

Rivenesque is a richly textured theme with window borders and titlebar buttons that look as if they are made out of weathered bronze. The active titlebar looks like wood, and the inactive title bar and panel background both have a rough stone texture. The theme (shown in Figure 18-10) even includes a background image for the KFM window that is reminiscent of a dark stone wall carved with a Celtic pattern. The full-sized wallpaper image looks like an image out of a dark fantasy.

Figure 18-10:
You can
almost feel
the textures
of the
Rivenesque
theme.

Part VI
Appendixes

The 5th Wave   By Rich Tennant

"YOU KNOW KIDS — YOU CAN'T BUY THEM JUST ANY WEB AUTHORING SOFTWARE."

In this part . . .

Nobody knows what the human appendix was originally for, but there's no doubt what this one's for — hooking you up to more resources for making contact with the KDE/Linux community. Here you'll find tips on how to get hold of and install KDE, where to find more know-how and know-who on the Internet, and a catalog of the goodies you'll find on the CD-ROM that accompanies this book. With these resources and *KDE For Linux For Dummies,* you're ready to rock.

Appendix A

Getting and Installing KDE

• •

In This Appendix

▶ Getting the KDE software

▶ Finding the packages you need

▶ Installing KDE from a Red Hat RPM package

▶ Installing KDE from a Debian deb package

▶ Installing KDE from source code

• •

*T*his book was written under the assumption that KDE is already installed on your computer. However, this may not be the case for all readers. Some Linux distributions, such as Corel, install KDE as the default interface, while others do not. Red Hat, an extremely popular distribution, uses a different desktop system called GNOME. Other distributions install some variant of the basic X Windows System and use a window manager such as AfterStep or fwvm. Still other distributions install no windowing system at all.

In any case, you need to install KDE before you can use it. Fortunately, this is not very difficult. After all, you already installed Linux! Compared to that, installing KDE is a piece of cake.

Getting the Software

Obviously, you need to have the software in order to install it. The very easiest way to do that is to use the CD-ROM that came with this book; it contains both Red Hat RPM packages and the basic source code packages for KDE and its ancillary programs.

Although you see distribution-specific packaging like the Red Hat RPM or the Debian deb in many file archives, you aren't limited to Red Hat or Debian to use the software. Make sure that you download the *source code* version instead of a specific package if you run a different distribution. Source code can be identified by the file extensions .tgz or .tar.gz. Distribution-specific packaging makes life a little easier for folks running those distributions, but rest assured that you can always install from source code. We tell you how in this appendix.

If, for some reason, you don't have the CD that accompanied this book or you'd like to install a later version of KDE (the CD contains KDE 1.1.2), you need to start searching. Your Linux distribution is a good place to start. If you installed Linux from a CD-ROM, look at the package listings and see if the KDE packages you need are listed there. If not, fire up your Web browser.

The most obvious place to look on the Web is the home site of the KDE project: www.kde.org. From the main page, click Download. You are asked to select the mirror site that is geographically closest to you. (The KDE Web site and FTP archives get so much traffic that in order to lighten the load, there are site mirrors all over the world. The mirror sites have the exact same content as the main KDE site; you're not missing anything by downloading software from a kde.org mirror. In fact, you're probably speeding your download quite a bit.)

When you've connected to the site, you see a file directory. This is the top level of the KDE FTP archive, and it's shown in Figure A-1. Use the following procedure to download the required packages and any optional packages you want to install at the same time.

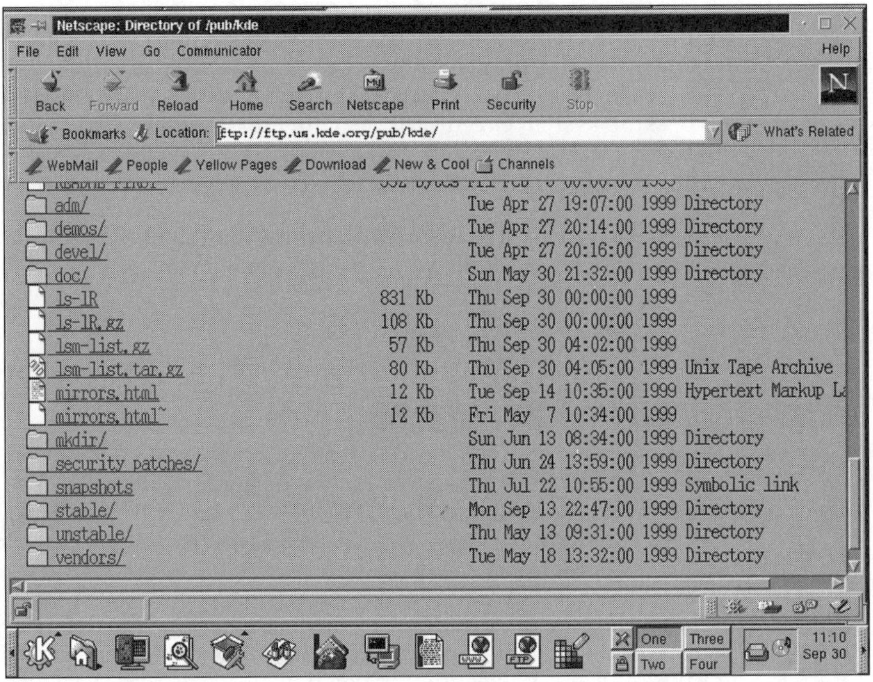

Figure A-1:
The entry screen for the KDE FTP archives.

1. **Click the file folder labeled** stable.

   The screen shifts to a view of the kde/stable directory. There are multiple subdirectories for the major releases of KDE in this directory. At the time of this writing, the most recent stable release was 1.1.2.

2. **Click the file folder for the distribution you want — probably the most recent.**

   The screen shifts to a view of the kde/stable/1.1.2 directory, shown in Figure A-2.

   The most recent stable release has the highest version number. This numbered list refers to that most recent version as 1.1.2, but releases may be well into the 2s by the time you pick up this book.

3. **Click the file folder labeled** distribution.

   The screen shifts to a view of the kde/stable/1.1.2/distribution directory. This directory, shown in Figure A-3, holds subdirectories for the major file types, as well as source code. If you prefer software packaged for your particular Linux distribution, open that subdirectory. It contains the same code as the other directories, but is packaged for ease of use with your distribution.

4. **Either find the packages appropriate to your Linux distribution or locate the source code versions.**

   Figure A-4 shows the complete directory of files you need to download.

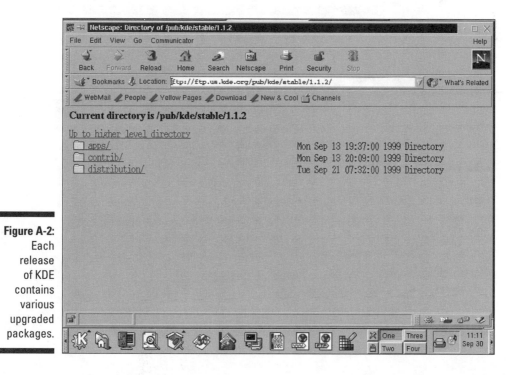

Figure A-2:
Each release of KDE contains various upgraded packages.

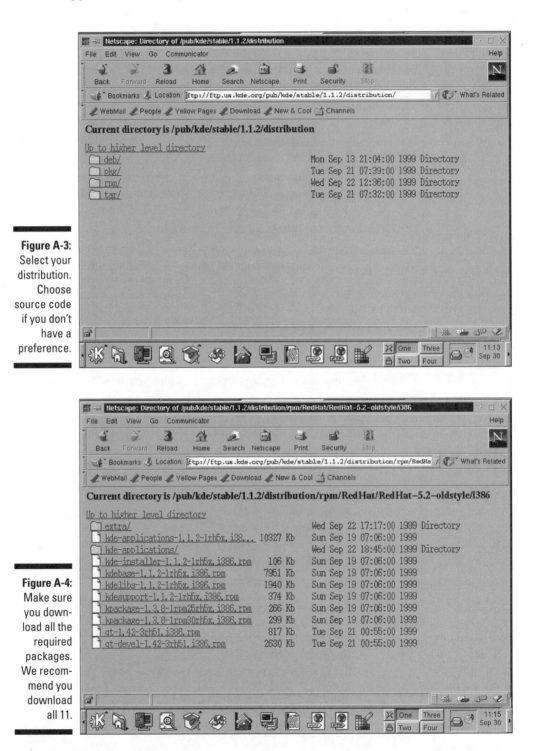

Figure A-3:
Select your
distribution.
Choose
source code
if you don't
have a
preference.

Figure A-4:
Make sure
you down-
load all the
required
packages.
We recom-
mend you
download
all 11.

5. **Download the files.**

   Use the process you're most comfortable with, whether that's Netscape's built-in downloading or a standard FTP program. A list of the packages follows; some you definitely need and some are optional. They are marked accordingly.

6. **After you've finished downloading, exit your browser or FTP program.**

Here are the 11 KDE packages:

✔ **kdebase (REQUIRED):** This package contains the main set of programs that form the KDE core. The window manager, the Control Center, the Panel, and other main functions are included in this package. Obviously, you need this package in order to do anything at all with KDE.

✔ **kdelibs (REQUIRED):** This package contains the library functions that were written especially for KDE. KDE will not function without these libraries.

Most software contains instructions that depend on certain standardized functions. These functions are contained in software *libraries*. All computers contain multiple libraries in their operating software.

✔ **kdesupport (RECOMMENDED):** This is a library package as well. It contains various libraries that are not exclusively part of KDE, but which KDE calls upon for various processes. If you already have these libraries on your system (look for libgif, libjpeg, libmime, libuu, and libgdbm), you do not need to download and install this package. If you're not sure, download and install. The worst thing that can happen is that you reinstall something you already had.

If you are running a Debian Linux distribution, you must install the kdesupport package. Debian does not utilize these libraries for its regular Linux operation, but you definitely need them for KDE.

✔ **kdenetwork (RECOMMENDED):** Although technically optional, all the Internet-related functions are in this package. The programs related to electronic mail, news, chat, and other network functions are contained in kdenetwork. Go ahead and install it. If you don't do it now, you'll just end up doing it later because you need to check your e-mail.

✔ **kdegraphics (RECOMMENDED):** This package contains programs that allow KDE to manage various kinds of graphic files, such as a PostScript viewer, a `.dvi` viewer, and a drawing program. These are all useful, and if you plan any work with graphics, you should probably have them installed.

✔ **kdeutils (RECOMMENDED):** This package contains some very useful things — various text editor programs and some other programs, such as a calculator or the KNotes utility.

- ✔ **kdemultimedia (RECOMMENDED):** In this package you find the various sound and multimedia-related applications. The sound utilities described in Chapter 11, such as Kscd, are in this package.

- ✔ **kdeadmin (RECOMMENDED):** These are the various system administration programs. More will be added to this package as KDE matures. It currently contains the user manager and the System V run level editor.

- ✔ **kdegames (RECOMMENDED):** If you want to play the games described at the end of Chapter 11, such as Asteroids or Mah-jongg, you need this package. Yes, it's optional on a purely technical level, but it's required for fun.

- ✔ **kdetoys (RECOMMENDED):** This package contains fun little surprises that don't do anything critical, but can get you to crack a smile on a bad day. For example, this package contains Mouspedometa, which is basically an odometer for your mouse. Odd, but funny.

- ✔ **kOrganizer (OPTIONAL):** If you want to take advantage of the KOrganizer, as described in Chapter 10, you need to install this package.

By now, you've probably figured out that the authors of this book think it's best to install everything at once. That way, you can work through the book at your own pace, but you won't ever have to delay trying something out until you find and install the requisite package.

Installing the Software

Now that you've downloaded all the packages, you can begin installing them. This section contains instructions for installing Red Hat .rpm files, Debian .deb packages, and straight source code.

Install kdesupport first, if you need it; then install kdelibs. You can install the remaining packages in any order, but they require functions from the libraries contained in the first two packages.

Installing KDE on a Red Hat Linux system

In order to install Red Hat RPM packages, you should run Red Hat Linux. Other distributions may have a utility that permits use of .rpm files, but when you're installing software that affects your operating system, it's best to be safe. Use the procedure described in this section to install KDE to a Red Hat system.

In order to install packages on a Red Hat Linux system, you need to be root. If you're logged into a user account, you need to log out and log again as root. You also need to be at a command prompt; if you're in some sort of windowed system, you need to either exit to a command prompt, or open a terminal window.

1. **At the command prompt, type the following command:**

   ```
   rpm -ivh <packagename>.rpm
   ```

   The v and h flags are optional, but they give you some visual feedback that lets you keep track of how your installation is going.

2. **Repeat the command for each package you want to install.**

3. **Log out of the root account.**

4. **Log back in to your user account.**

5. **Type** usekde **at the command prompt.**

   A couple of system messages show up on your screen while your computer sets KDE as your default user interface. As soon as the messages stop, you're ready to test.

6. **Type** startx **to start the X Window System.**

   If you're already running X Windows for some reason, shut it down and restart it.

   If KDE opens, you've successfully installed it! Congratulations!

If KDE is not running, something went wrong during the installation. Try reinstalling, following this procedure to the letter. If it still fails, go back a step, redownload the packages, and reinstall. If that doesn't work, consult Chapter 16 for more advanced sources of help.

Installing KDE on a Debian Linux system

Debian packages install according to the FHS, or File Hierarchy Standard.

As with Red Hat, Debian installations require that you work from a command line and that you be logged in as root. If you are currently logged into a user account, log out and back in again with your root password.

1. **At the command prompt, type the following command:**

   ```
   dpkg -i <packagename>.deb
   ```

2. **Repeat the command for each package you want to install.**

3. **Log out of the root account.**

4. **Log back into your user account.**

5. **Type** `usekde` **at the command prompt.**

   A couple of system messages appear on your screen while your computer sets KDE as your default user interface. When the messages stop, you're ready to test.

6. **Type** `startx` **to start the X Window System.**

   If you're already running X Windows for some reason, shut it down and restart it.

   If KDE opens, you've successfully installed it! Congratulations!

If KDE is not running, something went wrong during the installation. Try reinstalling, following this procedure to the letter. If it still fails, go back a step, redownload the packages, and reinstall. If that doesn't work, consult Chapter 16 for more advanced sources of help.

Installing KDE from source code

Installing KDE from source code is a bit more involved, but it's not at all difficult. In fact, you will probably find it helpful to understand how to install programs from source code packages. There will not necessarily be a specialized distribution-specific package for whatever distribution you use, for whatever program you want. Learning to install from source code means that you will always have the ability to get the software onto your computer from the basic format.

As Martha Stewart would say, "It's a good thing."

The process of installing from source code is a three-parter. First, unpack the source files; second, install them; third, start KDE. Follow along with the sequence given here to get KDE installed in a jiffy.

You need to be at a command-line prompt to use this method. If you're logged in to a window manager or another desktop program, exit it and work in regular text mode. You need to be logged in as root, so exit any user account you're using now and log in again as root.

1. **Locate the KDE packages you downloaded.**

   If you made a note of the location when you downloaded, good for you. You may also want to establish the habit of always downloading into the same directory, perhaps using the ingenious directory name of `download`. (If you upload a lot of files, you may want to create a sister directory called `upload` as the natural home for those items.)

2. **Move the package files into an appropriate directory.**

   The choice is yours, but common places for this are either `/tmp` or `/usr/src`.

3. **Type** `tar xvfz kdesupport.tgz` **at the prompt.**

   You must install the kdesupport package first in order to install libraries needed by future packages.

   When you use the `tar` command with the `xvfz` flags, you're decompressing the files. Source files usually come in compressed formats so that they take up less space during download and on the FTP server.

   The package creates its own subdirectory with the same name as the package: in this case, the subdirectory `kdesupport`.

4. **Type** `tar xvfz kdelibs.tgz` **at the prompt.**

   This unpacks the kdelibs libraries package and creates a kdelibs subdirectory.

5. **Continue to unpack the source packages with the command** `tar xvfz <packagename>.tgz`.

6. **Move into the subdirectory housing the kdesupport package.**

   To change directories, type `cd <packagename>`.

7. **Configure kdesupport by typing** `./configure` **at the prompt.**

8. **Type** `make` **at the prompt.**

   `make` is the main command that starts the compiler and builds the binary package. Many messages scroll up your screen as you do this; this is just the compiler letting you know what it's doing. You won't need to worry about this unless you get a rare error message.

   If you get an error message, read it. It will often alert you to what you need to do.

9. **Type** `make install` **at the prompt.**

   This command moves the binary packages into their new and proper directories.

10. **Return to the previous level of directories by typing** `cd ..` **at the prompt.**

11. **Move into the** `kdelibs` **subdirectory by typing** `cd kdelibs`.

12. **Configure kdelibs by typing** `./configure` **at the prompt.**

13. **Type** `make` **at the prompt.**

14. **Type** `make install` **at the prompt.**

    This command moves the binary packages into their new and proper directories.

15. **Return to the previous level of directories by typing** `cd ..` **at the prompt.**

16. **Move into the subdirectory housing the kdebase package by typing** `cd kdebase`.

17. **Learn about kdebase's options by typing** `./configure — help` **at the prompt.**

    The kdebase package has some special configuration options that may be applicable to your installation. When you've determined what options you want to use, move to the next step.

18. **Configure kdebase by typing** `./configure` **at the prompt.**

19. **Type** `make` **at the prompt.**

20. **Type** `make install` **at the prompt.**

21. **Return to the previous level of directories by typing** `cd ..` **at the prompt.**

22. **Use the same procedure for each of the recommended, but optional, packages that you want to install.**

23. **Change into the subdirectory containing the package by using** `cd <subdirectory-name>`.

24. **Configure the package by typing** `./configure` **at the prompt.**

    Check with `./configure — help` to see if there are special options for your particular installation.

25. **Type** `make` **at the prompt.**

26. **Type** `make install` **at the prompt.**

27. **Return to the previous level of directories by typing** `cd ..` **at the prompt.**

28. **Log out of the root account.**

29. **Log back in to your user account.**

30. **Type** `usekde` **at the command prompt.**

    There are a couple of system messages on your screen while your computer sets KDE as your default user interface. When the messages stop, you're ready to test.

31. **Type** `startx` **to start the X Window System.**

    If you're already running X Windows for some reason, shut it down and restart it.

    If KDE opens, you've successfully installed it! Congratulations!

If KDE is not running, something went wrong during the installation. Try reinstalling, following this procedure to the letter. If it still fails, go back a step, redownload the packages, and reinstall. If that doesn't work, consult Chapter 16 for more advanced sources of help.

Appendix B

Finding More Stuff on the Net

● ●

In This Appendix

▶ A guided tour of the official KDE Web site

▶ How to get non-English-speaking friends interested in KDE

▶ Lots and lots of programs for your KDE machine

▶ Where to go when you want to say what's on your mind

● ●

*A*fter you have the hang of KDE, you'll probably want to find more programs and additional general information. Like the help resources described in Chapter 16, almost all KDE information and resources are on the Web, due to the nature of the project.

You can find a great deal of help at the main KDE Web page, but there is also ample information available in languages other than English, as well as active Web discussion boards. Program archives have popped up in several places as well, so that you have several choices for downloading new gadgets or useful patches. We also point you to some resources for folks interested in becoming KDE developers, and where you may find the latest contributions.

Home Sweet Home: www.kde.org

The definitive online resource for KDE is the KDE project home page at www.kde.org. The Webmasters try to keep links updated, manage a busy FTP site, and provide news to the KDE community. Plus, it's overseen by a cute little dragon!

If you could have only one

If you don't have a lot of time, you can get the latest KDE information just by hitting the main page. A list of news updates is at the bottom of the page and links to the FAQ, the download area, and the dynamic news page are in a clickable bar at the top of the page. (If you really don't have a lot of time, install KWebwatch, described in Chapter 17 and included on this book's CD. You can set KWebwatch to notify you when the KDE home page is updated.)

Download commencing in 5. . .4. . .3. . .2. . .

Of course you want to download stuff. The KDE FTP site holds all programs that have been formally submitted to the KDE project. When you go to the FTP site at ftp://ftp.kde.org, you'll see the traditional file folder organization. Search for programs in either the stable or unstable folder.

Stability is determined by the program's author, not by the KDE project. A *stable program* is one the author claims works and installs well with KDE 1.0 (or any KDE 1.* release). An *unstable program,* which is usually a beta version, may not work well or may crash KDE. Then again, it may not. You must decide whether to take that risk. (Note that files in the stable directory are not guaranteed against crashing.)

Getting your news fix

In need of the latest KDE news? Head to www.kde.org/news_dyn.html or just click one of the News links on the main KDE page. The news is archived by month; each month's updates are on one page, so you can scroll through 30 days of information with one click.

One really useful touch is that the news wranglers post regular updates on new programs and applications that have been submitted to the download archives. You can also read updates on new releases of KDE itself, notices of awards, links to articles about KDE, and information about new books — like this one! If you have a news item to submit, e-mail it to the Webmaster.

Como se Dice KDE in Italiano?

Because KDE is an international project, it's not too surprising that KDE documentation is available in many languages. We provide links to some non-English Web pages that are recommended by other KDE users. (You may need to install certain fonts in order to view pages written in non-Roman characters.) The home for non-English information is www.kde.org/international. Table B-1 lists the URLs for KDE resources in languages other than English.

Do you speak English, another language, and KDE? If so, consider volunteering your expertise as a KDE project translator. Program documentation, general information, and news items all need translation into as many languages as possible, so that the reach KDE has is as global as are its users.

Table B-1	KDE Resources in Languages Other Than English
Language	**URL**
Chinese	http://mis.im.tku.edu.tw/~zbwei12b/kde/
Dutch	www.kde.nl/index.html
French	www.etu.info.unicaen.fr/~gduval/kde/index.shtml
German	www.kde.org/international/germany/index.html
Greek	http://users.hol.gr/~vrypan/cactus/kde.html
Italian	www.kde.org/international/italy/index.html
Japanese	www.tky.threewebnet.or.jp/~hmr/kde/
Polish	http://kde.fnet.com.pl/pl/
Portuguese	http://camoes.rnl.ist.utl.pt/~pmmm/kde
Russian	www.kde.org/international/russia/index.html
Slovakian	www.kde.org/international/slovakia/index.html

Treasures Waiting to Be Found

The KDE site is not the only place you can find new applications or upgrades of your KDE package. Most of the major Linux download sites now have areas for KDE programs, and some even have areas devoted to KDE themes.

freshmeat.net

When you're looking for Linux software, the best place to start your search is at Freshmeat, which you can find at www.freshmeat.net.

Freshmeat is the most popular repository for Linux programs on the Web. To narrow the archives to KDE-specific programs, just type **KDE** into the search box at the top of the home page and click Search.

linuxberg.com

Linuxberg is the Linux side of the most popular Windows software archive, Tucows. Find Linuxberg and its chilly penguins at www.linuxberg.com.

After you select your geographic region (to speed download times), you see the Linuxberg home page. Wander through the site, search for KDE programs, or look for packages that match your Linux distribution. Linuxberg even offers a full array of KDE themes, with subjects ranging from religious topics to military scenes. After you begin downloading, you'll find that it is faster than downloading from sites that use a single machine.

kde.tdyc.com

Looking for a KDE program packaged specifically for a Red Hat or Linux machine? Head to the KDE Linux Packaging Project at http://kde.tdyc.com.

The Packaging Project takes the files uploaded to various KDE file archives and reformats them. The result is a collection of KDE programs compressed in the formats most easily installed by Red Hat (.rpm) and Debian (.deb). This is a good place to look if you're having trouble installing a program that's not specifically packaged for your system.

kde.themes.org

This site contains nothing but KDE themes. You can find news about KDE themes, and the themes themselves at http://kde.themes.org.

If you make a theme you really like and want to share, upload it so that others can join in and use your creative idea. You can view screenshots from any of the themes before you begin to download; there's also an extensive how-to page, which includes a couple of automatic theme installation scripts.

Self-Proclaimed News for Nerds

The main source for Linux and Linux-related conversation on the Web is Slashdot, which you can find at www.slashdot.org. Any discussion about KDE on the Net is going to find its way to Slashdot sooner or later.

You don't have to be a geek to read Slashdot, but it helps. The volume of messages can be overwhelming; pick and choose what you want to read.

Appendix C

What's on the CD-ROM

In This Appendix

▶ Hardware you need

▶ Software you want

▶ Guidance you can't live without

*B*ecause we're such helpful folks, here's a little dog-and-pony show to tell you about that flying-saucer thingy at the back of the book. Enjoy!

System Requirements

Make sure your computer meets the minimum system requirements listed below.

- ✔ A PC with a 486 or faster processor.
- ✔ A working installation of Linux.
- ✔ A working installation of X Window System (this may have been installed when you installed Linux).
- ✔ At least 16MB of total RAM installed on your computer.

Because KDE is a graphical interface, it will work much better the more RAM you have installed, and the better chip you have. A Pentium, Pentium-II, or PentiumPro class processor with 64MB of RAM or more will work much better than the minimum requirements outlined above.

- ✔ At least 150MB of hard drive space available to install all the software from this CD.

You'll need less hard drive space if you don't install every program.

- ✔ A CD-ROM drive — double-speed (2x) or faster.
- ✔ A sound card.
- ✔ A monitor capable of displaying at least 256 colors or grayscale.

If you need more information on the basics, check out *PCs For Dummies,* 7th Edition, by Dan Gookin (IDG Books Worldwide, Inc.).

For more basic Linux information, you can also check out *Linux For Dummies,* 2nd Edition, by Jon "Maddog" Hall (IDG Books Worldwide, Inc.).

If your computer doesn't match up to most of these requirements, you may have problems in using the contents of the CD.

How to Use the CD

To install KDE or the other software on this CD, you will need to mount the CD-ROM drive. The installation process for KDE itself is described in Appendix A. To install the programs on this disk, use the following process and the information in Appendix A as complementary references.

General installation from source code

1. **Insert the CD-ROM into your computer's CD-ROM drive.**

2. **Make sure you are logged in as root.**

   If you are not logged in as root, you may log out of your user account and log back in as root, or use the Kfm superuser method described in Part IV.

3. **As root, issue the command** `mount -t iso9960 /dev/cdrom /mnt/cdrom`.

   This command mounts the CD-ROM drive, giving you access to the files on the book's CD.

4. **Issue the command** `mkdir /usr/src/KDE`.

   This command creates a new directory for your source code packages.

5. **Issue the command** `cp /mnt/cdrom/TGZ/* /usr/src/KDE`.

   This command copies the files from the CD-ROM drive to the directory you created in Step 4.

6. **Use the procedure in Appendix A to install the packages.**

Installation from .rpm (Red Hat and compatible distributions)

If your Linux distribution is either a Red Hat Linux distribution or uses the Red Hat .rpm packaging standard, you may use this process instead of the source code process described above.

1. **Insert the CD-ROM into your computer's CD-ROM drive.**

2. **Make sure you are logged in as root.**

   If you are not logged in as root, you may log out of your user account and log back in as root, or use the Kfm superuser method described in Part IV.

3. **As root, issue the command** mount -t iso9960 /dev/cdrom /mnt/cdrom.

   This command mounts the CD-ROM drive, giving you access to the files on the book's CD.

4. **Issue the command** cd /mnt/cdrom/RPM.

   This command moves you to the RPM directory.

5. **Use the .rpm procedure in Appendix A to install the packages.**

What You'll Find

All of these programs are freeware and released under either the GNU Public License (GPL) or Qt Public License (QPL). As a Linux user, you should be familiar with the GPL and its derivatives, and with the implications for your use of the software. Copyright ownership of, and distribution terms for, each program are stated in each program's primary directory and/or primary file archive. You can learn more about the GPL at http://www.gnu.org.

Where possible, we've mentioned each program's home page at the point where the package was discussed in the text. See especially Chapter 17 and Appendix A for more information about each of these packages.

Basic KDE packages

The basic KDE packages are described in Appendix A. The following packages are required in order to install KDE: kdebase, kdelibs, and kdesupport if you're running Debian Linux or don't have the included libraries already installed. The other KDE packages are recommended, because you'll need them in order to try out various things we describe throughout the book: kdeadmin, kdegames, kdegraphics, kdemultimedia, kdenetwork, kdeutils, and korganizer.

Non-KDE programs

You also find all the programs described in Chapter 17: WebMaker, Kstocks, Kpilot, Empath, Kuickshow, KVoicecontrol, KFortune, Katchit, Kwintv, and KWebwatch.

Koffice

As described in Part II, Koffice is an array of fully featured office programs. We've included Koffice on this disk; you'll probably want to download an updated version from http://www.kde.org if one is available, as Koffice is only available as an alpha release at the time of writing. The Koffice team predicts a beta release in the winter of 2000.

If You've Got Problems (Of the CD Kind)

If you follow the procedures outlined in Appendix A and in this appendix, you should have little trouble installing these programs. Of course, there is no guarantee of anything in the Linux world, especially when discussing youthful software like KDE and even younger programs like those written as additions to the basic KDE packages.

We selected programs for this CD that were generally regarded as stable enough for general user installation. You'll find a great many more programs written for KDE in various Internet archives; while we use some of them, we chose not to include those that may require a more advanced understanding of Linux or basic programming to operate safely on your individual computer.

If you have the basic minimum requirements described earlier in this appendix, these packages should work for you. Individual oddities can cause trouble, though; your computer may have an unusual architecture, or your Linux distribution may not like the packages very well. You may also simply need more RAM.

If you have bad luck with the CD, we suggest that you consider downloading the packages from http://www.kde.org directly; packages may have been improved or debugged in the time between this book's deadline and the day you purchased it. If you're having trouble with general Linux installation, you'll probably want to consult your local Linux guru or a good Linux reference text.

If you know that the trouble lies with installing the items from the CD, and not from KDE, please call the IDG Books Worldwide Customer Service phone number: 800-762-2974 (outside the United States: 317-572-3342).

Index

Notes

Notes

Notes

Notes

Notes

Notes

Notes

Notes

Notes

Notes

Notes

Notes

Notes

IDG Books Worldwide, Inc., End-User License Agreement

READ THIS. You should carefully read these terms and conditions before opening the software packet(s) included with this book ("Book"). This is a license agreement ("Agreement") between you and IDG Books Worldwide, Inc. ("IDGB"). By opening the accompanying software packet(s), you acknowledge that you have read and accept the following terms and conditions. If you do not agree and do not want to be bound by such terms and conditions, promptly return the Book and the unopened software packet(s) to the place you obtained them for a full refund.

1. **License Grant.** IDGB grants to you (either an individual or entity) a nonexclusive license to use one copy of the enclosed software program(s) (collectively, the "Software") solely for your own personal or business purposes on a single computer (whether a standard computer or a workstation component of a multiuser network). The Software is in use on a computer when it is loaded into temporary memory (RAM) or installed into permanent memory (hard disk, CD-ROM, or other storage device). IDGB reserves all rights not expressly granted herein.

2. **Ownership.** IDGB is the owner of all right, title, and interest, including copyright, in and to the compilation of the Software recorded on the disk(s) or CD-ROM ("Software Media"). Copyright to the individual programs recorded on the Software Media is owned by the author or other authorized copyright owner of each program. Ownership of the Software and all proprietary rights relating thereto remain with IDGB and its licensers.

3. **Restrictions on Use and Transfer.**

   (a) You may only (i) make one copy of the Software for backup or archival purposes, or (ii) transfer the Software to a single hard disk, provided that you keep the original for backup or archival purposes. You may not (i) rent or lease the Software, (ii) copy or reproduce the Software through a LAN or other network system or through any computer subscriber system or bulletin-board system, or (iii) modify, adapt, or create derivative works based on the Software.

   (b) You may not reverse engineer, decompile, or disassemble the Software. You may transfer the Software and user documentation on a permanent basis, provided that the transferee agrees to accept the terms and conditions of this Agreement and you retain no copies. If the Software is an update or has been updated, any transfer must include the most recent update and all prior versions.

4. **Restrictions on Use of Individual Programs.** You must follow the individual requirements and restrictions detailed for each individual program in Appendix C of this Book. These limitations are also contained in the individual license agreements recorded on the Software Media. These limitations may include a requirement that after using the program for a specified period of time, the user must pay a registration fee or discontinue use. By opening the Software packet(s), you will be agreeing to abide by the licenses and restrictions for these individual programs that are detailed in Appendix and on the Software Media. None of the material on this Software Media or listed in this Book may ever be redistributed, in original or modified form, for commercial purposes.

5. **Limited Warranty.**

   IDGB warrants that the Software and Software Media are free from defects in materials and workmanship under normal use for a period of sixty (60) days from the date of purchase of this Book. If IDGB receives notification within the warranty period of defects in materials or workmanship, IDGB will replace the defective Software Media.

   (b) IDGB AND THE AUTHOR OF THE BOOK DISCLAIM ALL OTHER WARRANTIES, EXPRESS OR IMPLIED, INCLUDING WITHOUT LIMITATION IMPLIED WARRANTIES OF MERCHANTABILITY AND FITNESS FOR A PARTICULAR PURPOSE, WITH RESPECT TO THE SOFTWARE, THE PROGRAMS, THE SOURCE CODE CONTAINED THEREIN, AND/OR THE TECHNIQUES DESCRIBED IN THIS BOOK. IDGB DOES NOT WARRANT THAT THE FUNCTIONS CONTAINED IN THE SOFTWARE WILL MEET YOUR REQUIREMENTS OR THAT THE OPERATION OF THE SOFTWARE WILL BE ERROR FREE.

   (c) This limited warranty gives you specific legal rights, and you may have other rights that vary from jurisdiction to jurisdiction.

6. **Remedies.**

   (a) IDGB's entire liability and your exclusive remedy for defects in materials and workmanship shall be limited to replacement of the Software Media, which may be returned to IDGB with a copy of your receipt at the following address: Software Media Fulfillment Department, Attn.: *KDE For Linux For Dummies*, IDG Books Worldwide, Inc., 10475 Crosspoint Boulevard, Indianapolis, IN 46256, or call 800-762-2974. Please allow three to four weeks for delivery. This Limited Warranty is void if failure of the Software Media has resulted from accident, abuse, or misapplication. Any replacement Software Media will be warranted for the remainder of the original warranty period or thirty (30) days, whichever is longer.

   (b) In no event shall IDGB or the author be liable for any damages whatsoever (including without limitation damages for loss of business profits, business interruption, loss of business information, or any other pecuniary loss) arising from the use of or inability to use the Book or the Software, even if IDGB has been advised of the possibility of such damages.

   (c) Because some jurisdictions do not allow the exclusion or limitation of liability for consequential or incidental damages, the above limitation or exclusion may not apply to you.

7. **U.S. Government Restricted Rights.** Use, duplication, or disclosure of the Software by the U.S. Government is subject to restrictions stated in paragraph (c)(1)(ii) of the Rights in Technical Data and Computer Software clause of DFARS 252.227-7013, and in subparagraphs (a) through (d) of the Commercial Computer–Restricted Rights clause at FAR 52.227-19, and in similar clauses in the NASA FAR supplement, when applicable.

8. **General.** This Agreement constitutes the entire understanding of the parties and revokes and supersedes all prior agreements, oral or written, between them and may not be modified or amended except in a writing signed by both parties hereto that specifically refers to this Agreement. This Agreement shall take precedence over any other documents that may be in conflict herewith. If any one or more provisions contained in this Agreement are held by any court or tribunal to be invalid, illegal, or otherwise unenforceable, each and every other provision shall remain in full force and effect.

Installation Instructions

To install KDE or the other software on this CD, you will need to mount the CD-ROM drive. The installation process for KDE itself is described in Appendix C. To install the programs on this disk, use the following process and the information in Appendix C as complementary references.

General installation from source code

1. **Insert the CD-ROM into your computer's CD-ROM drive.**

2. **Make sure you are logged in as root.**

3. **As root, issue the command** `mount -t iso9960 /dev/cdrom /mnt/cdrom`.

4. **Issue the command** `mkdir /usr/src/KDE`.

5. **Issue the command** `cp /mnt/cdrom/TGZ/* /usr/src/KDE`.

6. **Use the procedure in Appendix C to install the packages.**

Installation from .rpm

If your Linux distribution is either a Red Hat Linux distribution or uses the Red Hat .rpm packaging standard, you may use this process instead of the source code process described above.

1. **Insert the CD-ROM into your computer's CD-ROM drive.**

2. **Make sure you are logged in as root.**

3. **As root, issue the command** `mount -t iso9960 /dev/cdrom /mnt/cdrom`.

4. **Issue the command** `cd /mnt/cdrom/RPM`.

5. **Use the .rpm procedure in Appendix C to install the packages.**

Discover Dummies Online!

The Dummies Web Site is your fun and friendly online resource for the latest information about ...*For Dummies*® books and your favorite topics. The Web site is the place to communicate with us, exchange ideas with other ...*For Dummies* readers, chat with authors, and have fun!

Ten Fun and Useful Things You Can Do at www.dummies.com

1. Win free ...*For Dummies* books and more!
2. Register your book and be entered in a prize drawing.
3. Meet your favorite authors through the IDG Books Author Chat Series.
4. Exchange helpful information with other ...*For Dummies* readers.
5. Discover other great ...*For Dummies* books you must have!
6. Purchase Dummieswear™ exclusively from our Web site.
7. Buy ...*For Dummies* books online.
8. Talk to us. Make comments, ask questions, get answers!
9. Download free software.
10. Find additional useful resources from authors.

Link directly to these ten fun and useful things at http://www.dummies.com/10useful

For other technology titles from IDG Books Worldwide, go to
www.idgbooks.com

Not on the Web yet? It's easy to get started with *Dummies 101*®: *The Internet For Windows*® *98* or *The Internet For Dummies*®, 6th Edition, at local retailers everywhere.

Find other ...*For Dummies* books on these topics:

Business • Career • Databases • Food & Beverage • Games • Gardening • Graphics • Hardware
Health & Fitness • Internet and the World Wide Web • Networking • Office Suites
Operating Systems • Personal Finance • Pets • Programming • Recreation • Sports
Spreadsheets • Teacher Resources • Test Prep • Word Processing

IDG BOOKS WORLDWIDE
BOOK REGISTRATION

Register This Book and Win!

We want to hear from you!

Visit **http://my2cents.dummies.com** to register this book and tell us how you liked it!

- ✔ Get entered in our monthly prize giveaway.

- ✔ Give us feedback about this book — tell us what you like best, what you like least, or maybe what you'd like to ask the author and us to change!

- ✔ Let us know any other *...For Dummies*® topics that interest you.

Your feedback helps us determine what books to publish, tells us what coverage to add as we revise our books, and lets us know whether we're meeting your needs as a *...For Dummies* reader. You're our most valuable resource, and what you have to say is important to us!

Not on the Web yet? It's easy to get started with *Dummies 101*®: *The Internet For Windows*® *98* or *The Internet For Dummies*,® 6th Edition, at local retailers everywhere.

Or let us know what you think by sending us a letter at the following address:

...For Dummies Book Registration
Dummies Press
10475 Crosspoint Blvd.
Indianapolis, IN 46256

™

BESTSELLING BOOK SERIES